# THE BEST OF
## Gourmet

THE BEST OF

*Gourmet*

2001

FROM THE EDITORS OF GOURMET

CONDÉ NAST BOOKS • RANDOM HOUSE, NEW YORK

Copyright © 2000
The Condé Nast Publications Inc.
All rights reserved under International and Pan-
American Copyright Conventions. Published in the
United States by Random House, Inc., New York,
and simultaneously in Canada by Random House
of Canada Limited, Toronto.

ISBN 0-375-50604-7
ISSN 1046-1760

Random House website address:
www.atrandom.com

Most of the recipes in this work were published
previously in *Gourmet* magazine.

Printed in the United States of America on
acid-free paper

98765432
First Edition

Informative text in this book was written by
Diane Keitt and Ellen Morrissey.

The text of this book was set in Times Roman by
Bill SMITH STUDIO. The four-color separations
were done by American Color and Quad/Graphics, Inc.
The book was printed and bound at R. R. Donnelley
and Sons. Stock is Citation Web Gloss, Westvāco.

Front jacket: Peach Granita (page 227) and
Anise Biscotti (page 227)
Back jacket: Provence's Grand Aïoli (page 56)

**For Condé Nast Books**
Lisa Faith Phillips, Vice President/General Manager
Tom Downing, Direct Marketing Director
Deborah Williams, Associate Operations Director
Peter Immediato, Business Manager
Colleen P. Shire, Direct Marketing Manager
Catherine Punch, Direct Marketing Manager
Jennifer Zalewski, Direct Marketing Associate
Eric Levy, Inventory Assistant
Barbara Giordano, Direct Marketing Assistant
Alicia Hodroski, Direct Marketing Assistant
Richard B. Elman, Production Manager

**For *Gourmet* Books**
Diane Keitt, Director
Ellen Morrissey, Associate Editor

**For *Gourmet* Magazine**
Ruth Reichl, Editor in Chief

Zanne Early Stewart, Executive Food Editor
Kemp Miles Minifie, Senior Food Editor
Alexis M. Touchet, Associate Food Editor
Lori Walther Powell, Food Editor
Elizabeth Vought Greene, Food Editor
Katy Massam, Food Editor
Shelton Wiseman, Food Editor
Ruth Cousineau, Food Editor

Romulo A. Yanes, Photographer
Marjorie H. Webb, Style Director
Nancy Purdum, Senior Style Editor

Produced in association with
**JaBS Media**
Anne B. Wright, Project Editor
Jeffrey Rutzky, Production Manager
Karen Salsgiver, Design Consultant
Marilyn Flaig, Indexer

# ACKNOWLEDGMENTS

The editors of Gourmet Books would like to thank all those who worked on this volume, especially our dear friend, Beverly Charlton, whose lovely line drawings have appeared in *The Best of Gourmet* since 1991. Just last year, Beverly delighted us with a very large shipment of drawings; then, some months later came the sad news that she had died of cancer. It was so like her to think of others first and to be professional, always. This book, filled with many of Beverly's drawings, is dedicated to her. With the kind permission of her husband, Richard, we will continue to print Beverly's work for years to come. Other art this year is from Jean Chandler, Suzanne Dunaway, Maurie Harrington, Vicky Gonis, Elisa Mambrino, Jeanne Meinke, Bob Palevitz, Agni Saucier, Jim Saucier, Alexis Seabrook, Harley Seabrook, and Meg Shields.

We would also like to give thanks to Ruth Reichl, our editor in chief, who suggested that we feature Sicily in our Cuisines of the World section, and Zanne Stewart and Kemp Minifie, *Gourmet*'s executive food editor and senior food editor respectively, who tasted and critiqued all new recipes. Special thanks go to Mary Taylor Simeti, respected Sicilian food, travel, and Greek mythology writer, who acted as consultant and critiqued our menus and primers (usually via e-mail from Sicily). Exceptional travel photography came from Ernesto Bazan, Mark Ferri, and K.F. Schmidt, and fine line drawings were rendered by Laura Hartman Maestro. We would also like to thank *Gourmet* photographer, Romulo A. Yanes, for shooting all the Sicilian menus and Jeannie Oberholtzer for prop-styling them. The menus were developed in-house by the following food editors: Alexis Touchet (Summer Dinner in Palermo), Lori Powell (Carnival Dinner), and Tracey Seaman (A Sicilian Sweets Table). Gerald Asher, *Gourmet*'s wine editor, selected wines for each menu. Gina Miraglia helped out with cross-testing of recipes. Lori styled both the Carnival Dinner and the Palermo Dinner, including the jacket; Tracey styled her own Sweets menu.

Comfort food has always been a *Gourmet* favorite, and Shelley Wiseman and Ruth Cousineau offer twenty-four brand-new recipes in this volume on that very topic. Line drawings by Alexis Seabrook make this section even more homey and inviting.

This year was our first with JaBS Media. We would like to acknowledge Bill Smith, Jackie Ball, Jeffrey Rutzky, and Karen Salsgiver, with many thanks to Anne Wright for seeing to every detail. Meticulous editorial help came from Cheryl Brown and Kathleen Duffy Freud.

. . .

CONTENTS

*To Beverly Charlton, illustrator and friend*

# INTRODUCTION

As we begin a brand-new millennium, the food industry is thriving. Exceptional restaurants featuring clever young chefs continue to spring up all over the country; more new farmers markets open monthly; cookbooks of every stripe crowd bookstore shelves and kitchen countertops; and television food shows hosted by star chefs run every waking hour (and, for most of us, some sleeping ones, too). At *Gourmet,* this intense interest in food has been energizing, and we think you'll see the results in this "best" collection of 32 menus and 350 recipes, most of which appeared in our magazine during the year 2000. Now, in addition to cooking with only the freshest seasonal harvests, we've renewed our commitment to search out lesser-known delicious fruit and vegetable varieties and to show you how to cook with them. A quick glance at our newest recipes finds ever-so-tender flowering pea shoots in one vegetable dish and buttery mashed yuca in another; Gala apples in a wonderful brown Betty; even peppery-tasting nasturtiums in a lovely pasta starter. And, because more and more people are eating vegetarian today, we've included two menus for entertaining— an exotic Indian feast and a casual terrace dinner—that will please even your meat-loving guests. For weeknight cooking, we've expanded our everyday section of the magazine with plenty of quick and easy dishes to mix and match, including five-ingredients recipes, one-dish dinners, and low-fat menus. Many were chosen for this volume.

Our search for new flavors extends to the far corners of the globe. Throughout the past year, our food editors were busy traveling abroad, tasting extensively in the best restaurants, and attending cooking schools. They returned to *Gourmet's* test kitchens, sometimes with experts in tow, to create their own menus for the cuisines of India, Spain, Malaysia, France, and Italy. Each meal, found in the menu collection of this volume, contains dishes carefully honed to the home kitchen, yet each captures the true essence of these wonderful foreign kitchens. And, this year's Cuisines of the World section (page 218) turns to Sicily with three additional foreign menus: Summer Dinner in Palermo offers the season's best—a grilled tuna steak with mint-almond sauce and refreshing peach granita; a Carnival Dinner heartily fills you to the brim with pasta, sausages, meatballs, and braised beef; and A Sicilian Sweets Table, an extraordinary indulgence, stars a spectacular frozen hazelnut bombe, a *cassata alla Siciliana,* and much more. Twenty-four more new recipes appear in a special section highlighting comfort food. Who knew that old-fashioned chocolate pudding, or braised lamb shanks, or just a simple tuna melt could be better than any you've ever tasted?

Here at *Gourmet,* we keep saying that it can't get much better than this, but it has. Come enjoy all the new excitement, all the new flavors, of the ever-new *Best of Gourmet.*

The Editors of Gourmet

• • •

# THE MENU
# COLLECTION

The year 2000 proved to be one of ongoing enrichment for *Gourmet*'s ever-curious and tireless food editors. They traveled extensively in search of new flavors and invited talented guest chefs to share their culinary know-how. The bounty of all this hands-on learning is gathered here in 29 of *Gourmet*'s newest, best menus. The variety is impressive: There are portable little meals (including a picnic in the snow, a picnic in the park, and a beach-bound boxed lunch), more ambitious cookouts (for Father's Day, or for a warm summer evening in the country), and, as always, show-stopping holiday celebrations. But perhaps the most notable menus of the year are the dinner parties that celebrate foreign tables, including an Indian vegetarian feast; a Spanish meal featuring the flavors of Catalonia; a casual, quick-to-prepare Caribbean dinner complete with tropical fruit cocktails; and a three-in-one dish (chicken, rice, and soup) from Hainan, a tropical island off China's southern coast.

Plenty more outstanding breakfasts, lunches, and dinners offer entertaining ideas for the entire year. You'll delight in an Easter meal designed to highlight the season's finest blossoms in dishes such as *taglierini* with morels, asparagus, and nasturtiums; hibiscus-marinated leg of lamb; and lavender crème caramel tart. In the warmth of the summer sun, entertain poolside with a splashy party developed by chef Mary Sue Milliken. Treat your guests to charred tomatillo guacamole served with two types of crunchy tortilla triangles; chile-glazed salmon with orange salsa; seared rainbow chard with leeks; and raisin-studded cakes baked inside hollowed-out oranges. Later in the summer, gather friends and family around the table once more for a grand *aïoli* party—a feast of salt cod, shellfish, eggs, and assorted seasonal vegetables served with the thick, rich garlic mayonnaise for which Provence is famous—followed by simply gorgeous plum tarts. Then, as the days shorten, look forward to a spectacular Thanksgiving menu that finds new ways with old family favorites—cranberries transformed into chutney, beet soup served in whole roasted acorn squash, and green beans brightened with lemon. Of course there's a turkey, this one splendidly presented with apples, onions, fried sage leaves, and apple cider gravy.

Also included are two low-fat menus (a hearty winter dinner and a spicy cool one for summer) and two one-dish dinners (lobster salad and a Cornish hen and vegetable roast) from the magazine's popular Gourmet Every Day section. Like the entertaining menus, these simple meals reflect the myriad cultural influences of *Gourmet*'s food editors. They also prove that cooking from a global pantry can produce quick and easy everyday fare that's far from ordinary (and in many cases, lower in fat and calories).

*Gourmet*'s millennium begins as a culinary exploration of worldly flavors. We hope you enjoy the journey.

• • •

# Fragrant Feast: A Taste of India

*Serves 8*

FRIED PAPPADAMS
Crisp Lentil Wafers

THAKKALI RASAM, P. 107
Tomato Dal Soup

• • •

ELUMICHAMPAZHA SADAM, P. 155
Lemon Rice with Peanuts

PALAK PANEER, P. 170
Fresh Cheese with Spinach

BEANS PORIYAL, P. 159
Dry Curried Beans

VELLARIKKAI THAKKALI
VENGAYA PACHADI, P. 181
Cucumber, Tomato, and Onion Yogurt Salad

Iron Horse T-bar-T Fumé Blanc '98

• • •

PAAL PAYASAM, P. 212
Rice Pudding with Pistachios, Raisins, and Saffron

# A Picnic in the Snow

*Serves 8*

Mulled Wine, p. 216

• • •

SPICY RED PORK AND BEAN CHILI, P. 124

MANGO JÍCAMA CHOPPED SALAD, P. 177

Paulaner Premium Lager

• • •

CHEWY CARAMEL PECAN BARS, P. 191

Cinnamon Hot Chocolate, p. 217

Samuel Smith Oatmeal Stout

# THE GENEROUS TABLE:
## AN AMERICAN POTLUCK SUPPER

*Serves 20*

HUNDRED-CORNER SHRIMP BALLS, P. 92

HERBED LIMA BEAN HUMMUS, P. 96

CURRIED CHICKEN LIVER PÂTÉ, P. 96

Penfolds Eden Valley Reserve Riesling '99

• • •

FILLET OF BEEF WITH ASIAN SPICE RUB, P. 119

TOMATO AND MOZZARELLA LASAGNE, P. 150

CAJUN SHRIMP MIRLITON CASSEROLE, P. 117

MOROCCAN-SPICED ROASTED VEGETABLES, P. 172

WILD RICE SALAD, P. 185

ROSAURA'S FESTIVE SALAD, P. 176

GARLIC ROSEMARY FOCACCIA, P. 100

Delas-Frères Val Muzols Côtes-du-Ventoux '97

• • •

APPLE CRUMB TARTS, P. 194

HUNGARIAN CHOCOLATE MOUSSE
CAKE BARS, P. 190

Domaine de Durban Muscat de Beaumes-de-Venise '98

Fillet of Beef with Asian Spice Rub; Rosaura's Festive Salad

Apple Crumb Tart; Hungarian Chocolate Mousse Cake Bars

# Spain's Melting Pot

*Serves 6*

AMANIDA AMB ESPÀRREC I PERNIL, P. 174
Asparagus and Serrano Ham Salad with Toasted Almonds

• • •

ARROSSEJAT DE FIDEUS AMB LLAGOSTA, P. 147
Sautéed Pasta with Lobster

ESCALIVADA, P. 168
Roasted Peppers, Onion, and Eggplant

Carmenet Sangiacomo Vineyard Chardonnay '97

• • •

GELAT DE CREMA CATALANA
I XERÈS AMB MEL I FIGUES, P. 198
Sherry Crema Catalana Ice Cream with Honeyed Figs

TEULES DE TARONJA, P. 192
Candied-Orange Wafers

Asparagus and Serrano Ham Salad with Toasted Almonds

Sautéed Pasta with Lobster

# DINNER BY THE FIRE

*Serves 6*

Hot Cider with Rum, p. 216

HONEY-ROASTED PEPPERED PECANS, P. 88

• • •

CORIANDER- AND CHILE-RUBBED
LAMB CHOPS, P. 128

RICE AND LENTIL SALAD WITH
ORANGE AND DRIED CHERRIES, P. 185

SAUTÉED MUSTARD GREENS
WITH GARLIC, P. 166

Château Maucaillou Moulis '96

• • •

POACHED PEARS WITH
SPICED CARAMEL SAUCE, P. 202

# THE PROMISE OF
# EASTER BLOOMS

*Serves 8*

TAGLIERINI WITH MORELS, ASPARAGUS,
AND NASTURTIUMS, P. 152

Balduin von Hövel Riesling '98

• • •

HIBISCUS-MARINATED LEG OF LAMB, P. 126

SUGAR SNAPS WITH FLOWERING PEA SHOOTS,
PEAS, AND BABY ONIONS, P. 167

GOAT-CHEESE SCALLOPED POTATOES WITH
CHIVE BLOSSOMS, P. 169

Atlas Peak Vineyards Napa Valley Sangiovese '97

• • •

LAVENDER CRÈME-CARAMEL TART, P. 194

Lavender Crème-Caramel Tart

Hibiscus-Marinated Leg of Lamb, Sugar Snaps with Flowering Pea Shoots, Peas, and Baby Onions; Goat-Cheese Scalloped Potatoes with Chive Blossoms

# PARADISE AT HOME:
## A CASUAL CARIBBEAN DINNER

*Serves 6*

Frozen Papaya and Passion-Fruit Rum Cocktails, p. 216

CRAB AND COCONUT DIP WITH
PLANTAIN CHIPS, P. 97

• • •

SPICED PORK TENDERLOIN AND
PINEAPPLE-AVOCADO SALSA, P. 125

MASHED YUCA WITH GARLIC, P. 172

MacRostie Carneros Pinot Noir '97

Château Souverain Sonoma County
Chardonnay '98

• • •

MANGO FOOL WITH CHOCOLATE-ANISE
STRAWS, P. 211

# LA DOLCE VITA:
## AN ITALIAN FANTASY

*Serves 6*

CRISPY ARTICHOKE FLOWERS WITH
SALSA VERDE, P. 86

• • •

GREEN-PEA RAVIOLI IN LEMON BROTH, P. 104

• • •

ROASTED DOUBLE VEAL CHOPS, P. 122

CARROT AND SQUASH RIBBONS, P. 161

Vietti Tre Vigne Dolcetto D'Alba '98

• • •

GRAPPA SEMIFREDDO WITH
ESPRESSO SAUCE, P. 198

Grappa Semifreddo with Espresso Sauce

Roasted Double Veal Chops; Carrot and Squash Ribbons

# The Celebration Table

*Serves 16*

SHRIMP SATÉS WITH SPICED
PISTACHIO CHUTNEY, P. 92

• • •

MISO-MARINATED SALMON WITH
CITRUS AND SHIITAKES, P. 110

HARICOT VERT, EDAMAME, AND
PURPLE-POTATO SALAD, P. 179

SESAME FLATBREAD CRACKERS, P. 100

Amity Vineyards Willamette Valley Oregon
Pinot Blanc '98

• • •

MIXED-BERRY PAVLOVAS, P. 201

Robert Pecota Winery Napa Valley
Moscato d'Andrea '98

# HOT AND COOL COMFORT:
# A TASTE OF MALAYSIA

*Serves 6*

HAINANESE CHICKEN RICE, P. 132

Lockwood Monterey Sauvignon Blanc '98

• • •

TAPIOCA PUDDING WITH COCONUT CREAM
AND PALM-SUGAR SYRUP, P. 213

# Prime Time: Father's Day Cookout

*Serves 8*

ALASKA KING CRAB "NACHOS," P. 88

Shafer Vineyards "Red Shoulder Ranch"
Carneros Chardonnay '98

• • •

GRILLED SPICED RIB-EYE STEAKS, P. 119

FINGERLING-POTATO SALAD WITH
GREEN CHILE-CILANTRO SALSA, P. 182

RADICCHIO, RED CABBAGE, AND TOMATOES
WITH ORANGE VINAIGRETTE, P. 183

Voss Vineyards Napa Valley Shiraz '96

• • •

TROPICAL-FRUIT SPLITS WITH RUM SAUCE
AND CHILE-MACADAMIA BRITTLE, P. 204

# MEET US IN THE COUNTRY:
## FRIDAY NIGHT SUPPER

*Serves 8*

SAUTÉED SKIRT STEAK WITH FRISÉE AND
ROASTED-POTATO SALAD, p. 120

Merryvale Reserve Napa Valley Merlot '97

• • •

MANGO TART, p. 196

**GAME PLAN**
Timesaving preparations that can break up the
work before the cooking begins

**Before you leave:**
▶ Wash and dry all greens and keep chilled in
  sealable plastic bags
▶ Make tomato, caper, and olive vinaigrette
▶ Make hot pepper relish
▶ Make herb-garlic butter
▶ Make lime sugar
▶ Bake cookies or, if you prefer them freshly
  baked, prepare dough
▶ Measure out dry ingredients for scones,
  muffins, and coffeecake and put in labeled
  sealable plastic bags
▶ Grate and crumble cheeses and keep chilled
  in sealable plastic bags

**Friday night:**
▶ Make corn salad
▶ Cook beans

**Saturday morning:**
▶ Make blueberry coffeecake for Sunday

# Meet Us in the Country:
## Saturday Morning

*Serves 8*

**Peach Nectar with Lime,** p. 217

CHEDDAR-CHIVE SCONES, p. 102

SLICED PROSCIUTTO AND HONEYDEW MELON

RASPBERRY-LEMON CORN MUFFINS, p. 102

# Meet Us in the Country: Lunch: A Moveable Feast

*Serves 8*

POTATOES WITH VINEGAR AND SEA SALT, P. 169

CORN, TOMATO, AND SCALLION SALAD, P. 182

HARICOTS VERTS WITH
HOT PEPPER RELISH, P. 160

GRILLED CHICKEN AND PITAS, P. 131

Château Haut-Beauséjour
Saint-Estèphe '97

• • •

ASSORTED GRAPES ON ICE

# MEET US IN THE COUNTRY: THE BIG NIGHT

*Serves 8*

FETA AND RED BELL PEPPER PIZZA, P. 89

Boutari Santorini '99

• • •

GRILLED SEAFOOD WITH TOMATO, CAPER, AND
OLIVE VINAIGRETTE. P. 116

VEGETABLE BULGUR SALAD, P. 184

GRILLED HERBED GARLIC BREAD, P. 99

Joseph Phelps Napa Valley Viognier '98

• • •

LIME SUGAR COOKIES, P. 189

LIME ICE ON WATERMELON, P. 197

# MEET US IN THE COUNTRY:
## BRUNCH: THE LONG GOOD-BYE

*Serves 8*

Elderberry-Flower Mimosas, p. 216

PEACHES IN GINGER SYRUP, P. 203

BLUEBERRY-ALMOND COFFEECAKE, P. 189

SALMON-WRAPPED POACHED EGGS, P. 139

Alexander Valley Vineyards Chardonnay '98

# SUNDAY IN THE PARK

*Serves 2*

CHILLED ROASTED TOMATO AND
RED PEPPER SOUP WITH MINT, P. 108

• • •

MUSTARD-CRUSTED BEEF TENDERLOIN
WITH ARUGULA, RED ONION, AND
WAX BEAN SALAD, P. 118

Rex Hill Willamette Valley Pinot Noir '98

• • •

ALMOND CORNMEAL CAKE WITH
PEACH AND BERRY COMPOTE, P. 187

# Summer Splash:
# Poolside Dinner with
# Mary Sue Milliken

*Serves 8*

Pisco Sours, p. 215

CHILI-LIME TORTILLA TRIANGLES, P. 98

SEEDED TORTILLA TRIANGLES, P. 98

CHARRED TOMATILLO GUACAMOLE, P. 98

• • •

HEARTS OF ROMAINE WITH ROASTED PEPPERS
AND CABRALES DRESSING, P. 178

Viña Godeval Valdeorras '98

• • •

CHILE-GLAZED SALMON WITH ORANGE SALSA, P. 111

QUINOA-FENNEL PILAF, P. 153

SEARED RAINBOW CHARD WITH LEEKS, P. 162

Marqués de Cáceres Reserva Rioja '94

• • •

ROASTED ORANGE CAKES, P. 188

Malvasia Dulce El Grifo Lanzarote '98
Pedro Ximenez Don PX Reserva Sherry

# PROVENCE'S GRAND AÏOLI

*Serves 12*

CLASSIC AÏOLI, P. 158

STEAMED MUSSELS, P. 115

POACHED SALT COD, P. 110

HARD-BOILED EGGS

CHICKPEAS, P. 173

ROASTED BEETS AND ONIONS, P. 158

ARTICHOKES, P. 158

ASSORTED DIPPING VEGETABLES, P. 157

Château Routas "Rouvière" Rosé '99

• • •

PLUM TARTS, P. 196

Château de Fesles Bonnezeaux '97

# FROM THE TERRACE:
## A LATE SUMMER
## VEGETARIAN DINNER

*Serves 6*

SHREDDED COLLARD GREENS WITH
WALNUTS AND PICKLED APPLES, P. 178

EGGPLANT STEAKS WITH PUMPKIN, TOMATO,
AND MUSHROOM RAGOUT, P. 163

STEAMED COUSCOUS WITH
TOASTED PUMPKIN SEEDS, P. 148

Isole e Olena Chianti '98

• • •

OAT BISCUITS WITH TRIPLE-CRÈME CHEESE
AND GRAPES, P. 193

# DINNER IN FRANCE WITH KEN HOM

*Serves 8*

PUMPKIN-PEAR SOUP WITH CORIANDER, P. 108

. . .

"CRACKLING" SALMON WITH TRUFFLES, P. 90

Château Couhins-Lurton Pessac-Léognan '95

. . .

ORANGE PEKING DUCK, P. 136

VEGETABLE SALAD WITH
CURRY-SOY VINAIGRETTE, P. 183

SPICY FRIED BASMATI RICE, P. 154

Château Mouton-Rothschild Pauillac '83

. . .

WARM FRUIT COMPOTE WITH LEMON VERBENA
AND CRÈME FRAÎCHE, P. 206

Château Raymond-Lafon Sauternes '90

Warm Fruit Compote with Lemon Verbena and Crème Fraîche;
Opposite, clockwise from upper left: Pumpkin-Pear Soup with
Coriander; "Crackling" Salmon with Truffles; Vegetable Salad
with Curry-Soy Vinaigrette; Spicy Fried Basmati Rice; Orange
Peking Duck

65

# THANKSGIVING:
# AN AMERICAN GATHERING

*Serves 8*

BEET SOUP IN ROASTED ACORN SQUASH, P. 103

CORNMEAL-CAYENNE GRISSINI, P. 101

• • •

ROAST TURKEY WITH APPLES, ONIONS, FRIED
SAGE LEAVES, AND APPLE CIDER GRAVY, P. 136

WILD RICE DRESSING, P. 156

CRANBERRY CHUTNEY, P. 138

GREEN BEANS WITH LEMON, P. 164

RUTABAGA AND CARROT PURÉE, P. 169

Saintsbury Carneros Pinot Noir '99

• • •

GINGER-PECAN ROULADE WITH
HONEY-GLAZED PECANS, P. 186

PEAR AND DRIED-CHERRY TART, P. 195

Yalumba Old Sweet White "Museum Release"

# DEBORAH MADISON'S
# SANTA FE CHRISTMAS

*Serves 6*

HERBED RICOTTA AND ROASTED
POBLANOS ON ENDIVE, P. 91

Gruet NM Brut

• • •

FRISÉE, WATERCRESS, AND MINT SALAD, P. 179

• • •

ROAST CAPON WITH CHILE-CILANTRO RUB
AND ROASTED CARROTS, P. 131

OR

MUSHROOM BUDÍN, P. 165

POTATO-GREEN CHILE GRATIN, P. 168

CAVALO NERO WITH CILANTRO, P. 160

Kunde Sonoma Valley Zinfandel '98

• • •

DATE, DRIED-CHERRY, AND
CHOCOLATE TORTE, P. 188

BLOOD ORANGE JELLY WITH
BRANDIED WHIPPED CREAM, P. 213

Quady Essensia

Date, Dried-Cherry, and Chocolate Torte; Opposite, clockwise from upper left:
Cavalo Nero with Cilantro; Potato-Green Chile Gratin; Frisée, Watercress, and
Mint Salad; Blood Orange Jelly with Brandied Whipped Cream; Roast Capon
with Chile-Cilantro Rub and Roasted Carrots

73

# HOLIDAY COCKTAIL PARTY

*Serves 16 to 20*

Citron Martini with Black Sambuca, p. 215

Iron Horse Classic Vintage Brut '95

SESAME RICE BALLS WITH RED PEPPER
DIPPING SAUCE, P. 90

BRANDADE ON POPPY SEED CRACKERS, P. 94

CAVIAR MOONS, P. 94

TAPENADE ON JÍCAMA STARS, P. 95

SCALLOP CEVICHE ON BLACK PASTA CAKES
WITH CILANTRO SALSA, P. 95

TRUFFLED QUAIL EGGS, P. 89

PEPPERY BEEF KEBABS WITH
BRAISED PEARL ONIONS, P. 86

COCONUT MACADAMIA TRUFFLES, P. 207

CANDIED GRAPEFRUIT PEEL, P. 206

CHOCOLATE STAR ANISE TRUFFLES, P. 207

# ELEGANT HOLIDAY DINNER

*Serves 8*

SALMON CONSOMMÉ WITH CRÈME FRAÎCHE
AND SALMON CAVIAR, p. 106

BLACK PEPPER CORNMEAL CRISPS, p. 100

Deutz Blanc de Blancs Champagne '95

• • •

HERBED RIB ROAST, p. 118

PARMESAN ROASTED POTATOES, p. 167

CELERY AND FENNEL WITH BACON, p. 164

La Rioja Alta Viña Ardanza
Reserva Rioja '94

• • •

CRANBERRY COGNAC TRIFLE, p. 208

JELLIED QUINCES AND
MANCHEGO CHEESE, p. 205

Ramos-Pinto Quinta da Ervamoira
10-Year-Old Tawny Port

Jellied Quinces and Manchego Cheese; Cranberry Cognac Trifle

# LOW-FAT:
## HEARTY WINTER DINNER

*Serves 4*

**Each serving about 674 calories and 18 grams fat**

THREE-ONION SOUP, P. 105

• • •

CORNMEAL- AND CUMIN-COATED
PORK LOIN, P. 126

MAPLE-GINGER BUTTERNUT SQUASH, P. 171

SPICY BROCCOLI RABE, P. 161

• • •

CITRUS SALAD WITH STAR ANISE, P. 202

# LOW-FAT:
## SPICY COOL DINNER

*Serves 6*

Each serving about 652 calories and 20 grams fat

SPICY CUCUMBER-AVOCADO SOUP, P. 103

• • •

PERUVIAN-STYLE BEEF KEBABS WITH
GRILLED ONION AND ZUCCHINI, P. 122

QUINOA AND GRILLED-PEPPER SALAD, P. 184

• • •

MOJITO JELLY, P. 212

# ONE-DISH DINNER

*Serves 4*

LOBSTER, CORN, AND POTATO SALAD
WITH TARRAGON, P. 174

# ONE-DISH DINNER

*Serves 6*

PAPRIKA-ROASTED CORNISH HENS
AND VEGETABLES, p. 135

# A RECIPE
# COMPENDIUM

Each and every month, *Gourmet* readers look forward to the Gourmet Entertains
section for splendid menus filled with new recipes. Whatever the occasion—whether it's
an elegant dinner for eight or an intimate outdoor lunch for two—each menu is developed
with utmost flavor and accessibility in mind. Yet the bulk of the magazine's recipes come
from the Gourmet Every Day section, which is filled with inspired ideas for quick, casual
cooking. Invariably, they include delicious dishes to celebrate the changing seasons and
many low-fat variations of your favorites, but often there are outstanding "five ingredients"
recipes and amazing one-dish dinners, too. On the following pages, you'll find more than
350 recipes, most of which appeared in *Gourmet* during 2000. Many of these recipes can be
used as entertaining menu substitutions as you mix and match courses according to your
own tastes. You might love everything about the grand *aïoli* party (page 56) except the
dessert. In this case, you can easily make broiled peaches with crème fraîche instead of the
plum tarts. Or you may decide to serve sage buttermilk biscuits with sausage and cheddar
instead of salmon-wrapped poached eggs for a leisurely summer brunch. Or maybe you'd
prefer to design a brunch, lunch, or dinner menu entirely on your own—whatever you
choose, your guests will be pampered in style.

Throughout the year, *Gourmet*'s food editors emphasized making the most of fresh ingredients as they appeared in the market. Recipes for butternut squash, ramps, berries, peaches,
corn, and a handful of other seasonal favorites were all featured, and a number of the most
spirited recipes are collected here. Bring the garden inside with anise-spiced squash soup
with fennel chips; corn and okra stew; and an absolutely delicious peach soup. Breakfast
recipes also are in abundance. Morning delicacies from around the world include Mexican
fried eggs on corn tortillas with two sauces, French raisin brioche pastries, and Chinese rice
soup with pumpkin, otherwise known as *congee*, among other exotic offerings.

Plenty of the dishes that follow can go from stovetop to tabletop in no time flat. When time
is tight, turn to the index and look for the clock symbol ☺. These recipes can be prepared
in 45 minutes or less. Or if low-fat foods are what you have in mind, look for the feather
symbol ✐. Then, to help you plan meals more efficiently, we include two times—active
time and start-to-finish time—beneath each of the recipe titles. These will provide a realistic
idea of how much time each dish requires, allowing you to manage more recipes while food
cooks or chills or rests at room temperature, unattended.

This year's collection is perhaps one of the most eclectic—meaning more choice for you, the
cook. Take some time to read through the recipes, then try the ones that pique your interest.
You'll be amazed at the sheer variety of memorable meals at hand.

• • •

## CRISPY ARTICHOKE FLOWERS WITH SALSA VERDE

**Serves 6**
Active time: 40 min   Start to finish: 55 min

2 lemons, halved
6 (4-oz) small (not baby) artichokes
4 cups olive oil
*For salsa verde*
1 tablespoon fresh lemon juice
⅛ teaspoon anchovy paste
3 tablespoons extra-virgin olive oil
1 tablespoon chopped shallot
1 tablespoon capers, drained and chopped
2 tablespoons chopped fresh flat-leaf parsley

*Trim and fry artichokes:*
Fill a large bowl with 6 cups cold water and squeeze juice from 1 lemon into bowl.

Cut stems of artichokes flush with base. Bend back outer leaves of 1 artichoke until they snap off close to base, then discard several more layers of leaves in same manner until exposed leaves are pale green at top and yellow at base. Cut off pale-green top of artichoke. Carefully spread leaves and scrape out purple leaves and hairy choke with a melon-ball cutter or spoon. Trim fibrous parts from base and rub artichoke all over with a lemon half. Place in bowl of lemon water, then repeat trimming process with remaining artichokes.

Drain artichokes well, stem ends up. Heat oil in a deep 2-quart saucepan over moderate heat until a deep-fat thermometer registers about 200°F, then submerge artichokes with tongs, stem ends down, in oil. Simmer until artichokes are tender, about 10 minutes. Transfer to paper towels to drain.

Reheat olive oil over moderate heat until deep-fat thermometer registers 365°F. Spear 1 artichoke, through center of stem end, with a long kitchen fork and immerse (still on fork) into oil. Fry until leaves are open, browned, and crisp, 30 to 40 seconds. Drain well, stem end up, on paper towels and repeat frying process with remaining artichokes. Return oil to 365°F for each artichoke.

*Make salsa verde:*
Whisk together lemon juice, anchovy paste, and oil. Stir in shallot, capers, and parsley and season with salt and pepper.

Serve artichokes hot, warm, or at room temperature with sauce.

PHOTO ON PAGE 33

## PEPPERY BEEF KEBABS WITH BRAISED PEARL ONIONS

**Makes 60 hors d'oeuvres**
Active time: 2 hr   Start to finish: 2¾ hr

60 small white pearl onions (1 lb)
1 tablespoon unsalted butter
1 tablespoon coarsely ground black pepper
1 teaspoon finely chopped fresh rosemary
1 tablespoon minced garlic
2 teaspoons kosher salt
1½ lb (½-inch-thick) boneless sirloin steaks, trimmed of excess fat
20 (4-inch-long) rosemary branches, stripped of all but 1½ inches of top leaves and bottoms cut diagonally to a point
40 (6-inch) bamboo skewers, soaked in water 1 hour

Blanch onions in a large pot of boiling water 1 minute and drain, then cool under cold running water. Trim root ends and peel. Cook onions in butter in a 10-inch heavy skillet over moderate heat, stirring, 3 minutes (onions will not brown). Add salt and regular-grind pepper to taste and enough water to just cover onions and boil, partially covered, stirring occasionally, until onions are tender but not falling apart, about 15 minutes. Transfer onions to a bowl with a slotted spoon and if necessary boil juices until reduced to about ¼ cup. Toss onions with juices.

Combine coarsely ground pepper, chopped rosemary, garlic, and salt, then rub into both sides of steak. Cut meat into ¾-inch cubes.

Put 1 onion, then 1 steak cube (thread through unpeppered sides) on each rosemary branch or skewer to make 60 kebabs.

Preheat broiler.

Arrange some of kebabs in a row, a peppered side facing up, along 1 long side of oiled rack of a broiler pan so that leaf ends of rosemary branches and blunt ends of skewers point toward middle of pan. Cover exposed skewer or branch ends with a sheet of foil (don't cover beef or onions). Arrange another row of kebabs over foil, covering exposed ends in same manner. Continue adding rows of kebabs and layers of foil until pan is full, making sure exposed ends of last row of branches or skewers are covered with foil. (To broil kebabs in batches, keep remaining kebabs on a tray, covered with plastic wrap and chilled.)

Broil kebabs 2 inches from heat until beef is seared on 1 side but still medium-rare, 2 to 3 minutes. Serve immediately.

Cooks' notes:
· Onions may be braised 2 days ahead and chilled, with juices, in a sealed bag.
· You can chill raw kebabs, covered, on broiler pan or a tray 4 hours.
· Although all kebabs will fit on 1 broiler pan, you may prefer to broil kebabs in batches so they are not all ready at once.

PHOTO ON PAGE 75

## SWEET CORN FLANS WITH TOMATO-CORN RELISH

*Serves 4*
Active time: 40 min   Start to finish: 3½ hr

*For flans*
3 ears fresh corn, shucked
⅔ cup 1% milk
2 large eggs
½ teaspoon salt
⅛ teaspoon cayenne
*For relish*
¾ cup corn reserved from flans
6 oz grape or cherry tomatoes, cut into
    small dice (¾ cup)
⅓ cup chopped red onion
1 tablespoon chopped fresh basil
2 teaspoons extra-virgin olive oil
1 teaspoon red-wine vinegar

*Special equipment:* 4 (4- to 6-oz) ramekins

*Make flans:*
Preheat oven to 350°F.

Cook corn in a pot of boiling water until tender, about 5 minutes. Drain and cool.

Cut off kernels with a sharp knife into a bowl, scraping ears. Reserve ¾ cup for relish and purée remainder in a blender with milk until smooth. Force purée through a fine sieve into a bowl, discarding skins.

Whisk together eggs, salt, and cayenne, then whisk in corn purée. Pour into lightly oiled ramekins and bake in a hot-water bath just until set, about 40 minutes. Remove ramekins from water bath and cool on a rack. Chill until cold, about 2 hours.

*Make relish:*
Stir together corn, tomatoes, onion, and basil. Stir in oil and vinegar and season with salt and pepper.

Run a thin knife around edge of each flan, then invert onto plates. Spoon relish over them.

Cooks' note:
· Flans and reserved corn for relish may be chilled, covered, up to 1 day.

each serving about 146 calories and 6 grams fat

## SPICED PISTACHIOS

**Makes 2 cups**
Active time: 15 min   Start to finish: 15 min

*These pistachios make an unusual but addictive cocktail snack. The recipe was inspired by some versions we tried at Restaurant Sent Soví, in Saratoga, California.*

¼ cup sugar
½ teaspoon salt
1 tablespoon curry powder
2 teaspoons ground coriander
½ teaspoon ground cumin
⅛ teaspoon ground cinnamon
⅛ teaspoon ground ginger
2 cups unsalted shelled pistachios
2 tablespoons olive oil

Line a shallow baking pan with wax paper or parchment paper. Stir together sugar, salt, and spices in a small bowl.

Cook pistachios in oil in a 12-inch nonstick skillet over moderate heat, stirring occasionally, until a shade darker, about 5 minutes. Stir sugar mixture into nuts and cook over moderate heat, stirring constantly, until sugar begins to melt and coats nuts evenly, 2 to 3 minutes. Immediately transfer nuts to baking pan and cool.

## ALASKA KING CRAB "NACHOS"

**Makes 24 hors d'oeuvres**
Active time: 30 min   Start to finish: 40 min

24 won ton wrappers (sources on page 264)
1 tablespoon vegetable oil
*For filling*
1 ripe California avocado
1½ tablespoons finely chopped shallot
2 tablespoons fresh lime juice
½ to ¾ teaspoon *wasabi* paste (sources on
   page 264)
¾ lb cooked Alaska king crab leg in shell (1 leg),
   thawed if frozen and split lengthwise

*Special equipment:* 2 mini-muffin pans

*Make won ton cups:*
Preheat oven to 375°F.

Stack 12 won ton wrappers together and trim stack into a 3-inch square. Repeat with remaining won tons. Transfer 1 won ton to an oiled work surface and brush top lightly with some oil. Top with another won ton and brush lightly with oil. Repeat with remaining won tons (this way both sides become lightly oiled).

Put 1 won ton into cup of a muffin pan, pressing it gently into bottom and side to form a cup. Repeat with remaining won tons and sprinkle with salt to taste.

Bake won ton cups in middle of oven until crisp and golden brown, 7 to 10 minutes. Transfer won ton cups to racks to cool (they will continue to crisp).
*Make filling:*
Scoop flesh from avocado and mash coarsely with a fork. Stir in shallot, 1 tablespoon lime juice, and *wasabi* to taste. Season with salt and pepper.

Remove crab meat from shell and cut into ½-inch cubes. Toss crab with remaining tablespoon lime juice and salt to taste. Spoon guacamole into won ton cups and top with crab.

Cooks' notes:
· **Won ton cups can be made 2 days ahead and kept in an airtight container at cool room temperature.**
· **Guacamole may be made 4 hours ahead. Chill and cover surface with plastic wrap.**

PHOTO ON PAGE 41

## HONEY-ROASTED PEPPERED PECANS

**Serves 6**
Active time: 10 min   Start to finish: 30 min

¼ cup honey
2 teaspoons black pepper
1 teaspoon salt
¼ teaspoon ground allspice
8 oz pecan halves (2 cups)
2 tablespoons sugar

Preheat oven to 350°F.

Stir together honey, pepper, salt, and allspice, then add pecans, tossing to coat well. Spread pecans in 1 layer in a shallow (1-inch-deep) baking pan and sprinkle with sugar. Bake in middle of oven 15 minutes, then stir pecans and bake 5 minutes more. Transfer to a sheet of wax or parchment paper to cool and, working quickly, separate pecans with a fork while still warm. Serve at room temperature.

## FETA AND RED BELL PEPPER PIZZA

*Serves 8*
Active time: 15 min   Start to finish: 40 min

1 lb fresh or thawed frozen pizza dough
All-purpose flour for dusting
2 garlic cloves, finely chopped
4 tablespoons extra-virgin olive oil
2 red bell peppers, cut into short, thin strips
5 oz feta, coarsely crumbled
2 tablespoons finely chopped fresh oregano

*Prepare grill:*

Open vents in lid and bottom of a kettle grill and put 25 briquets on each of 2 opposite sides of bottom, leaving middle clear. Oil rack and position it with flaps over briquets (for adding more briquets), 5 to 6 inches above them. Light briquets. (They're ready when grayish white, 20 to 30 minutes.)

*Shape pizza dough while grill heats:*

Halve dough and form each half into a disk. Dust dough and your hands with flour. Holding 1 edge of 1 piece of dough in the air with both hands and letting bottom touch work surface, move hands around edge (like turning a steering wheel), allowing weight of dough to stretch round to roughly 6 inches. Flour your fists and with them stretch dough from center of underside, turning dough to maintain a rough circle, until about 10 inches in diameter.

Put round on a lightly floured foil-lined baking sheet, then lightly flour top of dough and cover with another sheet of foil. Repeat shaping with remaining piece of dough and stack on top of first round, lightly flouring and covering with foil.

*Make pizzas:*

Stir garlic into oil. Discard foil from top crust and lightly brush with 1 tablespoon garlic oil.

Holding foil underneath, flip crust, oiled side down, onto rack of grill. Repeat with remaining crust. Cover grill and cook until undersides of crusts are golden brown, about 4 minutes.

Flip crusts with 2 metal spatulas, then brush each with 1 tablespoon garlic oil and sprinkle with bell peppers, feta, oregano, and salt and pepper to taste. Cover grill and cook 5 to 7 minutes more, or until undersides are golden brown and cheese is slightly melted.

PHOTO ON PAGE 49

## TRUFFLED QUAIL EGGS

*Makes 48 hors d'oeuvres*
Active time: 2 hr   Start to finish: 2 hr

50 g (1½ oz) fresh or preserved black
    winter truffles
¼ cup hazelnut oil
1 tablespoon fresh lemon juice
24 quail eggs
1 tablespoon finely chopped fresh chives

*Garnish:* finely chopped fresh chives
*Special equipment:* a ¾-inch round cutter
    (sources on page 264) and a pastry bag
    fitted with a ¼-inch plain tip

Very thinly slice truffles with a truffle slicer or other small manual slicer or with a sharp thin knife. Cut out 48 circles from slices with round cutter. Mince enough scraps to measure 1 tablespoon and reserve with 2 teaspoons juice from jar if using preserved truffles.

Whisk oil into lemon juice in a small bowl and season with salt and pepper. Spoon 1½ tablespoons of vinaigrette into another small bowl and add truffle circles. Marinate truffle circles, covered and chilled, 1 hour, or until ready to use.

While truffle circles are marinating, cover quail eggs with water by 1 inch in a small saucepan. Simmer, covered, 5 minutes, then refresh under cold water to stop cooking. Peel eggs and halve lengthwise. Carefully push out yolks and mash with chives, minced truffles (and any juice if using preserved truffles), and remaining vinaigrette to create a paste. Season with salt and pepper and transfer mixture to pastry bag fitted with tip. Chill deviled yolks in bag until ready to use.

Arrange egg white halves on a platter and pipe in just enough deviled yolks to fill holes (do not mound). Cover each yolk with a truffle circle.

Cooks' notes:
· Truffles, vinaigrette, egg white halves, and deviled yolks may be prepared 1 day ahead and chilled separately. (Cover whites with plastic wrap.)
· Although best assembled right before serving, hors d'oeuvres can be chilled, covered with plastic wrap, up to 2 hours.

PHOTO ON PAGE 74

## SESAME RICE BALLS WITH RED PEPPER DIPPING SAUCE

**Makes about 40 hors d'oeuvres**
Active time: 2 hr   Start to finish: 2 hr

*For information on specialty ingredients, see sources on page 264.*

*For dipping sauce*
1 red bell pepper, coarsely chopped
¾ cup seasoned rice vinegar
2 tablespoons sugar
½ teaspoon dried hot red pepper flakes
*For rice balls*
2 cups Japanese short-grain rice
2 cups water
¼ cup seasoned rice vinegar
⅓ cup minced pickled ginger
1 tablespoon *wasabi* paste, or 1½ tablespoons
   *wasabi* powder stirred to a paste with
   2 teaspoons water
20 frozen *edamame* (soybeans in the pod), thawed
¼ cup toasted black sesame seeds

*Make dipping sauce:*
Purée bell pepper with rice vinegar and sugar in a blender until smooth. Transfer to a small heavy saucepan and stir in red pepper flakes. Simmer 5 minutes, then pour through a fine sieve into a bowl, pressing on solids.

*Make rice balls:*
Rinse rice in a bowl in several changes of cold water until water is almost clear; drain well in a large sieve. Combine rice and 2 cups water in a 3-quart heavy saucepan and let stand 10 minutes. Cover with a tight-fitting lid and bring to a boil over high heat. Cook at a rapid boil (lid will rattle and foam may drip down outside of pan) 5 minutes, or until water is absorbed. Remove from heat and let stand, covered, 10 minutes.

Transfer warm rice to a large wooden bowl and sprinkle vinegar over it, a little at a time, while gently tossing with a flat wooden paddle or spoon so vinegar is absorbed and rice cools as it is aerated. Cool to room temperature.

Stir together ginger and *wasabi* paste and remove *edamame* beans from pods.

Have ready a bowl of warm water (for dipping hands and spoon) and a double-thickness 12-inch square

of plastic wrap. Holding plastic in palm of 1 hand, put an *edamame* bean in center and invert a packed tablespoon of rice on top of bean. Gather plastic up around rice and twist tightly to form a ball (bean should still be visible). Unwrap, leaving plastic in your hand, and, going in from side opposite bean, poke a dampened finger into center of ball and fill with ¼ teaspoon ginger mixture. Close rice over mixture and twist plastic tightly to reform ball, then flatten slightly. Remove rice ball from plastic. Sprinkle sesame seeds over top and sides of rice ball, pressing lightly to adhere (do not coat bean with seeds). Transfer rice ball, bean side up, to a plate. Make more rice balls in same manner.

Serve rice balls with dipping sauce.

Cooks' notes:
· If you use fresh *edamame*, cook the pods briefly in boiling water.
· Dipping sauce may be made 1 day ahead and rice balls 4 hours ahead and chilled, covered tightly with plastic wrap.

PHOTO ON PAGE 74

## "CRACKLING" SALMON WITH TRUFFLES

**Serves 8 (first course)**
Active time: 35 min   Start to finish: 1 hr

*This salmon is wrapped in rice paper, which gets very crisp when sautéed.*

2 oz fresh or canned black truffles, very thinly
   sliced (sources on page 264)
1 (2-lb) center-cut salmon fillet, skinned and cut
   crosswise into 8 pieces
2 teaspoons fine sea salt
1 teaspoon freshly ground mixed or black
   peppercorns
8 (8-inch) rice-paper rounds (sources on page 264)
8 fresh chives, trimmed to 4 inches
3 tablespoons extra-virgin olive oil
Truffle oil to taste (sources on page 264)

Reserve 8 of the best-looking truffle slices.

Butterfly each salmon piece horizontally with a sharp knife. Arrange 1 layer of truffle slices on bottom halves and replace tops to cover truffles. Sprinkle with sea salt and pepper.

Spread a kitchen towel on a work surface and fill a large bowl with warm water. Soak 1 rice-paper round (make sure there are no holes) in water until pliable, 1 to 1½ minutes, then transfer to kitchen towel. Arrange 1 chive and 1 reserved truffle slice in center of round and top with 1 salmon piece, rounded side down. Fold rice paper over short sides of salmon, then over long sides to enclose salmon, trimming excess with scissors if necessary. (Truffle slice and chive will show through.) Transfer, seam sides down, to a tray and keep covered with plastic wrap. Wrap and cover remaining salmon in same manner.

Heat 1½ tablespoons olive oil in a 12-inch heavy skillet over moderately high heat until hot but not smoking, then sauté 4 salmon packages, seam sides up, until golden brown, about 3 minutes. Turn salmon over and reduce heat to moderate. Cook until sides of salmon are firm to the touch, 4 to 6 minutes more, then transfer with a spatula to plates. Cook remaining salmon in same manner.

Lightly brush with some truffle oil.

Cooks' note:
· Salmon may be prepared up to the point of wrapping in rice paper 4 hours ahead and chilled, covered tightly with plastic wrap.

PHOTO ON PAGE 64

### Herbed Ricotta and Roasted Poblanos on Endive

*Serves 6 (hors d'oeuvre)*
Active time: 30 min   Start to finish: 30 min

2 fresh *poblano* chiles (sources on page 264)
¾ cup whole-milk ricotta (preferably fresh)
¼ cup chopped scallion greens or chives
2 tablespoons finely chopped fresh cilantro
1 tablespoon finely chopped fresh mint
¾ teaspoon kosher salt, or to taste
2 Belgian endives, trimmed and leaves separated

*Garnish:* thinly sliced radishes and fresh cilantro

Lay chiles on their sides on rack of a gas burner and turn flame on high. (Or put chiles on rack of broiler pan about 2 inches from heat.) Roast chiles, turning with tongs, until skins are blackened, 5 to 8 minutes. Transfer chiles to a bowl and let stand, covered, 15 minutes.

While chiles stand, stir together ricotta, scallions, cilantro, mint, and salt.

Rub skins off chiles with paper towels and discard stems and seeds (if desired, devein to further reduce heat). Finely chop chiles and stir into ricotta mixture. Spoon some of mixture onto base of each endive leaf.

Cooks' note:
· Ricotta mixture can be made 4 hours ahead and chilled, covered.

PHOTO ON PAGE 71

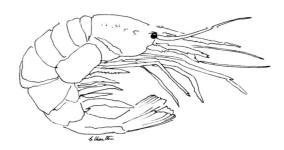

### Mexican Shrimp Cocktail

*Serves 4*
Active time: 20 min   Start to finish: 40 min

12 large shrimp (½ lb)
2 plum tomatoes, finely diced
1 scallion, thinly sliced
1 small garlic clove, minced
1 tablespoon fresh lemon juice
1 tablespoon fresh lime juice
1 teaspoon salt
½ teaspoon black pepper
½ California avocado

*Garnish:* lime wedges

Cook shrimp in boiling salted water, stirring occasionally, until just cooked through, about 3 minutes. Drain, cool, and then shell, leaving tail shells attached if desired. Chill until cold, at least 15 minutes.

Stir together tomatoes, scallion, garlic, lemon and lime juices, salt, and pepper.

Just before serving, finely dice avocado and stir into tomato salsa. Spoon salsa into 4 serving dishes and arrange shrimp on top.

Cooks' note:
· Salsa can be made 1 hour ahead and kept at room temperature. Add avocado just before serving.

each serving about 109 calories and 5 grams fat

## SHRIMP SATÉS WITH SPICED PISTACHIO CHUTNEY

### Makes about 65 hors d'oeuvres
Active time: 45 min   Start to finish: 2 hr

2½ lb shrimp (65), shelled and
    deveined
1 tablespoon minced garlic
3 tablespoons olive oil
2 tablespoons fresh lime juice
*For chutney*
1 (16-oz) container plain yogurt
2 teaspoons ground coriander
1 teaspoon ground cumin
1 tablespoon olive oil
4 fresh jalapeño chiles, 3 with seeds and ribs
    removed
2 cups fresh cilantro sprigs
2 tablespoons fresh lime juice
1 cup shelled natural pistachios, toasted and
    finely ground

*Special equipment:* about 65 (6- to 8-inch)
    bamboo skewers

*Marinate shrimp:*
Butterfly shrimp by cutting almost, but not all the
way, through backs. Toss with garlic, oil, lime juice,
and salt to taste. Marinate, chilled, 1 hour.

*Make chutney:*
Drain yogurt in a fine-mesh sieve set over a bowl,
chilled, 1 hour. Cook coriander and cumin in oil in a
small skillet over moderate heat, stirring occasionally,
until fragrant. Coarsely chop chiles, then purée in a
blender with drained yogurt, coriander mixture, and
cilantro until smooth. Stir in lime juice, pistachios, and
salt to taste.

*Make satés:*
Preheat broiler.

Gently press 1 shrimp open and thread lengthwise
onto a skewer near pointed end. Repeat with remaining
shrimp and skewers.

Arrange *satés* in a row on 1 long side of a broiler
pan so blunt ends of skewers point toward middle of
pan. Cover exposed portions of skewers with a sheet of
foil (don't cover shrimp). Arrange another row of *satés*
over foil. Continue adding rows of *satés* and layers of
foil until pan is full, making sure exposed skewer ends

of last row of *satés* are covered with foil. Broil until
shrimp are just cooked through, 3 to 4 minutes. Serve
*satés* with chutney for dipping.

Cooks' note:
· You can marinate shrimp and make chutney 1 day ahead
  and chill, covered.

PHOTO ON PAGE 36

## HUNDRED-CORNER SHRIMP BALLS

### Makes 80 hors d'oeuvres (serving 20)
Active time: 1 hr   Start to finish: 1 hr

*This hors d'oeuvre is adapted from a recipe by Chinese
cooking authority Nina Simonds.*

1½ lb large shrimp (30), peeled and deveined
1 (8-oz) can water chestnuts (1 cup), rinsed and
    finely chopped
1 large egg white, lightly beaten
3 tablespoons finely chopped chilled fresh
    pork fat or lard
1½ tablespoons Chinese rice wine or Scotch
1 tablespoon grated peeled fresh ginger
2 tablespoons finely chopped scallion greens
2¼ teaspoons kosher salt
2 tablespoons cornstarch
3 cups *panko* (Japanese bread crumbs;
    sources on page 264)
About 8 cups vegetable oil

*Accompaniment:* apricot dipping sauce
    (recipe follows)

Pulse shrimp in a food processor until finely chopped. Transfer to a large bowl, then stir in water chestnuts,
egg white, pork fat, rice wine, ginger, scallions, salt, and
cornstarch. Beat shrimp mixture vigorously with a
wooden spoon and throw it against side of bowl until
combined well and compacted. Wet your hands with
cold water and form teaspoons of shrimp mixture into
balls, arranging in 1 layer on a wax-paper-lined tray.
Coat balls, 1 at a time, in *panko*, then arrange in 1 layer
on another wax-paper-lined tray.

Preheat oven to 425°F.

Heat oil in a 5-quart heavy pot until a deep-fat thermometer registers 375°F, then fry balls in 4 batches,
turning, 1 to 1½ minutes, or until golden and just

cooked through. (Return oil to 375°F between batches.) Transfer with a slotted spoon to paper towels to drain. When all shrimp balls are fried, reheat on a rack set in a shallow baking pan in middle of oven until just hot, about 2 minutes.

Cooks' note:
• Shrimp balls may be coated and fried 1 day ahead, cooled completely, then chilled, covered. Bring to room temperature before reheating.

PHOTO ON PAGE 17

## APRICOT DIPPING SAUCE

**Makes about 2 cups**
Active time: 7 min   Start to finish: 7 min

1¾ cups apricot jam
2 tablespoons soy sauce, or to taste
3 tablespoons finely chopped scallion greens
1 tablespoon fresh lime juice, or to taste
Dash of Tabasco, or to taste

Melt jam in a small saucepan. Stir in remaining ingredients and salt and pepper to taste and serve warm.

Cooks' note:
• Sauce may be made 2 days ahead, cooled, then chilled, covered. Reheat sauce over low heat, stirring.

## SESAME TEMPURA GREEN BEANS WITH SOY DIPPING SAUCE

**Serves 6**
Active time: 20 min   Start to finish: 20 min

About 4 cups vegetable oil
2 tablespoons soy sauce
2 teaspoons fresh lime juice
1 teaspoon superfine granulated sugar
1 cup all-purpose flour
¼ cup sesame seeds
1 cup beer (not dark)
¾ lb green beans, trimmed

Heat 2 inches oil in a 4-quart heavy pot over moderate heat until a deep-fat thermometer registers 365°F.

While oil is heating, make dipping sauce by stirring together soy sauce, lime juice, and sugar until sugar is dissolved.

Whisk together flour and sesame seeds and whisk in beer until batter is smooth.

Toss about 10 beans in batter until coated. Add to oil 1 at a time (to keep separate) and fry, turning, until golden, about 1½ minutes. Transfer with tongs to paper towels to drain and sprinkle with salt to taste. Coat and fry remaining beans in same manner.

Serve beans with dipping sauce.

CANAPÉS

## ARTICHOKE BRUSCHETTA

**Serves 6**
Active time: 30 min   Start to finish: 30 min

*Though these bruschetta are a terrific first course for almost any meal, they'd make a great lunch as well—just think of them as open-faced sandwiches.*

6 (⅓-inch-thick) slices from a round country loaf
6 tablespoons extra-virgin olive oil
2 (6½-oz) jars marinated artichoke hearts, drained
1 (2-oz) piece prosciutto or ham
1 small red onion, chopped
1 (10-oz) package frozen peas, thawed
2 scallions (greens only), coarsely chopped
3 tablespoons chopped fresh mint
¼ cup parmesan shavings

Preheat broiler.

Arrange bread in 1 layer on a baking sheet, then brush tops with 2 tablespoons oil and season with salt and pepper. Broil until golden and transfer to a rack.

Cut artichokes lengthwise into ¼-inch-thick slices and cut prosciutto into matchsticks. Cook artichokes and prosciutto in 3 tablespoons oil in a 10-inch heavy skillet over moderately high heat, stirring, until artichokes are golden, about 4 minutes. Add onion and cook, stirring, until softened. Add peas and cook, stirring, until tender, about 2 minutes. Stir in scallions, mint, and salt and pepper to taste.

Spoon mixture over toasts. Drizzle with remaining tablespoon oil and top with parmesan.

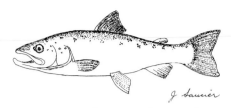

## BRANDADE ON POPPY SEED CRACKERS

**Makes about 60 hors d'oeuvres**
Active time: 1½ hr   Start to finish: 25½ hr

¼ lb choice-grade skinless boneless salt cod
1 large russet (baking) potato
½ cup heavy cream
3 large garlic cloves, thinly sliced
1 bay leaf (not California)
1 fresh thyme sprig
1 whole clove
2 tablespoons extra-virgin olive oil
Poppy seed crackers (recipe follows)

*Garnish:* celery leaves

Rinse salt cod well to remove external salt. Cover with cold water by 2 inches in a bowl and soak, chilled, changing water 3 times, about 24 hours.

Peel potato and cut into 1-inch pieces. Put in a 2-quart saucepan with salted water to cover by 1 inch. Bring to a boil and simmer potato until very tender, about 15 minutes. (Do not drain until ready to whip.)

While potato is cooking, bring cream to a simmer with garlic, bay leaf, thyme, and clove in a very small heavy saucepan, then simmer gently, partially covered, until garlic is tender, about 15 minutes. Discard bay leaf, thyme, and clove and purée garlic with cream in a blender until smooth.

Meanwhile, drain salt cod and transfer to another 2-quart saucepan with water to cover. Bring just to a simmer and remove from heat. (Cod will just flake; do not boil or it will become tough.)

Drain cod and potatoes in a colander and, while still warm, combine in a large bowl with cream mixture. Beat with an electric mixer at low speed until combined well. Add oil in a slow stream, beating, and season with salt and white pepper.

Top crackers with warm *brandade* and serve.

**Cooks' note:**
- *Brandade* keeps, covered and chilled, 1 week. Before serving, reheat *brandade*, covered, in a 350°F oven, stirring once or twice, until heated through, about 20 minutes.

## POPPY SEED CRACKERS

**Makes about 60 crackers**
Active time: 30 min   Start to finish: 1 hr

1 large egg
2 tablespoons cold water
1 teaspoon salt
8 (6- to 7-inch) flour tortillas
½ cup poppy seeds (2.6-oz jar)

*Special equipment:* a 2-inch star cookie cutter

Preheat oven to 350°F.

Stir together egg, water, and salt. Brush each tortilla on 1 side with egg wash, then, holding over a bowl, sprinkle with poppy seeds to cover completely.

Cut out 7 or 8 stars from each coated tortilla (you'll have to press hard; use a pot holder to protect your hands), transferring to 2 baking sheets, seeded sides up. Bake, 1 sheet at a time, in middle of oven until crisp, about 15 minutes. Cool crackers on a rack.

**Cooks' note:**
- Crackers keep, layered between wax paper, in an airtight container 3 days.

## CAVIAR MOONS

**Makes 40 hors d'oeuvres**
Active time: 30 min   Start to finish: 30 min

10 very thin slices firm white sandwich bread
2 tablespoons unsalted butter, melted
½ cup sour cream
100 g (3½ oz) caviar (preferably osetra)

*Special equipment:* a 2-inch crescent-moon cookie
  cutter

Preheat oven to 350°F.

Brush white bread with melted butter and cut out 40 moons. Arrange, buttered sides up, on a large baking sheet and bake in middle of oven until pale golden, about 10 minutes. Cool completely.

Serve toasts topped with sour cream and caviar.

**Cooks' note:**
- Toasts may be made 1 day ahead and kept in an airtight container at room temperature.

PHOTO ON PAGE 75

## SCALLOP CEVICHE ON BLACK PASTA CAKES WITH CILANTRO SALSA

**_Makes 48 hors d'oeuvres_**
Active time: 1½ hr   Start to finish: 5 hr

*For ceviche*
½ cup thinly sliced white onion
1 cup fresh orange juice
1 cup fresh lime juice
1 fresh jalapeño chile, sliced, including seeds
2 tablespoons kosher salt
24 medium sea scallops (1¼ lb), tough muscles
   removed from sides if necessary and scallops
   halved horizontally
*For pasta cakes*
6 oz black (squid ink) angel's hair pasta
1 teaspoon extra-virgin olive oil
About 1 cup olive or vegetable oil
*For cilantro salsa*
½ cup minced white onion
½ cup chopped fresh cilantro
½ cup finely chopped fresh tomatillos
½ cup finely chopped tomato
1 tablespoon minced fresh jalapeño chile,
   including seeds
1 teaspoon kosher salt

*Make ceviche:*

Combine onion, juices, jalapeño, and salt in a bowl.
Poach scallops in 4 quarts of simmering salted water, stirring occasionally, until just cooked through (scallops should be opaque with centers slightly pink), about 1 minute. Drain and gently toss with marinade. Marinate scallops, covered and chilled, 3 hours.

*Make pasta cakes:*

Boil pasta in a large pot of boiling salted water until just cooked through, 1 to 2 minutes. Reserve 1 cup cooking water, then drain pasta in a colander. Rinse briefly under cold running water to stop cooking (don't cool pasta completely) and drain well. Toss pasta with extra-virgin olive oil.

Heat ¼ inch olive or vegetable oil in a 10-inch non-stick skillet over moderate heat until hot but not smoking. Form cakes by dropping a few strands of loosely squiggled pasta into a 1-tablespoon measure to fill it and inverting tablespoon into oil, flattening cake slightly if necessary. (If strands in bowl become too sticky to handle, stir in a little reserved pasta water, 1

teaspoon at a time. You need some starch from pasta to hold cake together, but you don't want strands to become wet.) Cook cakes, 4 at a time, until crisp, 45 seconds to 1 minute per side, and drain on paper towels. Season cakes with salt.

*Make salsa:*

Soak onion in cold water to cover 20 minutes, then drain and rinse well. Stir together onion, cilantro, tomatillos, tomato, jalapeño, and salt and chill, covered, until ready to use.

*Assemble hors d'oeuvres:*

Lift scallops out of marinade and put 1 on top of each pasta cake. Top with salsa and serve immediately.

**Cooks' notes:**
· **Pasta cakes may be made 1 day ahead and kept between sheets of wax paper in an airtight container at room temperature.**
· ***Ceviche* can be made 1 day ahead and chilled, covered.**
· **Salsa is best when made no more than 2 hours before serving.**

PHOTO ON PAGE 75

## TAPENADE ON JÍCAMA STARS

**_Makes about 45 hors d'oeuvres_**
Active time: 1 hr   Start to finish: 1 hr

2 lb *jícama* (1 large or 2 medium), peeled
2 tablespoons fresh lemon juice
About 45 small fresh flat-leaf parsley leaves
½ cup *tapenade* or other olive paste (4-oz jar)

*Special equipment:* a 2-inch star cookie cutter

Cut *jícama* crosswise into 1-inch-thick slices (make slices thinner if your cookie cutter is shallow). Lay 1 slice flat and cut out as many star-shaped chunks as possible. Cut chunks into ⅛-inch-thick stars using a *mandoline* or other manual slicer or a sharp thin knife.

Sprinkle stars with lemon juice and arrange a parsley leaf on each. Drop ¼ teaspoon *tapenade* onto center of each star, partially covering leaf.

**Cooks' note:**
· **You can cut *jícama* stars 1 day ahead and chill, tossed with lemon juice, in a sealable plastic bag.**

PHOTO ON PAGE 75

## CURRIED CHICKEN LIVER PÂTÉ

*Makes about 3½ cups*
Active time: 30 min   Start to finish: 3½ hr

1 onion, thinly sliced
2¼ sticks unsalted butter, cut into 1-tablespoon
   pieces
1 lb chicken livers, trimmed and rinsed
2 teaspoons curry powder
2 teaspoons paprika
1¼ teaspoons salt, or to taste
½ teaspoon black pepper
3 tablespoons brandy

*Accompaniment:* baguette slices oven-toasted
   with olive oil, salt, and pepper

Cook onion in 4 tablespoons butter in a large heavy skillet over moderate heat, stirring, until softened. Stir in livers, curry powder, paprika, salt, and pepper and cook, covered, over moderately low heat, stirring occasionally, until livers are barely pink inside, about 10 minutes. Remove from heat and add brandy.

Purée warm mixture in a food processor with remaining butter until smooth. Pour into a 3½-cup terrine and cover surface with plastic wrap. Chill until firm, at least 3 hours.

Cooks' note:
· **Pâté is best the day after it's made and keeps, covered and chilled, 1 week.**

## HERBED LIMA BEAN HUMMUS

*Makes about 4 cups*
Active time: 25 min   Start to finish: 1 hr

*This dip was inspired by a recipe for bissara, a garlicky purée from Egypt made from dried broad beans, in Claudia Roden's* Mediterranean Cookery.

2 (10-oz) packages frozen baby lima beans
1 large onion, chopped
5 garlic cloves, smashed with side of a large knife
1 teaspoon salt

2 cups water
¼ cup chopped fresh cilantro
¼ cup chopped fresh flat-leaf parsley
1 teaspoon ground cumin
¼ teaspoon cayenne, or to taste
3 to 4 tablespoons fresh lemon juice
5 tablespoons extra-virgin olive oil
2 tablespoons chopped fresh dill
2 tablespoons chopped fresh mint

*Accompaniment:* sesame won ton crisps (recipe
   follows) or toasted pita wedges

Simmer beans, onion, garlic, salt, and water in a 3-quart saucepan, covered, until beans are tender, about 8 minutes. Stir in cilantro and parsley and let stand, uncovered, 5 minutes.

Drain bean mixture in a sieve and transfer to a food processor. Add cumin, cayenne, 3 tablespoons lemon juice, 4 tablespoons oil, dill, and mint and purée until smooth. Transfer to a bowl and cool to room temperature, stirring occasionally. Stir in salt, pepper, and lemon juice to taste.

Serve drizzled with remaining tablespoon oil.

Cooks' note:
· **Dip keeps, covered and chilled, 3 days.**

PHOTO ON PAGE 17

## SESAME WON TON CRISPS

*Makes 40 crisps*
Active time: 30 min   Start to finish: 30 min

1 cup sesame seeds, toasted
1 tablespoon kosher salt
1 teaspoon sugar
½ teaspoon cayenne
5 tablespoons water
2 tablespoons cornstarch
5 cups vegetable oil
40 won ton wrappers (sources on page 264)

Stir together seeds, salt, sugar, and cayenne in a small bowl. Stir together water and cornstarch in another bowl.

Heat oil in a 5-quart heavy pot over moderate heat until a deep-fat thermometer registers 360°F. Brush 1 side of 2 wrappers with cornstarch mixture and sprinkle with seed mixture. Shake off any excess seeds and drop wrappers into oil, seeded sides down. Fry, turning over once with tongs, until golden, about 10 seconds total. (Some seeds will fall off during frying.) Transfer crisps to paper towels to drain, then make more, 2 at a time, in same manner.

Cooks' note:
• You can make crisps 3 days ahead and keep in an airtight container at room temperature.

PHOTO ON PAGE 17

## CRAB AND COCONUT DIP WITH PLANTAIN CHIPS

*Serves 6*
Active time: 20 min   Start to finish: 20 min

⅓ cup well-stirred unsweetened canned coconut milk
3 scallions, chopped
1 teaspoon chopped fresh jalapeño chile, including seeds
½ cup chopped fresh cilantro
½ cup mayonnaise
3 tablespoons fresh lime juice, or to taste
1 lb jumbo lump crab meat, picked over and coarsely shredded

*Accompaniment:* plantain chips (recipe follows)

Blend coconut milk, scallions, jalapeño, and ¼ cup cilantro in a blender until smooth and pour into a bowl. Whisk in mayonnaise, lime juice, and remaining ¼ cup cilantro until just combined. Stir in crab and salt to taste and serve spooned on plantain chips.

Cooks' note:
• Dip can be made 6 hours ahead and chilled, covered. Stir before serving.

PHOTO ON PAGE 30

## PLANTAIN CHIPS

*Serves 6*
Active time: 30 min   Start to finish: 30 min

1½ teaspoons finely grated fresh lime zest, chopped
1½ teaspoons salt
¼ teaspoon cayenne
6 cups vegetable oil
4 green plantains (1½ lb)

Stir together zest, salt, and cayenne.

Heat oil in a 5-quart heavy pot over moderate heat until a deep-fat thermometer registers 375°F. While oil is heating, cut ends from plantains and score skin of each plantain 5 times lengthwise, avoiding ridges. Soak in hot tap water 5 minutes and peel. Cut plantains lengthwise with a U-shaped peeler or manual slicer into very thin strips (about ¹⁄₁₆ inch thick). Fry strips 6 at a time, turning frequently, until golden, 30 to 45 seconds. Transfer with tongs to paper towels and sprinkle crisps immediately with salt mixture.

Cooks' note:
• You can make plantain crisps 2 days ahead and keep in an airtight container at room temperature.

## CHARRED TOMATILLO GUACAMOLE

**Makes about 3½ cups**
Active time: 30 min   Start to finish: 30 min

6 oz tomatillos (6 or 7), husked and rinsed
½ small red onion, finely chopped
3 to 4 fresh *serrano* chiles, seeded (optional)
   and finely chopped
½ cup finely chopped fresh cilantro
1 teaspoon salt
½ teaspoon black pepper
2 large California avocados (1 lb total)

*Accompaniments:* chili-lime tortilla triangles and
   seeded tortilla triangles (recipes follow)

Preheat broiler.

Broil tomatillos in a flameproof shallow baking pan about 4 inches from heat until tops are charred, 7 to 10 minutes. Turn tomatillos over with tongs and broil until charred, about 5 minutes more.

Combine onion, chiles, cilantro, salt, and pepper in a large bowl. Add tomatillos 2 at a time, mashing with a fork or pestle to form a coarse paste.

Pit and peel avocados. Add avocados to mixture and continue mashing until incorporated but still chunky.

Cooks' notes:
- Seed about half of chiles for moderately spicy guacamole, all of them for mild.
- Guacamole may be made 8 hours ahead and chilled, covered. Bring to room temperature before serving.

PHOTO ON PAGE 55

## CHILI-LIME TORTILLA TRIANGLES

**Makes about 32 triangles**
Active time: 15 min   Start to finish: 40 min

1½ teaspoons paprika
1 teaspoon Mexican *achiote* (annatto) paste
   (sources on page 264)
¼ teaspoon cayenne
1 teaspoon salt
3 tablespoons fresh lime juice

⅓ cup vegetable oil
4 (10- to 12-inch) flour tortillas

Preheat oven to 350°F.

Stir together paprika, *achiote*, cayenne, salt, lime juice, and oil. Put 1 tortilla on each of 2 baking sheets and brush with oil mixture. Cut each tortilla into long thin triangles with a sharp knife.

Bake in upper and lower thirds of oven, switching position of sheets halfway through baking, until crisp and lightly golden, 15 to 20 minutes total. Transfer to racks to cool. Repeat with remaining 2 tortillas.

Cooks' note:
- Triangles may be made 1 day ahead and kept in an airtight container at room temperature.

PHOTO ON PAGE 55

## SEEDED TORTILLA TRIANGLES

**Makes about 32 triangles**
Active time: 15 min   Start to finish: 40 min

¼ cup flax seeds (sources on page 264)
¼ cup sesame seeds
¼ cup poppy seeds
4 (10- to 12-inch) flour tortillas
1 large egg beaten with 2 tablespoons cold water
   and 1 teaspoon salt

Preheat oven to 350°F.

Stir together flax, sesame, and poppy seeds. Put 1 tortilla on each of 2 baking sheets and brush with some egg mixture. Sprinkle with seeds to coat, then cut each tortilla into long thin triangles with a sharp knife.

Bake in upper and lower thirds of oven, switching position of sheets halfway through baking, until crisp and lightly golden, 15 to 20 minutes total. Transfer to racks to cool. Repeat with remaining 2 tortillas.

Cooks' note:
- Triangles may be made 1 day ahead and kept in an airtight container at room temperature. If triangles lose crispness, recrisp in a 350°F oven about 5 minutes.

PHOTO ON PAGE 55

## GRILLED HERBED GARLIC BREAD

**Serves 8**
Active time: 15 min   Start to finish: 20 min

2 sticks (1 cup) unsalted butter, cut into pieces
4 garlic cloves, minced
1 tablespoon kosher salt
½ cup finely chopped fresh flat-leaf parsley
2 large round loaves of crusty bread,
     halved horizontally

Prepare grill for cooking.

Heat butter with garlic and salt over moderate heat, stirring, until melted. Transfer to a bowl and cool. Stir in parsley and pepper to taste.

Brush cut sides of bread with half of garlic butter. Grill bread, cut sides down, 5 to 6 inches over glowing coals 2 minutes. Turn bread over and brush with remaining garlic butter. Grill until golden brown, 2 to 3 minutes more.

PHOTO ON PAGE 49

## SEEDED BREADSTICKS

**Makes 16 breadsticks**
Active time: 45 min   Start to finish: 2¼ hr

¾ cup 1% milk, warmed (105–115°F)
1 tablespoon olive oil
1 teaspoon sugar
1 teaspoon active dry yeast (from one
     ¼-oz package)
1 cup whole-wheat flour
1 cup all-purpose flour plus additional
¾ teaspoon salt
Cornmeal for sprinkling
1 large egg white, lightly beaten
1 tablespoon nigella (black onion) seeds (sources
     on page 264) or mixed white and black sesame
     seeds
Kosher salt for sprinkling

Stir together milk, oil, sugar, and yeast in a large bowl until blended. Let stand until foamy, about 5 minutes. Stir in both flours (except additional all-purpose flour) and salt.

Turn dough out onto a floured work surface and knead until smooth and elastic, 8 to 10 minutes, adding just enough additional all-purpose flour to keep dough from sticking.

Transfer dough to a lightly oiled bowl and turn to coat. Cover bowl with plastic wrap and let dough rise in a warm place until doubled in bulk, about 1 hour.

Punch down dough and turn out onto work surface. Cut dough into 16 equal pieces and roll each into a 15- to 16-inch rope. Arrange ropes 1 inch apart on 2 greased baking sheets sprinkled with cornmeal and let stand, uncovered, 15 minutes.

Preheat oven to 400°F.

Brush breadsticks with egg white and sprinkle with seeds and kosher salt, pressing to adhere. Bake in upper and lower thirds of oven, switching position of sheets halfway through baking, until golden brown, about 20 minutes total. Transfer to racks to cool.

**Cooks' note:**
• **Baked breadsticks may be frozen, in sealable plastic bags, 1 week. Reheat in a 350°F oven until crisp.**

each serving (2 breadsticks) about 156 calories and 2 grams fat

## BLACK PEPPER CORNMEAL CRISPS

**Makes about 30 wafers**
Active time: 40 min   Start to finish: 1½ hr

¾ cup all-purpose flour
¼ cup yellow cornmeal
1 tablespoon sugar
1 teaspoon baking powder
1 teaspoon salt
½ stick (¼ cup) unsalted butter, softened
1 large egg at room temperature
1 cup whole milk at room temperature
¾ teaspoon coarsely ground black pepper

*Special equipment:* 2 nonstick baking sheets or pans

Preheat oven to 350°F.

Sift together flour, cornmeal, sugar, baking powder, and salt. Mix together butter and egg in a blender. Add whole milk, pepper, and flour mixture and blend just until smooth.

Drop 6 scant tablespoons batter about 5 inches apart onto a buttered baking sheet. Spread each dollop of batter with back of a spoon into a 5-inch round.

Bake 1 sheet of wafers in middle of oven until golden brown, 6 to 8 minutes, then transfer wafers to a rack to cool. Form 6 more wafers on second sheet while first is baking, then continue to make wafers, 1 sheet at a time. (Sheets should be cooled but not cleaned between batches.)

Cooks' notes:
• Wafers keep in an airtight container at room temperature 2 days.
• You can also make these wafers on regular baking sheets sprayed with vegetable cooking spray.

PHOTO ON PAGE 76

## SESAME FLATBREAD CRACKERS

**Serves 16**
Active time: 1 hr   Start to finish: 2 hr

3 cups all-purpose flour
2 teaspoons baking powder
2 teaspoons salt
1 stick (½ cup) unsalted butter, cut into pieces
1 cup plain yogurt
1¼ cups sesame seeds, toasted

2 large eggs
2 tablespoons sugar
1 tablespoon soy sauce

*Make dough:*

Pulse together flour, baking powder, and salt in a food processor. Add butter and pulse until mixture resembles coarse meal. (Alternatively, whisk together dry ingredients and cut in butter with a pastry blender.) Transfer to a bowl and stir in yogurt and 1 cup sesame seeds until mixture forms a dough. Quarter dough, wrapping each piece in plastic wrap. Chill 10 minutes.

Preheat oven to 350°F.

*Make glaze:*

Stir together eggs, sugar, and soy sauce with a fork until sugar is dissolved.

*Roll out dough:*

Divide 1 dough quarter into 12 equal portions and form each into a 4-inch log with your hands. With a floured rolling pin, roll out each log into a 12- to 14-inch strip on a lightly floured surface. Transfer strips to 2 greased baking sheets. Brush strips with glaze and sprinkle with one fourth of remaining sesame seeds. Make more strips in same manner.

*Bake crackers:*

Bake in upper and lower thirds of oven, switching position of sheets halfway through baking, 20 minutes total, or until glaze is golden brown and crackers are crisp. Transfer to racks to cool. Bake more crackers in same manner.

Cooks' note:
• You can make crackers 1 week ahead and keep in an airtight container at room temperature.

## GARLIC ROSEMARY FOCACCIA

**Makes a 17- by 11-inch loaf**
Active time: 40 min   Start to finish: 4¼ hr

6 large garlic cloves, halved lengthwise
⅔ cup olive oil
3 (¼-oz) packages active dry yeast
   (7½ teaspoons)
2¼ cups warm water (95°–105°F)
7 cups all-purpose flour plus additional
1 tablespoon table salt
1 tablespoon coarsely chopped fresh
   rosemary

Coarse salt for sprinkling
Black pepper for sprinkling

Preheat oven to 300°F.

Combine garlic and oil in a very small metal bowl and set on a baking sheet. Bake in lower third of oven 1 hour. Cool on a rack 30 minutes. Pour oil through a small sieve into another bowl and discard garlic.

Whisk together yeast and warm water in bowl of a standing mixer and let stand 5 minutes, or until creamy.

Stir ⅓ cup garlic oil into yeast mixture. Whisk together 7 cups flour and table salt and stir half of flour into yeast mixture. Fit mixer with dough-hook attachment. Add remaining flour and mix at low speed 3 minutes, or until dough pulls away from side of bowl, adding more flour if necessary. Knead dough with dough hook at medium-high speed, scraping down hook and side of bowl as needed, 5 minutes, or until dough is soft and slightly sticky. Transfer dough to a large oiled bowl, turning with floured hands to coat with oil. Cover bowl with plastic wrap and let dough rise in a warm place until doubled in bulk, about 1 hour.

Preheat oven to 450°F.

Oil a 17- by 11-inch baking pan with some garlic oil. Gently press dough into pan, allowing dough to rest 5 minutes if difficult to work with. Cover dough with oiled plastic wrap and let rise in a warm place until doubled in bulk, about 30 minutes.

Make indentations in dough at 1-inch intervals with oiled fingertips. Drizzle with remaining garlic oil and sprinkle with rosemary, coarse salt, and pepper. Bake in lower third of oven until deep golden on top and pale golden on bottom, 25 to 30 minutes. Transfer bread to a rack and serve warm or at room temperature.

PHOTO ON PAGE 16

## CORNMEAL-CAYENNE GRISSINI

**Makes about 50 breadsticks**
Active time: 1 hr   Start to finish: 2¾ hr

1 cup warm water (105°F–110°F)
1 (¼-oz) package active dry yeast (2½ teaspoons)
2 cups all-purpose flour
1¼ cups yellow cornmeal
½ teaspoon table salt
¼ teaspoon cayenne
¼ cup olive oil plus additional for brushing
2 tablespoons kosher salt

Stir together warm water and yeast and let stand until foamy, about 5 minutes.

Stir together flour, cornmeal, table salt, and cayenne in a large bowl, then stir in yeast mixture and oil just until a dough forms. Turn out dough onto an unfloured work surface and knead until smooth and elastic, 8 to 10 minutes. Transfer dough to an oiled bowl and turn to coat. Cover bowl with plastic wrap and let dough rise in a warm place 1 hour, or until doubled in bulk.

Preheat oven to 350°F.

Punch down dough and turn out onto unfloured work surface. Roll 2-teaspoon portions of dough into 10-inch-long sticks and arrange about ¾ inch apart on greased baking sheets. Brush sticks lightly with oil and sprinkle with kosher salt.

Bake in batches in upper and lower thirds of oven, switching position of sheets halfway through baking, until sticks are crisp and ends are golden, 22 to 25 minutes total. Transfer to racks to cool.

Cooks' note:
• Grissini keep in an airtight container at room temperature 1 week.

PHOTO ON PAGE 67

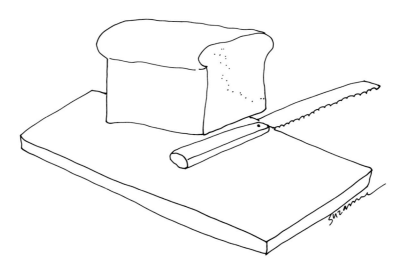

## RASPBERRY-LEMON CORN MUFFINS

*Makes 15 muffins*
Active time: 25 min   Start to finish: 35 min

1 cup all-purpose flour
1 cup yellow cornmeal
¾ cup granulated sugar
1 tablespoon baking powder
½ teaspoon salt
1½ tablespoons finely grated fresh lemon zest
1½ sticks (¾ cup) unsalted butter, melted and
    cooled
¾ cup whole milk
2 large egg yolks
1 whole large egg
1½ cups raspberries (6 oz)
2 to 3 tablespoons sanding (coarse) or
    granulated sugar

*Special equipment:* paper or foil muffin-cup liners

Preheat oven to 400°F. Line 15 (⅓-cup) muffin cups with liners, dividing evenly between 2 pans (muffins cook more evenly with empty cups among them).

Whisk together flour, cornmeal, granulated sugar, baking powder, salt, and zest in a large bowl. Whisk together butter, milk, yolks, and whole egg and stir into flour mixture until just combined.

Gently stir in raspberries and divide batter evenly among cups (each cup will be about three fourths full). Bake in middle of oven (or upper and lower thirds if necessary) 10 minutes, then sprinkle tops evenly with sanding sugar. Bake muffins until tops are golden and a tester comes out clean, about 7 minutes more. Remove muffins from pans and cool on a rack.

PHOTO ON PAGE 45

## CHEDDAR-CHIVE SCONES

*Makes 16 scones*
Active time: 25 min   Start to finish: 45 min

3 cups all-purpose flour
1 tablespoon baking powder
1 tablespoon sugar
2 teaspoons salt
½ cup finely chopped fresh chives
5 oz extra-sharp Cheddar, coarsely grated (1½ cups)
2 cups heavy cream plus additional for brushing

*Accompaniments:* sliced prosciutto and honeydew
    melon

Preheat oven to 400°F.

Whisk together flour, baking powder, sugar, and salt. Add chives and Cheddar, tossing to combine. Stir in cream with a fork until a sticky dough forms.

Turn dough out onto a lightly floured surface and knead 8 times with floured hands. Halve dough and form each half into a 7-inch round. Brush tops of rounds with additional cream and cut each into 8 wedges.

Arrange wedges about ½ inch apart on an ungreased large baking sheet and bake in middle of oven until golden brown, about 20 minutes. Cool on a rack.

PHOTO ON PAGE 45

# SOUPS

## BEET SOUP IN ROASTED ACORN SQUASH

### Serves 8 (makes about 10 cups)
Active time: 45 min  Start to finish: 1½ hr

*The roasted acorn squash tastes fabulous when scooped up with spoonfuls of the beet soup. But if oven space is limited, simply serve the soup in bowls.*

*For roasted squash*
8 (1- to 1¼-lb) acorn squash
3 tablespoons vegetable oil
1 tablespoon kosher salt
*For soup*
1 large red onion, chopped
1½ tablespoons vegetable oil
5 medium beets (2 lb without greens), peeled
    and cut into 1-inch pieces
1 red apple such as Gala or Braeburn, peeled
    and cut into 1-inch pieces
2 garlic cloves, minced
4 cups chicken or vegetable broth
4 to 5 cups water
2 tablespoons cider vinegar
1 tablespoon packed light brown sugar

*Accompaniment*: cornmeal-cayenne *grissini*
    (page 101)

*Roast squash:*
Preheat oven to 375°F.
Cut off "tops" of squash (about 1 inch from stem end) and reserve. Scoop out seeds and discard. Cut a very thin slice off bottoms of squash to create a stable base. Brush "bowls" and tops all over with oil and sprinkle salt inside. Arrange squash bowls, with tops alongside, stem ends up, in 2 large shallow baking pans.

Roast squash in upper and lower thirds of oven, switching position of pans halfway through baking, until flesh of squash is just tender, about 1¼ hours total.

*Make soup while squash roast:*
Cook onion in oil in a 5-quart heavy saucepan over moderate heat, stirring occasionally, until softened. Add beets and apple and cook, stirring occasionally, 5 minutes. Add garlic and cook, stirring, 30 seconds.

Add broth and 4 cups water, then simmer, uncovered, until beets are tender, about 40 minutes. Stir in vinegar and brown sugar.

Purée beet soup in 3 batches in a blender until very smooth, at least 1 minute per batch (use caution when blending hot liquids), transferring to a bowl. Return soup to pan, then season with salt and pepper and reheat. If soup is too thick, add enough water to thin to desired consistency.

Serve soup in squash bowls.

Cooks' notes:
· Squash flesh shrinks during baking; if a small hole forms, serve soup in squash but set in a soup bowl.
· Soup can be made 3 days ahead and chilled, covered.

PHOTO ON PAGE 67

## SPICY CUCUMBER-AVOCADO SOUP

### Serves 6
Active time: 10 min  Start to finish: 10 min

½ firm-ripe California avocado
1¾ English cucumbers (1½ lb), cut into
    ½-inch pieces
1 (8-oz) container plain low-fat yogurt
3 tablespoons chopped fresh chives
1 teaspoon fresh lime juice
1 teaspoon salt, or to taste
½ teaspoon chopped fresh jalapeño chile
    with seeds
1 cup small ice cubes

*Garnish:* diced avocado and chopped chives

Peel and pit avocado. Blend all ingredients in a blender until very smooth, about 1 minute.

each serving about 81 calories and 1 gram fat

PHOTO ON PAGE 81

## HARIRA

### MOROCCAN CHICKPEA SOUP

**Serves 6 (main course)**
Active time: 45 min   Start to finish: 12½ hr

1½ cups dried chickpeas
8 cups water
1 (35-oz) can whole tomatoes, drained
1 large onion, finely chopped
1 small celery rib (including leaves),
   finely chopped
3 tablespoons unsalted butter
1 teaspoon turmeric
1 teaspoon black pepper
½ teaspoon cinnamon
⅔ cup chopped fresh cilantro
4 cups vegetable broth (preferably organic)
   or chicken broth
1 cup lentils
2 oz dried *capellini*, broken into 1-inch
   pieces, or fine egg noodles (¾ cup)
½ cup chopped fresh parsley

*Accompaniment:* lemon wedges

*Prepare chickpeas:*
Soak chickpeas in water to cover by 2 inches for
8 to 12 hours.

Drain chickpeas and rinse well. Transfer to a large
saucepan and add 8 cups water. Bring to a boil, then
reduce heat and simmer, uncovered, until tender, 1¼ to
1½ hours. Cool chickpeas and drain, reserving cooking
liquid. You should have about 2½ cups liquid (if not,
add more water).

Coarsely purée tomatoes in a food processor.

Cook onion and celery in butter in a 4-quart heavy
pot over moderately low heat, stirring occasionally,
until softened. Add turmeric, pepper, and cinnamon and
cook, stirring, 3 minutes.

Stir in tomato purée, ⅓ cup cilantro, chickpeas with
reserved liquid, vegetable broth, and lentils. Bring to a
boil, then reduce heat and simmer, uncovered, until
lentils are tender, about 35 minutes.

Stir in pasta and cook, stirring, until tender, about 3
minutes. Stir in parsley, remaining ⅓ cup cilantro, and
salt to taste.

## GREEN-PEA RAVIOLI IN LEMON BROTH

**Serves 6 (first course)**
Active time: 35 min   Start to finish: 35 min

*For filling*
1 cup thawed baby peas
1 small shallot, finely chopped
1½ teaspoons olive oil
3 tablespoons freshly grated parmesan
3 tablespoons fine fresh bread crumbs

18 won ton wrappers (sources on page 264)
1 qt chicken broth
1 garlic clove, smashed
1 teaspoon finely grated fresh lemon zest

*Garnish:* fresh chervil or parsley and cooked peas

*Make filling:*
Force peas through the fine disk of a food mill into
a bowl to remove skins.

Cook shallot in olive oil in a small skillet over moderately low heat, stirring occasionally, until softened.
Remove from heat and stir into pea purée with parmesan and crumbs. Season with salt and pepper.
*Fill ravioli:*
Put 1 won ton wrapper on a lightly floured surface,
keeping remaining wrappers covered with plastic wrap,
and mound a level teaspoon of filling onto center. Lightly dampen edges of wrapper with a fingertip dipped in
water and fold over to form a triangle, pressing down
around filling to force air out and pressing edges together firmly to seal. Moisten 1 end of long side of triangle
and fold opposite end over, creating a little hat shape,
then pinch ends together to seal. Transfer to a dry kitch-
en towel and make 17 more ravioli in same manner.
*Cook ravioli:*
Bring broth, garlic, zest, and salt and pepper to taste
to a simmer in a saucepan. Cook ravioli in a large pot of
boiling salted water until al dente, 2 to 3 minutes, then
drain in a colander.

Divide ravioli among soup plates (3 each) and ladle
broth over them, discarding garlic.

**Cooks' note:**
· **Ravioli may be made, but not cooked, 1 day ahead and**
  **chilled, covered, in a pan lined with a dry kitchen towel.**

PHOTO ON PAGE 32

## THREE-ONION SOUP

**Serves 4 (makes about 4 cups)**
Active time: 20 min   Start to finish: 55 min

4 medium leeks
1 teaspoon olive oil
1 small onion (¼ lb), thinly sliced
2 large shallots (¼ lb), thinly sliced
1½ cups water
1 large boiling potato (6 oz) such as Yukon Gold
1 cup nonfat chicken broth
½ cup grated Gruyère (2 oz)
2 teaspoons balsamic vinegar

Chop enough white and pale green parts of leeks to measure 2 cups. Wash leeks well in a large bowl of cold water. Lift from water and drain in a colander.

Heat oil in a 10-inch nonstick skillet over moderate heat until hot but not smoking, then cook chopped leeks, onion, and shallots with salt and pepper to taste, stirring frequently, until edges are golden brown, about 15 minutes. Add ½ cup water and deglaze skillet, stirring and scraping up brown bits. Transfer mixture to a saucepan.

Peel potato and cut into ½-inch cubes. Add potato, chicken broth, and remaining cup water to onion mixture, then simmer, covered, stirring occasionally, until potatoes are very tender.

Purée 1½ cups soup in a blender (use caution when blending hot liquids) and stir into remaining soup. Season with salt and pepper.

Serve soup sprinkled with Gruyère and drizzled with vinegar.

Cooks' note:
• Soup may be made 1 day ahead and cooled completely before being chilled, covered. Reheat, covered, over low heat.

each serving about 172 calories and 6 grams fat

## ANISE-SPICED SQUASH SOUP WITH FENNEL CHIPS

**Makes about 9 cups**
Active time: 1¼ hr   Start to finish: 2¾ hr

*For soup*
1 large fennel bulb (sometimes called anise; 1 lb), trimmed and bulb cut into ½-inch pieces
1 (3-lb) butternut squash, peeled, seeded, and cut into ½-inch pieces
1 medium onion, chopped
¼ teaspoon anise seeds
2 tablespoons unsalted butter
5 cups water
*For fennel chips*
1 cup water
½ cup sugar
2 tablespoons fresh lemon juice
1 small fennel bulb (½ lb), trimmed

*Special equipment:* Silpat or Exopat nonstick reusable baking-sheet liner (sources on page 264)
*Garnish:* sour cream

*Make soup:*
Cook fennel, squash, onion, and anise seeds in butter in a 6- to 8-quart pot over moderate heat, covered, stirring occasionally, 15 minutes. Add water and simmer, covered, until squash is very tender, 25 to 30 minutes. Purée soup in batches in a blender (use caution when blending hot liquids). Season with salt and pepper.

*Make fennel chips:*
Preheat oven to 225°F.

Boil water and sugar in a small saucepan, stirring until sugar is dissolved. Remove from heat and add lemon juice. Cut fennel bulb lengthwise into paper-thin slices using a *mandoline* or other manual slicer. Pour sugar mixture over fennel slices in a bowl and let stand 5 minutes.

Put Silpat or Exopat pad on a baking sheet. Shake off excess liquid from fennel slices and arrange on pad in 1 layer (don't let slices touch). Bake in middle of oven 1 hour, or until dry and crisp. Working quickly, carefully peel chips off liner and transfer to a rack to cool. Top soup with chips.

Cooks' note:
• Soup may be made 2 days ahead and chilled, covered.

## SALMON CONSOMMÉ WITH CRÈME FRAÎCHE AND SALMON CAVIAR

### *Makes about 8 cups*
Active time: 1 hr   Start to finish: 2¼ hr

*For consommé*
5 to 5½ lb of salmon carcasses
   (heads, bones, and tails)
4 large leeks (white and pale green parts only),
   halved lengthwise and sliced crosswise
3 celery ribs, chopped
2 onions, chopped
2 carrots, chopped
3 garlic cloves, chopped
1 (1-inch) piece fresh ginger, sliced
6 fresh parsley stems (without leaves)
1 fresh thyme sprig
5 coriander seeds
1 bay leaf (not California)
½ teaspoon salt
1 (750-ml) bottle dry white wine
3½ qt cold water
5 large egg whites, shells reserved
*For topping*
½ cup crème fraîche
3 tablespoons water
2 oz salmon caviar (roe) or other caviar

*Garnish:* fresh dill sprigs
*Accompaniment:* black pepper cornmeal crisps
   (page 100)
*Special equipment:* cheesecloth

*Make consommé:*

Rinse salmon carcasses under cold water. Remove any blood spots and discard any gills (they look like the underside of a mushroom cap). Transfer salmon to a 10- to 12-quart pot.

Wash leeks well in a large bowl of cold water and lift from water to a colander to drain. Add leeks and remaining consommé ingredients except egg whites and eggshells to pot with salmon. Bring to a boil, covered, then reduce heat and simmer, uncovered, skimming any foam, 40 minutes.

Pour stock through a sieve lined with a triple thickness of cheesecloth into a 6-quart saucepan. Boil until reduced to about 9 cups, 15 to 20 minutes, and skim any fat from surface.

Whisk egg whites in a large bowl until foamy. Crumble reserved shells into whites and slowly whisk in half of hot stock. Gradually whisk egg white mixture into stock in saucepan and bring to a steady boil over moderate heat, whisking constantly. Boil, undisturbed, until all of whites rise to top and stock is clear, about 10 minutes. Remove from heat and let stand 3 minutes.

Pour stock through a cheesecloth-lined sieve into a bowl. Then pour stock through a paper towel-lined sieve into a 3-quart saucepan. (You'll have about 8 cups.) Reheat and season with salt.

*Make topping:*

Whisk together crème fraîche and water in a small bowl set over a larger bowl of hot water until it reaches room temperature, then continue whisking until smooth and forms soft mounds.

Serve consommé with dollops of crème fraîche and salmon caviar.

Cooks' notes:
· We recommend calling your fish market a few days ahead to order the salmon carcasses.
· Consommé can be made 3 days ahead. Cool completely before chilling, covered, or freeze 1 month.
· The crème fraîche topping melts fast, so to make the most of its fabulous taste and texture, add it just before eating.

PHOTO ON PAGE 76

## CARDAMOM PEA SOUP

### *Makes about 6½ cups*
Active time: 15 min   Start to finish: 35 min

1 large onion, coarsely chopped
2 teaspoons minced peeled fresh ginger
2 tablespoons unsalted butter
¾ teaspoon ground cardamom
2 (14- to 15-oz) cans chicken broth
2 (10-oz) packages frozen peas

Cook onion and ginger in butter in a 3- to 4-quart heavy sauepan over moderate heat, stirring occasionally, until onion is softened. Add cardamom and cook, stirring, 30 seconds. Add broth and bring to a boil. Add peas and simmer, uncovered, until very tender, about 10 minutes. Purée soup in 3 batches in a blender until very smooth, at least 1 minute per batch (use caution when blending hot liquids). Return to pan, then season with salt and pepper and reheat.

## CLEAR SEA BROTH WITH CLAMS AND SNOW PEAS

### Serves 4
Active time: 10 min   Start to finish: 15 min

¼ lb snow peas, trimmed
4 cups *dashi* (page 121)
28 cockles or 20 littleneck clams measuring
   1½ inches across
1 tablespoon sake
1 teaspoon soy sauce

Blanch snow peas in a saucepan of boiling salted water 30 seconds. Drain in a colander and rinse under cold water to stop cooking. Cut diagonally in half.

Bring *dashi* to a boil with cockles in a large saucepan; simmer until cockles are opened (discard any unopened cockles after 5 minutes; if using clams, discard after 7 minutes). Stir in sake and soy sauce and scatter with snow peas.

## THAKKALI RASAM

TOMATO DAL SOUP

### Makes about 5 cups (serving 6)
Active time: 25 min   Start to finish: 1½ hr

*We liked this soup on its own, but in India it is frequently served over rice and topped with a spoonful of warm ghee. For information on specialty ingredients, see sources on page 264.*

5 tablespoons picked-over split skinned *toovar dal*
4 cups water
1½ tablespoons *ghee* (recipe follows or see sources)
1½ teaspoons black mustard seeds
1 fresh hot red chile such as *serrano* or Thai,
   halved lengthwise
1½ lb plum tomatoes, seeded and chopped
2 tablespoons finely chopped peeled fresh ginger
1 teaspoon ground coriander
1 teaspoon tamarind concentrate
¾ teaspoon turmeric
½ teaspoon ground cumin
½ teaspoon *asafetida* powder
3 fresh hot green chiles such as *serrano* or Thai,
   halved lengthwise

*Garnish:* fresh cilantro sprigs

Wash *dal* in several changes of water until water runs clear and drain well in a sieve. Cook *dal* at a bare simmer in 1½ cups water in a 3-quart saucepan until most of water is evaporated and *dal* has consistency of a paste, 40 to 45 minutes, stirring frequently during last 15 minutes to prevent scorching.

Heat *ghee* in a 6-quart heavy saucepan over moderately high heat until hot but not smoking, then cook mustard seeds and red chile, stirring, until seeds begin to pop. Add 1½ cups water and remaining ingredients (not *dal* paste). Bring to a boil and simmer, stirring occasionally, until tomatoes are softened, 6 to 8 minutes. Stir in *dal* paste and remaining cup water. Bring *rasam* to a boil, stirring occasionally, and season with salt.

Cooks' note:
· *Rasam* may be made 2 days ahead and chilled, covered.
  Add water to thin, if necessary, before reheating.

PHOTO ON PAGE 12

## GHEE

INDIAN CLARIFIED BUTTER

### Makes about ¾ cup
Active time: 10 min   Start to finish: 20 min

2 sticks unsalted butter, cut into 1-inch
   pieces

*Special equipment:* cheesecloth

Bring butter to a boil in a small heavy saucepan over moderate heat. Once foam completely covers butter, reduce heat to very low. Continue to cook butter, stirring occasionally, until a thin crust begins to form on surface and milky white solids fall to bottom of pan, about 8 minutes. Continue to cook butter, watching constantly and stirring occasionally to prevent burning, until solids turn light brown and butter deepens to golden and turns translucent and fragrant, about 3 minutes. Remove *ghee* from heat and pour through a sieve lined with a triple layer of cheesecloth into a jar.

Cooks' note:
· *Ghee* keeps, covered and chilled, 2 months.

## PUMPKIN-PEAR SOUP WITH CORIANDER

**Serves 8**
Active time: 30 min   Start to finish: 45 min

3 tablespoons extra-virgin olive oil
3 scallions, finely chopped
3 large shallots, finely chopped
1 medium onion, finely chopped
1 lb fresh sugar pumpkin or butternut squash,
   peeled, seeded, and cut into 1-inch pieces
½ lb yellow-fleshed potatoes such as Yukon Gold,
   peeled and cut into 1-inch pieces
4 cups chicken or vegetable stock or 2 cups chicken
   broth mixed with 2 cups water
1 tablespoon sugar
2 teaspoons ground coriander seeds
2 teaspoons fine sea salt
Freshly ground mixed or black peppercorns
1 ripe Bartlett pear
2 tablespoons unsalted butter, cut into pieces

*Garnish:* finely chopped fresh cilantro and fresh
   chives

Heat oil in a 3-quart heavy saucepan over moderate heat until hot but not smoking, then cook scallions, shallots, and onion, stirring, until softened but not browned. Add pumpkin, potatoes, stock, sugar, coriander, salt, and pepper to taste, then simmer, covered, until pumpkin is very tender, 15 to 20 minutes.

While soup is simmering, peel and core pear and cut into 1-inch pieces. Stir pear into soup and remove from heat. Cool 10 minutes and pureé in a blender in batches, transferring to a bowl (use caution when blending hot liquids).

Return to pan and add butter. Reheat over moderate heat, stirring, until butter is melted. Season with salt and pepper and, if desired, thin soup with water to desired consistency.

Cooks' note:
• Soup may be made 1 day ahead and chilled, covered.

PHOTO ON PAGE 64

## CHILLED ROASTED TOMATO AND RED PEPPER SOUP WITH MINT

**Makes about 4 cups (serving 2)**
Active time: 45 min   Start to finish: 3¼ hr

*We love this soup chilled, but it's just as delicious hot.*

2 red bell peppers, quartered and seeded
4 medium tomatoes, halved and cored
1 small onion, cut into ½-inch-thick slices
2 large garlic cloves, halved
1½ tablespoons olive oil
½ teaspoon ground coriander
¾ cup water
2 tablespoons heavy cream
1 teaspoon fresh lemon juice
1½ teaspoons salt
¼ teaspoon sugar
2 tablespoons finely chopped fresh mint, or to taste

Preheat broiler.

Toss bell peppers, tomatoes, onion, and garlic with oil and coriander in a large roasting pan and broil about 4 inches from heat until edges of vegetables are charred, about 7 minutes. Stir vegetables, then broil until vegetables are tender, about 3 minutes more.

Pureé vegetables with any pan juices in batches in a blender until smooth. Stir in remaining ingredients except mint.

Cool soup, uncovered, 30 minutes, then chill, covered, until cold, at least 2 hours. Just before serving, stir in mint.

Cooks' note:
• Soup can be made 2 days ahead and kept chilled, covered.

PHOTO ON PAGE 52

# FISH AND SHELLFISH

## CUMIN-DUSTED SEA BASS ON GREEN RICE

### Serves 4
Active time: 45 min   Start to finish: 45 min

*For rice*
1¼ cups water
⅔ cup long-grain rice
1 small onion, chopped
2 garlic cloves, minced
1 bay leaf
¾ teaspoon salt
2 tablespoons chopped fresh cilantro
2 tablespoons chopped fresh flat-leaf parsley
*For fish*
2 (1-inch-thick) skinned Chilean sea bass,
    monkfish, or halibut fillets (18 oz total)
1 teaspoon ground cumin
¼ teaspoon olive oil
*For sauce*
⅔ cup fat-free chicken broth
¼ cup fresh lime juice
2 tablespoons molasses
1 teaspoon cornstarch

Preheat oven to 500°F.
*Prepare rice:*
Bring water to a boil in a 2-quart saucepan, then add rice, onion, garlic, bay leaf, salt, and pepper to taste. Return to a boil, cover, and reduce heat to low. Cook until rice is tender and liquid is absorbed, 15 to 17 minutes. Fluff rice with a fork and let stand, covered, 5 minutes. Stir in herbs just before serving.
*Cook fish while rice cooks:*
Pat fillets dry and sprinkle with cumin and salt and pepper to taste on both sides. Heat oil in a well-seasoned 10-inch cast-iron skillet over high heat until hot but not

smoking, then sear fillets until browned on 1 side, about 5 minutes. Turn fillets over and put skillet in oven. Roast fillets in upper third of oven until just cooked through, 6 to 8 minutes.
*Make sauce while rice stands:*
Whisk together broth, lime juice, molasses, and cornstarch in a small skillet and simmer, whisking, until slightly thickened, 4 to 5 minutes. Halve each fillet crosswise and serve over rice. Spoon sauce over and around fish.

each serving, including rice, about 301 calories and 4 grams fat

## SEARED SALMON WITH BALSAMIC GLAZE

### Serves 4
Active time: 10 min   Start to finish: 15 min

¼ cup balsamic vinegar
¼ cup water
1½ tablespoons fresh lemon juice
4 teaspoons packed light brown sugar
4 (6-oz) center-cut salmon fillets
2 teaspoons vegetable oil

Stir together balsamic vinegar, water, lemon juice, and brown sugar.

Pat salmon dry and season with salt and pepper.

Heat oil in a 12-inch nonstick skillet over moderately high heat until hot but not smoking. Increase heat to high and sear salmon, skin sides up, until well browned, about 4 minutes. Turn fish over and sear until just cooked through, 3 to 4 minutes more.

Transfer salmon to plates and carefully add vinegar mixture to skillet (liquid will bubble vigorously and steam). Simmer, stirring, until thickened and reduced to about ⅓ cup, about 2 minutes.

Spoon glaze over salmon.

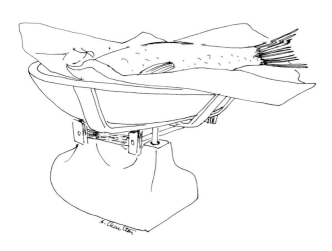

## POACHED SALT COD

**Serves 12 (as part of aïoli menu)**
Active time: 30 min   Start to finish: 2 days

4 lb center-cut skinless boneless salt cod,
   rinsed well
3 qt water
1 medium onion, halved
3 sprigs fresh thyme
2 bay leaves
½ teaspoon whole black peppercorns

Divide cod between 2 large bowls and cover with
cold water by 2 inches. Soak cod, chilled, changing
water 3 times a day, up to 3 days (see cooks' note
below). Refrigerate until ready to use.

Drain cod and transfer to a 6- to 8-quart pot with
water, onion, thyme, bay leaves, and peppercorns. Bring
just to a simmer and remove from heat. (Cod will just
flake; do not boil or it will become tough.)

Gently transfer cod with a slotted spoon to a platter,
discarding cooking liquid and seasonings. Serve warm
or at room temperature.

Cooks' note:
• Brands of cod differ in their degree of saltiness: A less
salty variety may only need 1 day of soaking, while
another could require up to 3. To test it, simply taste a
small piece after 1 day; you want it to be pleasantly salty
but not overwhelming.

## BROILED GROUPER FILLETS WITH ROMESCO SAUCE

**Serves 4**
Active time: 30 min   Start to finish: 30 min

*For romesco sauce*
⅓ cup whole blanched almonds, toasted
1 slice firm white sandwich bread, crust discarded
   and bread torn into pieces
2 large garlic cloves
½ teaspoon dried hot red pepper flakes
½ cup coarsely chopped drained bottled roasted
   red peppers
2 tablespoons red-wine vinegar
½ teaspoon salt, or to taste
¼ cup extra-virgin olive oil

4 (6-oz) pieces grouper fillet
1 to 2 tablespoons olive oil

*Make sauce:*
Finely grind almonds, bread, garlic, and red pepper
flakes in a food processor. Add roasted peppers, vinegar, and salt, then purée, adding oil in a slow stream.
Season with black pepper.
*Prepare fish:*
Preheat broiler.
Put fish on a lightly oiled shallow (1-inch-deep)
baking pan, skin sides down. Brush fish with oil and
season with salt and pepper. Broil 3 inches from heat,
without turning, until fish is just cooked through, about
7 minutes.
Serve fish with sauce.

## MISO-MARINATED SALMON WITH CITRUS AND SHIITAKES

**Serves 16**
Active time: 45 min   Start to finish: 25 hr

2 (3-lb) whole salmon fillets with skin, any small
   bones removed with tweezers
500 grams *shiro miso* (white fermented-soybean
   paste) (about 2 cups; sources on page 264)
2 tablespoons sake or white wine
*For shiitakes with citrus zests*
3 tablespoons plus ½ cup olive oil

1 lb fresh shiitake mushrooms, stems discarded
    and caps thinly sliced
3 navel oranges
3 large lemons
1 cup fresh cilantro
½ cup (½-inch) lengths of fresh chives

½ cup fresh orange juice (preferably from juice
    oranges)
3 tablespoons fresh lemon juice

*Marinate salmon:*

Line a large shallow (1-inch-deep) baking pan with plastic wrap and arrange salmon fillets, skin sides down, in it. Stir together *miso* and sake and spread over flesh sides of salmon to completely cover. Cover with plastic wrap and chill 24 to 48 hours.

*Make shiitakes with citrus zests:*

Heat 3 tablespoons oil in a 12-inch nonstick skillet over high heat until hot but not smoking, then sauté shiitakes with salt to taste, stirring occasionally, until golden brown and nearly dry, 15 to 20 minutes. Transfer to paper towels.

While mushrooms are cooking, remove zest from navel oranges and lemons in long, thin strips, preferably with a 5-holed citrus zester.

Heat remaining ½ cup oil in a 10-inch skillet over moderately low heat until hot but not smoking, then cook zests in 4 batches, stirring frequently, until curly and crisp, about 1 minute.

Transfer to paper towels with mushrooms. When mushrooms and zests are cool, transfer to a bowl. Just before serving, toss together with cilantro and chives.

*Roast salmon:*

Preheat oven to 500°F.

Gently scrape *miso* from salmon with a rubber spatula and discard *miso.* Arrange salmon fillets, skin sides down, in 2 well-greased large shallow (1-inch-deep) baking pans (tail ends may hang over ends of pans slightly). Roast salmon in upper and lower thirds of oven, switching position of pans after 10 minutes, until edges begin to brown and salmon is just cooked through, 15 to 20 minutes total.

Transfer each salmon fillet to a platter using 2 large metal spatulas. (If fillets break as you're transferring them, simply piece them together on the platter.) Pour orange and lemon juices over salmon and sprinkle with shiitake mixture.

Cooks' notes:
- We like the tangy flavor the juice oranges bring to the salmon, but you can use the juice from navel oranges for a sweeter note.
- Shiitakes and zests may be cooked 1 day ahead and kept, covered, at room temperature.

PHOTO ON PAGE 36

## CHILE-GLAZED SALMON WITH ORANGE SALSA

**Serves 8**
Active time: 40 min    Start to finish: 1¼ hr

*For salsa*
4 oranges
½ cup coarsely chopped fresh cilantro
1 small fresh jalapeño chile, seeded and finely
    chopped
½ small red onion, thinly sliced
¼ cup olive oil
¼ cup red-wine vinegar
1 teaspoon salt
½ teaspoon black pepper
*For salmon*
8 (6-oz) pieces salmon fillet with skin (3 lb total)
1 cup chile glaze (recipe on page 112)
2 tablespoons fennel seeds
2 tablespoons whole black peppercorns, coarsely
    crushed

*Make salsa:*

Cut peel and any white pith from oranges with a sharp knife, then cut sections free from membranes, letting them drop into a bowl. Stir in remaining salsa ingredients.

*Prepare salmon:*

Preheat broiler.

Season salmon with salt on all sides. Arrange on rack of a broiler pan, skin sides down, and broil about 4 inches from heat 4 minutes. Spoon glaze on top and spread onto sides, then sprinkle with fennel seeds and cracked pepper. Broil until glaze is bubbly and fish is just cooked through, 2 to 3 minutes more.

Serve salmon with salsa.

PHOTO ON PAGE 55

## CHILE GLAZE

**Makes about 1½ cups**
Active time: 20 min   Start to finish: 30 min

6 dried *panco* chiles or 3 dried *ancho* chiles,
   seeded (sources on page 264)
1 cup hot water
3 tablespoons tamarind paste (from a pliable
   block; sources on page 264)
½ cup fresh orange juice
1½ tablespoons fresh lemon juice
2 garlic cloves, coarsely chopped
2 tablespoons red-wine vinegar
2 tablespoons extra-virgin olive oil
1½ teaspoons dry mustard
¼ cup honey

Tear chiles into large pieces and toast in a dry heavy skillet over moderate heat, about 30 seconds on each side. Soak chiles in ½ cup hot water in a 1-cup glass measure to soften.

Mash tamarind paste with remaining ½ cup hot water to soften and force through a sieve into a bowl, discarding solids.

Purée chiles with soaking water, orange and lemon juices, garlic, vinegar, oil, and mustard in a blender. Add tamarind mixture and honey and blend well. Pour purée through sieve into a small saucepan and simmer, partially covered (mixture will spatter) and stirring occasionally, until thickened, 5 to 10 minutes. Season with salt and pepper.

**Cooks' note:**
• Glaze may be made 2 days ahead and chilled, covered.

## SALMON FILLETS IN DILL-PEPERONCINI CREAM SAUCE

**Serves 4**
Active time: 20 min   Start to finish: 20 min

4 (6-oz) salmon fillets, skinned
1 tablespoon vegetable oil
1 shallot, finely chopped
1½ tablespoons *peperoncini* (3), seeded
   and minced
1 cup half-and-half
1 tablespoon chopped fresh flat-leaf parsley
2 tablespoons chopped fresh dill
4 lemon wedges

Pat salmon dry and season with salt and pepper. Heat oil in a large nonstick skillet over moderately high heat until hot but not smoking, then cook salmon, turning once, until just cooked through, about 7 minutes. Transfer to a platter.

Cook shallot in skillet over moderate heat, stirring, until softened. Stir in *peperoncini*, half-and-half, parsley, and 1 tablespoon dill and simmer until sauce is slightly thickened, about 3 minutes. Stir in remaining tablespoon dill and salt and pepper to taste.

Pour cream sauce over salmon and serve with lemon wedges.

## SALMON PAPILLOTES WITH FENNEL, POTATOES, AND OLIVES

**Serves 4**
Active time: 1 hr   Start to finish: 1¼ hr

1 small fennel bulb, stalks discarded
3 medium carrots (½ lb)
½ lb small red potatoes
½ cup Kalamata or other brine-cured black
   olives, slivered
2 teaspoons finely grated fresh lemon zest
4 teaspoons fresh thyme
2 large garlic cloves, minced
3 tablespoons extra-virgin olive oil
1 (1½-lb) piece center-cut salmon fillet,
   skinned and cut into 4 square pieces

*Special equipment:* a *mandoline* or other manual
   slicer, 4 (15-inch) squares parchment paper,
   kitchen string

Place a large baking sheet on bottom rack of oven and remove any other racks. Preheat oven to 400°F.

Trim fennel stalks flush with bulb and discard stalks. Halve bulb lengthwise and remove most of core, leaving enough intact to keep layers together when sliced. Using *mandoline*, cut fennel bulb (lengthwise), carrots (diagonally), and potatoes into ⅛-inch-thick slices, keeping vegetables separate.

Blanch vegetables separately in salted boiling water: fennel 2 minutes, carrots 1 minute, potatoes 2 minutes.

Transfer fennel and carrots with a slotted spoon to a bowl of ice water, then drain well. Drain potatoes well.

Toss fennel and carrots with olives, zest, thyme, half of garlic, 2 tablespoons olive oil, and salt and pepper to taste. Toss potatoes with remaining oil and garlic and salt and pepper to taste.

Divide potato mixture among centers of parchment squares. Season salmon with salt and pepper and put on top of potatoes, then top salmon with fennel mixture. Gather sides of parchment up over fennel mixture to form a pouch, leaving no openings, and tie tightly with kitchen string.

Put packages directly on hot baking sheet in oven and bake 20 minutes. Serve immediately.

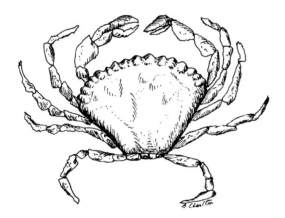

## CRAB-MEAT-STUFFED SOLE

*Serves 4*
Active time: 25 min   Start to finish: 45 min

*For crab stuffing and fish*
4 oz jumbo lump crab meat (1 cup)
1½ tablespoons reduced-fat (not low-fat)
   mayonnaise
¼ cup finely diced yellow bell pepper
1 tablespoon chopped fresh flat-leaf parsley
4 (4-oz) gray sole fillets
*For garlic bread crumbs*
1 small garlic clove, minced
2 teaspoons extra-virgin olive oil
¼ cup fine fresh bread crumbs (preferably
   from a baguette)
1 teaspoon finely grated fresh lemon zest

*Prepare stuffing and fish:*
Preheat oven to 450°F.

Stir together crab, mayonnaise, bell pepper, parsley, and salt and pepper to taste.

Lay sole fillets flat, darker sides up, and season with salt and pepper. Divide stuffing among fillets, mounding on thicker half of each. Fold thinner half of fillet over stuffing, tucking end under to form a packet.

Arrange stuffed fillets in a lightly oiled 9-inch pie plate. Cover with a round of parchment paper, then cover pie plate tightly with foil. Bake in upper third of oven until just cooked through, about 20 minutes.

*Make bread crumbs while sole bakes:*
Cook garlic in oil in a small skillet over moderate heat, stirring, until fragrant, about 30 seconds. Add bread crumbs and cook, stirring, until golden brown, 4 to 5 minutes. Remove from heat, then stir in zest and salt and pepper to taste.

Transfer sole to plates and pour pan juices through a fine sieve into a small bowl. Spoon some of juices over fish and sprinkle with bread crumbs.

each serving about 207 calories and 6 grams fat

## OVEN-POACHED FISH IN OLIVE OIL

*Serves 4*
Active time: 15 min   Start to finish: 1½ hr

¼ cup capers (preferably in salt), rinsed
2½ lb (1-inch-thick) scrod or halibut fillets
1½ teaspoons salt
½ teaspoon black pepper
1½ large lemons, thinly sliced crosswise
¼ cup fresh flat-leaf parsley
2 cups extra-virgin olive oil

Preheat oven to 250°F.

Chop half of capers and pat fish dry. Sprinkle fish with salt and pepper and let stand 10 minutes at room temperature. Arrange half of lemon slices in 1 layer in an 8-inch square glass baking dish and arrange fish in 1 layer over lemon. Top with all of capers, remaining lemon slices, and 3 tablespoons parsley, then pour oil over fish. Bake in middle of oven, uncovered, until fish just flakes and is cooked through, about 1 to 1¼ hours.

Serve fish with some of lemon slices, capers, and olive oil spooned over. Sprinkle with remaining tablespoon parsley.

## BROILED SEA TROUT WITH BASIL SAUCE

*Serves 2*
Active time: 15 min   Start to finish: 25 min

1 cup fresh basil
¼ cup fresh flat-leaf parsley
1 large garlic clove
4 tablespoons extra-virgin olive oil
1 tablespoon water
1 tablespoon fresh lemon juice
4 (6- to 8-oz) sea trout, bluefish, or mackerel
   fillets, with skin

*Accompaniment:* lemon wedges

Preheat broiler.

Finely chop basil, parsley, and garlic together in a blender. Add 3 tablespoons oil and purée, then blend in water, lemon juice, and salt and pepper to taste. If desired, thin with more water.

Arrange fillets, skin sides down, in an oiled shallow (1-inch-deep) baking pan. Brush fish with remaining tablespoon oil and season with salt and pepper. Broil fish 5 to 6 inches from heat until just cooked through, about 7 minutes. Serve fish with sauce.

## HAZELNUT-CRUSTED TROUT

*Serves 2*
Active time: 25 min   Start to finish: 25 min

½ cup hazelnuts
2 (10- to 12-oz) brook trout, cleaned
1 large egg
2 tablespoons vegetable oil
1 tablespoon unsalted butter
1 teaspoon fresh lemon juice
1 tablespoon chopped fresh flat-leaf parsley

Pulse nuts in a food processor until finely ground. Rinse trout and pat dry. Season with salt inside and out.

Beat egg in a pie plate. Spread ground nuts on a dinner plate. Dip both sides of trout first in egg and then nuts. Heat oil in a 12-inch heavy skillet over moderate heat until hot but not smoking, then cook trout, shaking skillet to prevent sticking and turning once with a metal spatula, until browned on both sides and just cooked through, about 12 minutes total.

While trout is cooking, melt butter in a small saucepan and stir in lemon juice. Season with salt and pepper and keep warm. Pour over trout and sprinkle with parsley.

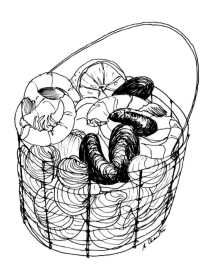

SHELLFISH

## SEARED CUMIN SEA SCALLOPS WITH CAULIFLOWER AND LEEKS

*Serves 4*
Active time: 30 min   Start to finish: 30 min

2 leeks, cut crosswise into ½-inch-thick slices
1¼ lb sea scallops, halved horizontally and
   patted dry
1 teaspoon cumin seeds
2 tablespoons olive oil
½ medium head cauliflower, cut into 1½-inch
   florets
3 tablespoons dry white wine
¼ cup water
½ cup heavy cream
¼ cup fresh cilantro, chopped
1 tablespoon fresh lemon juice

Wash sliced leeks in a large bowl of water, then lift out and pat dry.

Toss scallops with cumin seeds and salt and pepper to taste. Heat 1 tablespoon oil in a 12-inch nonstick skillet over moderately high heat until hot but not smoking, then sear scallops until golden, about 2 minutes on each side. Transfer to a bowl with tongs.

Heat remaining tablespoon oil in skillet (do not clean) until hot but not smoking, then sauté cauliflower and leeks with salt to taste, stirring until golden. Add wine and water and simmer, covered, until vegetables are almost tender, 5 to 7 minutes. Add heavy cream and scallops with juices in bowl and simmer, uncovered, until liquid is slightly thickened, about 3 minutes more. Stir in cilantro and lemon juice and season with salt and pepper.

## STEAMED MUSSELS

### Serves 12 (as part of aïoli menu)
Active time: 45 min   Start to finish: 45 min

½ medium onion, chopped
1 tablespoon olive oil
1 cup dry white wine
3 lb mussels (preferably cultivated), scrubbed
　　and beards removed

*Garnish:* fresh flat-leaf parsley sprigs and lemon
　　wedges

Cook onion in oil in a 5- to 6-quart pot over moderate heat, stirring, until softened, 3 to 5 minutes. Add wine and mussels and bring to a boil. Cover and cook, shaking pot occasionally, until mussels are opened, 4 to 5 minutes. (Discard any unopened ones.)

Transfer mussels to a platter with a slotted spoon, discarding steaming liquid.

PHOTO ON PAGE 59

## MUSSELS WITH POTATOES AND SPINACH

### Serves 2
Active time: 35 min   Start to finish: 35 min

1 lb small red boiling potatoes
3 tablespoons olive oil
1 tablespoon minced garlic
2 lb mussels (preferably cultivated), scrubbed
　　and beards removed
¼ cup water
½ lb baby spinach, trimmed

Simmer potatoes in enough salted water to cover by 1 inch until just tender, about 15 minutes. Drain and rinse under cold water until cool enough to handle. Pat dry and cut in half (quarter larger potatoes).

Heat 2 tablespoons oil in a large heavy skillet over moderately high heat until hot but not smoking, then sauté potatoes with salt to taste, turning occasionally, until golden brown, about 10 minutes.

While potatoes are sautéing, cook garlic in remaining tablespoon oil in a 5- to 6-quart pot over moderately high heat, stirring, until fragrant. Add mussels and water and cook, covered, until mussels are opened, 3 to 5 minutes. (Discard any unopened ones.)

Add spinach to potatoes, tossing until just wilted. Serve potatoes and spinach with mussels.

## SEARED CURRIED SCALLOPS WITH ZUCCHINI

### Serves 2
Active time: 20 min   Start to finish: 20 min

1 lb sea scallops
1 teaspoon curry powder
1½ to 2 tablespoons vegetable oil
1 teaspoon finely grated peeled fresh ginger
1 garlic clove, minced
2 medium zucchini (¾ lb total), halved lengthwise
　　and cut diagonally into ½-inch-thick slices

*Garnish:* fresh cilantro sprigs and lime wedges

Remove tough muscle from side of each scallop if necessary. Pat scallops dry and sprinkle with curry powder and salt and pepper to taste. Heat ½ tablespoon oil in a large nonstick skillet over moderately high heat until hot but not smoking, then sear scallops in 2 batches, adding another ½ tablespoon oil if necessary, until golden, 1 to 2 minutes on each side. Transfer to a plate.

Add remaining tablespoon oil to skillet, then cook ginger and garlic over moderate heat, stirring, until fragrant, about 30 seconds. Add zucchini and salt and pepper to taste, then cook, stirring frequently, until crisp-tender, 4 to 5 minutes.

Return scallops to skillet with any juices accumulated on plate and toss with zucchini just until heated through, about 1 minute.

## GRILLED SEAFOOD WITH TOMATO, CAPER, AND OLIVE VINAIGRETTE

### Serves 8
Active time: 30 min   Start to finish: 2 hr

2 (1¼-lb) live lobsters
1½ lb small hard-shelled clams (16), well scrubbed
5 tablespoons olive oil
1 lb jumbo shrimp (8 to 12), with shells
1 lb large sea scallops (10 to 12)
2 (2-lb) whole red snappers, cleaned and heads removed
Vegetable bulgur salad (page 184)
1¾ cups tomato, caper, and olive vinaigrette (recipe follows)
½ cup pine nuts, toasted and salted

*Accompaniment:* lemon wedges

Prepare grill for cooking.

Plunge live lobsters headfirst into an 8-quart pot of boiling salted water. Cook, covered, 4 minutes from time they enter water (lobsters will be only partially cooked) and transfer with tongs to a colander to drain and cool.

Twist tails off each lobster and break off claws at body, discarding body. Halve tails lengthwise (including shells) with kitchen shears and lightly crack claws. (Do not remove tail or claw meat from shells.)

Put clams in a disposable aluminum pie plate and drizzle with 1 tablespoon oil. Snip shells of shrimp down center of backs with kitchen shears, from wide end down to last tail section, and devein. Pat lobsters, shrimp, scallops, and fish dry, then brush with remaining 4 tablespoons oil and season with salt and pepper.

Put lobster claws and tails (cut sides up), shrimp, and clams (in pie plate) on rack of grill, 5 to 6 inches over glowing coals, and cover grill. Cook, turning once, until just cooked through, about 5 minutes for claws (liquid will bubble at open ends), 5 to 6 minutes for tails and shrimp (meat will be opaque), and 6 to 8 minutes for clams, or until opened (discard any unopened ones). Transfer as cooked to a platter and keep warm, covered.

Put scallops and fish in center of rack and cover grill. Cook, turning once, until just cooked through and meat is opaque, about 4 minutes for scallops and about 12 minutes for fish. Transfer with a large metal spatula to platter.

Mound bulgur salad in center of 8 plates and arrange seafood on top and around it. Spoon over some vinaigrette (serve remainder on the side) and sprinkle seafood and bulgur with pine nuts.

PHOTO ON PAGE 49

## TOMATO, CAPER, AND OLIVE VINAIGRETTE

### Makes about 2 cups
Active time: 20 min   Start to finish: 20 min

½ cup fresh lemon juice
2 teaspoons Dijon mustard
¾ cup extra-virgin olive oil
1 cup cherry tomatoes, quartered
⅔ cup Kalamata or other brine-cured black olives, pitted and halved
2 tablespoons drained capers, rinsed

Whisk together lemon juice and mustard. Add oil in a slow stream, whisking until emulsified. Stir in tomatoes, olives, capers, and salt and pepper to taste.

## BUTTER-BRAISED OYSTERS ON GREENS

### Serves 4 (lunch main course)
Active time: 20 min   Start to finish: 20 min

5 tablespoons unsalted butter
4 (½-inch-thick) diagonal slices French bread
2 cups mesclun (mixed baby salad greens)
1 shallot, finely chopped
3 tablespoons Sherry vinegar
1 pint shucked medium-size oysters (about 2 dozen in the shell), rinsed and picked over

Heat 1 tablespoon butter in a 12-inch skillet over moderately high heat until foam subsides, then lightly brown bread in butter on both sides. Put toasts on plates and top with mesclun.

Add 1 tablespoon butter to skillet, then cook shallot, stirring, over moderate heat until softened and beginning to brown, 2 to 3 minutes. Add vinegar and cook, swirling skillet frequently, until vinegar is reduced to about 1 tablespoon. Add oysters and remaining 3 tablespoons butter and cook, swirling skillet frequently, until oysters are plumped and butter is incorporated into sauce, about 2 minutes.

Remove from heat and season with salt and pepper. Spoon oysters and sauce over mesclun.

## CAJUN SHRIMP MIRLITON CASSEROLE

*Serves 8 to 10*
Active time: 1½ hr   Start to finish: 1¾ hr

*This rich, savory dish (pronounced shrimp* mah-*lih-tone) is pure Cajun comfort food. In Louisiana it's often served as a side dish; it also works as a first course.*

7 medium mirlitons (also called chayotes;
    sources on page 264)
2 medium onions, chopped
2 green bell peppers, chopped
1 stick unsalted butter
3 large garlic cloves, minced
24 saltines, finely ground (¾ cup)
2 lb large shrimp, shelled, deveined, and cut
    into ½-inch pieces
¼ teaspoon cayenne, or to taste
2 tablespoons fine dry bread crumbs

Simmer mirlitons in water to cover by 2 inches in an 8-quart pot, partially covered, until very tender, about 1 hour. Drain mirlitons, then halve and peel, discarding pits. Coarsely chop in a food processor.
Preheat oven to 400°F.
Cook onions and bell peppers in 6 tablespoons butter in a 6- to 7-quart wide heavy pot over moderately low heat, stirring occasionally, until softened. Add garlic and cook, stirring, 1 minute. Add mirlitons and cook,

stirring occasionally, until most of liquid is evaporated, about 5 minutes. (Do not let vegetables brown.) Stir in cracker crumbs, shrimp, cayenne, and salt and pepper to taste and cook, stirring, 1 minute.

Spoon into a shallow 3-quart baking dish and sprinkle with dry bread crumbs. Dot with remaining 2 tablespoons butter and bake in upper third of oven until crumbs are just golden, 12 to 15 minutes.

PHOTO ON PAGE 16

## BAKED SHRIMP IN CHIPOTLE SAUCE

*Serves 4*
Active time: 10 min   Start to finish: 25 min

½ stick (¼ cup) unsalted butter
¼ cup dry red wine
1½ tablespoons Worcestershire sauce
1 to 2 canned *chipotle* chiles in *adobo*, minced,
    plus 2 to 3 teaspoons *adobo* sauce (sources on
    page 264)
1 large garlic clove, minced
1½ teaspoons salt
1½ lb medium shrimp,
    with shells

*Accompaniment:* baguette

Preheat oven to 400°F.
Melt butter in a saucepan and stir in red wine, Worcestershire sauce, *chipotles, adobo* sauce, garlic, and salt. Toss shrimp in sauce in a large shallow baking dish and bake in middle of oven until shrimp are just cooked through, 10 to 12 minutes.

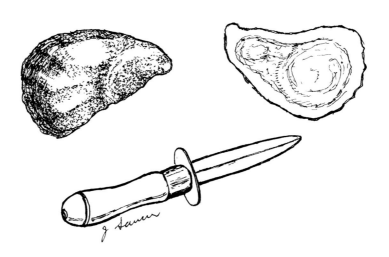

`BEEF`

### HERBED RIB ROAST

*Serves 8*
Active time: 30 min   Start to finish: 11 hr

*For roast*
1 (7- to 8-lb) prime rib roast (sometimes
　called standing rib roast; 3 or 4 ribs)
1 tablespoon whole black peppercorns
2 bay leaves (not California)
1 tablespoon kosher salt
3 garlic cloves
1 teaspoon chopped fresh thyme
1 teaspoon chopped fresh rosemary
1 tablespoon olive oil
*For jus*
2 cups beef broth
1 small fresh rosemary sprig
1 small fresh thyme sprig
1 garlic clove, smashed

*Prepare roast:*
Trim all but a thin layer of fat from roast. Grind peppercorns and bay leaves with salt to a powder in an electric coffee/spice grinder, then transfer to a mortar. Add garlic, thyme, and rosemary, then pound to a smooth paste with pestle. Stir in olive oil. Rub paste all over roast.

Transfer roast to a rack set in a small flameproof roasting pan. Marinate roast, covered and chilled, at least 8 hours and up to 24.

*Cook roast:*
Let roast stand at room temperature 1 hour. Preheat oven to 450°F.

Roast beef in middle of oven 20 minutes. Reduce temperature to 350°F and roast beef until a thermometer inserted into center of meat registers 110°F, 1½ to 1¾ hours more. Transfer to a large platter and let stand,

uncovered, 25 minutes. (Meat will continue to cook, reaching about 130°F for medium-rare.)

*Make jus:*
Skim fat from pan juices. Add broth, rosemary, thyme, and garlic and deglaze pan by simmering on top of stove over moderate heat, stirring and scraping up brown bits. Transfer to a small saucepan and add any juices that have collected on platter. Gently simmer 10 minutes. Skim fat and season *jus* with salt and pepper.

Cut slices from roast and serve with *jus.*

PHOTO ON PAGE 77

### MUSTARD-CRUSTED BEEF TENDERLOIN WITH ARUGULA, RED ONION, AND WAX BEAN SALAD

*Serves 2*
Active time: 20 min   Start to finish: 2 hr

*For beef*
¼ cup coarse-grained mustard
¾ teaspoon dry mustard
2¼ teaspoons packed dark brown sugar
¾ teaspoon coarsely ground black pepper
½ teaspoon finely grated fresh lemon zest
1 (1-lb) trimmed beef tenderloin roast, tied
1 tablespoon vegetable oil
*For salad*
1 small red onion, thinly sliced
½ lb wax or green beans, cut diagonally
　into 2-inch pieces
4 oz baby arugula (4 cups)
*For dressing*
1½ tablespoons balsamic vinegar
1 tablespoon fresh lemon juice
¼ teaspoon Dijon mustard
¼ cup olive oil

*Prepare beef:*
Preheat oven to 425°F.

Stir together mustards, brown sugar, pepper, and lemon zest.

Pat beef dry and season generously with salt. Heat oil in a heavy skillet over moderately high heat until just beginning to smoke, then brown beef on all sides, about 2 minutes total. Transfer to an oiled shallow baking pan and coat with mustard mixture.

Roast beef in middle of oven until a thermometer inserted 2 inches into thickest part of meat registers 125°F for medium-rare, 15 to 20 minutes. Transfer to a board and let stand until cool, at least 45 minutes.

*Prepare salad while beef roasts:*

Chill onion slices in water to cover 30 minutes.

Cook beans in boiling salted water until crisp-tender, about 5 minutes. Drain beans in a colander and rinse under cold water to stop cooking, then transfer to a large bowl. Add arugula to beans. Drain onion slices and pat dry.

*Make dressing and toss salad:*

Whisk together vinegar, lemon juice, mustard, and salt and pepper to taste. Add oil in a slow stream, whisking until emulsified.

Cut beef into thin slices.

Add onion slices, beef slices, and enough dressing to arugula and beans to just coat and toss to combine well.

PHOTO ON PAGE 53

## GRILLED SPICED RIB-EYE STEAKS

**Serves 8**
Active time: 15 min   Start to finish: 45 min

8 (1-inch-thick) bone-in rib-eye steaks
  (1 lb each)
¼ teaspoon ground allspice
1 teaspoon ground cumin
2 tablespoons kosher salt

Prepare grill for cooking.

Let steaks stand at room temperature 30 minutes. Stir together allspice, cumin, and salt. Pat steaks dry and sprinkle spice mixture onto both sides of steaks to lightly coat, pressing to adhere.

Grill steaks in 2 batches on an oiled rack set 5 to 6 inches over glowing coals 4 to 5 minutes on each side, or until an instant-read thermometer inserted horizontally 2 inches into thickest part of meat registers 130°F for medium-rare. Transfer steaks to a platter and let stand 10 minutes.

PHOTO ON PAGE 40

## FILLET OF BEEF WITH ASIAN SPICE RUB

**Serves 8 to 10**
Active time: 20 min   Start to finish: 1¼ hr

2 tablespoons Sichuan peppercorns (sources on
  page 264)
1 tablespoon anise seeds
4 teaspoons kosher salt
1 teaspoon Chinese five-spice powder
1 teaspoon ground ginger
1 (4- to 5-lb) beef tenderloin roast, trimmed
  and tied
4 tablespoons vegetable oil

*Garnish:* snipped fresh chives and tarragon sprigs

Preheat oven to 425°F.

Toast peppercorns and anise seeds in a dry large heavy skillet over moderate heat, stirring, until fragrant, about 1 minute. Finely grind toasted mixture in an electric coffee/spice grinder or with a mortar and pestle. Sift mixture through a coarse sieve into a bowl and stir in salt, five-spice powder, and ginger.

Halve beef crosswise and sprinkle rub all over both pieces, pressing to adhere.

Heat 2 tablespoons oil in skillet over moderately high heat until just smoking, then brown 1 piece of beef on all sides, about 1 minute. Transfer to a large roasting pan. Wipe skillet clean with paper towels and brown remaining beef in same manner. Arrange beef pieces 2 inches apart in roasting pan.

Roast in middle of oven 25 to 35 minutes, or until a thermometer inserted diagonally 2 inches into centers of beef pieces registers 120°F. Let beef stand in pan on a rack 25 minutes. Beef will continue to cook as it stands, reaching 130°F (medium-rare). Discard string and slice roast beef.

Serve at room temperature.

PHOTO ON PAGE 18

## Sliced Steak with Roasted-Corn Salsa

*Serves 4*
Active time: 20 min   Start to finish: 35 min

3 cups fresh corn kernels (3 ears)
4 scallions, white and green parts thinly
   sliced separately
2 tablespoons unsalted butter
2 garlic cloves, minced
1½ teaspoons kosher salt
1½ teaspoons ground cumin
1 teaspoon chili powder
½ teaspoon black pepper
2 plum tomatoes, finely diced
1 to 2 fresh jalapeño chiles, finely diced
   (including seeds)
1 (2-lb) trimmed boneless sirloin steak
   (about 1½ inches thick)
¼ cup finely chopped fresh cilantro

*Accompaniment:* lime wedges

Prepare grill for cooking.
*Make corn salsa:*

Heat a dry large cast-iron skillet over moderately high heat until hot, then pan-roast corn, stirring occasionally, until golden brown, 8 to 10 minutes. Transfer to a bowl.

Cook white part of scallions in butter with garlic, 1 teaspoon salt, ½ teaspoon each cumin and chili powder, and ¼ teaspoon pepper in skillet over moderate heat, stirring, until scallions are tender, 3 to 4 minutes. Remove from heat and stir in corn, tomatoes, and jalapeño.

*Grill steak:*

Combine remaining ½ teaspoon salt, 1 teaspoon cumin, ½ teaspoon chili powder, and ¼ teaspoon pepper and sprinkle on both sides of steak. Grill, turning once, until an instant-read thermometer inserted horizontally into thickest part of meat registers 130°F, 18 to 20 minutes total for medium-rare. Transfer to a grooved cutting board and let stand 5 to 10 minutes before slicing.

While steak is standing, reheat corn mixture over moderate heat, stirring occasionally. Stir in cilantro and scallion greens.

Spoon corn on top of sliced steak and pour over any accumulated juices.

## Sautéed Skirt Steak with Frisée and Roasted-Potato Salad

*Serves 8*
Active time: 45 min   Start to finish: 45 min

3 lb skirt steak, cut into 8 pieces
1½ tablespoons Worcestershire sauce
1½ lb small boiling potatoes, cut into
   wedges
1 large garlic clove, finely chopped
8½ tablespoons olive oil
1 shallot, finely chopped
1½ tablespoons Sherry vinegar or red-wine vinegar
1½ teaspoons Dijon mustard
1 teaspoon kosher salt
¾ lb mixed greens such as frisée (French curly
   endive), *mizuna*, baby spinach, and mesclun,
   coarse stems discarded
3 tomatoes, halved horizontally, seeded, and cut
   into thin wedges
¼ cup finely grated Parmigiano Reggiano

Preheat oven to 450°F.
Brush skirt steak with Worcestershire and marinate 15 minutes.

*Roast potatoes while steak marinates:*

Toss potatoes with garlic, 2 tablespoons oil, and salt and pepper to taste. Arrange wedges in 1 layer in an oiled shallow (1-inch) baking pan. Roast in upper third of oven 15 minutes, then turn over. Roast until golden and cooked through, about 5 minutes more.

*Sauté steaks:*

Lightly pat steaks dry and season well with salt. Heat ½ tablespoon oil in each of 2 (12-inch) nonstick or heavy skillets over moderately high heat until hot but not smoking, then sauté steaks in batches, without crowding, about 3 minutes on each side for medium-rare. Transfer steaks to a platter and let stand, loosely covered, 5 minutes.

*Make salad while steaks stand:*

Whisk together shallot, vinegar, mustard, kosher salt, and pepper to taste. Add remaining 4½ tablespoons oil in a slow stream, whisking until emulsified.

Toss together greens, potatoes, tomatoes, three fourths of Parmigiano Reggiano, and enough vinaigrette to coat. Sprinkle remaining Parmigiano Reggiano over salad and serve with steaks.

PHOTO ON PAGE 43

## JAPANESE BEEF STEW

**Serves 4**
Active time: 30 min   Start to finish: 1½ hr

*Trimming all corners and ragged edges from the carrots and potatoes is very Japanese; rounded edges also ensure even cooking.*

1½ lb boneless beef chuck, cut into
    1½-inch pieces
2 tablespoons vegetable oil
1 cup *dashi* (recipe follows)
½ cup sake
1 bunch scallions, white parts trimmed
    and greens sliced
2½ tablespoons sugar
12 (1½-inch) small boiling potatoes (1 lb)
2 large carrots (1 lb)
3 tablespoons soy sauce

*Prepare beef:*
Pat beef dry. Heat oil in a 5-quart heavy pot until hot but not smoking, then brown beef on all sides. Add *dashi*, sake, and white parts of scallions and simmer, covered, skimming froth and turning beef occasionally, until meat is very tender, 1¼ to 1½ hours. (Check pot periodically and add a few tablespoons water if beef becomes less than half submerged.) Add sugar and simmer, covered, 15 minutes longer (more liquid may evaporate at this point, but that's fine).

*Prepare vegetables while beef simmers:*
Peel potatoes, halving and trimming into ovals if large, and steam, covered, over boiling water until barely tender, about 10 minutes.

Cut carrots crosswise into ½-inch-thick slices. Trim slices with a paring knife to create rounded edges. Steam carrots, covered, over boiling water until barely tender, about 7 minutes.

*Finish stew:*
Add carrots and potatoes to beef and simmer, tossing occasionally, 5 minutes, or until vegetables are tender. Add soy sauce and bring to a boil. Discard white parts of scallions.

Serve beef stew in small bowls sprinkled with scallion greens.

## DASHI

### JAPANESE SEA STOCK

**Makes about 6 cups**
Active time: 5 min   Start to finish: 10 min

*Kombu comes packaged in dried lengths that are most easily cut with scissors.*

6 cups cold water
1 oz (30 grams) *kombu* (dried kelp; sources on page
    264), about 20 square inches
2 (5-gram) packages *katsuo bushi* (dried bonito
    flakes; sources on page 264), about 1 cup

Bring cold water and *kombu* just to a boil in a large saucepan over high heat. Remove from heat and remove *kombu* (saving it for pickled Napa cabbage, page 161). Sprinkle *katsuo bushi* over liquid; let stand 3 minutes and, if necessary, stir to make *katsuo bushi* sink. Pour through a cheesecloth-lined sieve or a coffee filter into a bowl. Reserve *katsuo bushi* for rice with soy-glazed bonito flakes and sesame seeds, page 156.

Cooks' note:
• Sea stock keeps 4 days. Cool, uncovered, before chilling,
  covered.

## RIB-EYE STEAKS WITH CURRIED SALT

**Serves 2**
Active time: 10 min   Start to finish: 20 min

1½ teaspoons kosher salt
1¾ teaspoons curry powder
2 (¾-inch-thick) beef rib-eye steaks
¼ cup water

Stir together salt and curry powder. Pat steaks dry and sprinkle both sides evenly with curried salt.

Heat a well-seasoned 10-inch cast-iron skillet over moderately high heat until hot but not smoking, then sear steaks 4 to 5 minutes on each side, or until an instant-read thermometer inserted horizontally into thickest part of meat registers 130°F for medium-rare. Transfer steaks to a plate and let stand 5 minutes. Add water to skillet and deglaze pan by boiling, scraping up brown bits, until reduced to about 2 tablespoons. Spoon juices over meat.

## PERUVIAN-STYLE BEEF KEBABS WITH GRILLED ONION AND ZUCCHINI

**Serves 6**
Active time: 35 min   Start to finish: 1½ hr

1¾ lb beef tenderloin roast, trimmed
2 tablespoons soy sauce
2 tablespoons fresh lime juice
2 teaspoons kosher salt
1 teaspoon ground cumin
6 (¼-inch-thick) rounds of red onion
2 teaspoons olive oil
3 medium zucchini (1 lb), sliced ¼ inch thick
   lengthwise

*Special equipment:* 6 (8-inch) bamboo skewers

Soak skewers in water while marinating beef.

Cut beef into 24 (1-inch) cubes. Stir together soy sauce, lime juice, salt, and cumin in a bowl and add beef, tossing to coat well. Marinate beef, covered, at room temperature 1 hour.

Prepare grill for cooking.

After beef has been marinating 45 minutes, lightly brush onion rounds with oil and season with salt and pepper. Grill onion on a well-oiled rack set 5 to 6 inches over glowing coals, carefully turning once with a metal spatula, until lightly charred and tender, 3 to 4 minutes on each side. Transfer to a platter and keep warm.

Grill zucchini until lightly charred and just tender, about 1 minute on each side. Transfer to platter and season with salt.

Pat beef dry with paper towels and toss with remaining oil. (Discard marinade.) Thread 4 pieces beef onto each skewer and grill, turning occasionally, until charred, about 5 minutes total for medium-rare.

Serve kebabs with onion and zucchini.

**Cooks' note:**
· **Instead of the grill, you can cook the vegetables and beef in a hot well-seasoned ridged grill pan over moderately high heat.**

each serving about 263 calories and 15 grams fat

PHOTO ON PAGE 81

**VEAL**

## ROASTED DOUBLE VEAL CHOPS

**Serves 6**
Active time: 20 min   Start to finish: 1½ hr

*You'll need to order this cut of veal, a two-rib chop, from your butcher. When the meat is carved, the first one or two slices may contain gristle, but after that the veal will be beautifully tender.*

1½ oz sliced *pancetta*, cut into ¼-inch-thick
   strips
1 to 2 tablespoons olive oil
2 (2-rib) veal chops (4 lb total)
*For sauce*
1 garlic clove, minced
½ cup dry white wine
1 cup veal stock or chicken broth
2 teaspoons unsalted butter
1 tablespoon finely chopped fresh parsley
1 teaspoon finely chopped fresh thyme

*Cook pancetta and chops:*
Preheat oven to 400°F.

Cook *pancetta* in 1 tablespoon oil over moderately low heat in a large heavy skillet, stirring occasionally, until browned and fat is rendered. Transfer to paper towels to drain, reserving fat in skillet.

Pat chops dry and season with salt and pepper. Increase heat under skillet to moderately high, then brown chops in fat on all sides, adding more oil if necessary. Transfer chops to a small flameproof roasting pan, bone sides down, and set skillet aside.

Roast chops in middle of oven until an instant-read thermometer inserted 2 inches into center of meat (without touching bone) registers 135°F for medium, about 1 hour. Transfer chops to a cutting board and let stand, covered loosely with foil, 15 minutes (internal temperature will rise to about 140°F).

*Begin sauce while chops roast:*

Discard all but about 1 tablespoon fat from skillet. Heat over moderate heat until hot but not smoking, then cook garlic, stirring, until fragrant, 30 seconds. Add wine to skillet and deglaze by boiling over high heat, stirring and scraping up brown bits. Add stock and boil until mixture is reduced to about ¾ cup.

*Finish sauce while chops stand:*

Deglaze roasting pan with wine mixture. Transfer to a small saucepan and skim off any fat. Reheat and swirl in butter, parsley, and thyme. Stir in any juices accumulated on cutting board, *pancetta*, and pepper to taste.

With chops on their sides, cut parallel to bones into thin slices, then serve with sauce.

PHOTO ON PAGE 34

## VEAL, MUSHROOM, AND RED PEPPER GOULASH

### Serves 6
Active time: 1 hr   Start to finish: 2¼ hr

*We like this stew with egg noodles (12 ounces of dried pasta), cooked and tossed with two tablespoons of reduced-fat sour cream and a quarter cup of chopped fresh dill.*

½ oz dried mushrooms
2½ cups hot water
1 (1¼-lb) boneless veal shoulder, cut into
    1-inch cubes
3 teaspoons olive oil
1 large onion, halved and sliced lengthwise
    ¼ inch thick
2 large garlic cloves, minced
1½ tablespoons all-purpose flour

1 tablespoon sweet Hungarian paprika
1 teaspoon tomato paste
2 red bell peppers
1 lb fresh *cremini* mushrooms, trimmed and
    halved (quartered if large)

Soak dried mushrooms in hot water until softened, about 30 minutes. Remove mushrooms from liquid, reserving it, and rinse mushrooms. Squeeze out excess moisture and coarsely chop. Pour reserved mushroom liquid through a paper towel–lined sieve into a bowl to remove grit. Return mushrooms to liquid.

Pat veal dry and season with salt and pepper. Heat 1 teaspoon oil in a 4- to 5-quart heavy pot over moderate heat until hot but not smoking, then brown veal in batches. Transfer as browned to a bowl.

Add 1 teaspoon oil and onion to pot and cook over moderately low heat, stirring frequently, until softened. Add garlic and cook, stirring, until fragrant, about 1 minute. Stir in flour and paprika and cook, stirring, 1 minute. Whisk in soaked mushrooms with liquid, scraping up any brown bits, and tomato paste, then bring to a simmer, whisking. Add browned veal with any juices. Cover and simmer over low heat until veal is tender, about 1¼ hours.

While meat is simmering, lay peppers on their sides on racks of gas burners and turn flames on high. Roast peppers, turning with tongs, until skins are blistered and blackened in spots, 4 to 5 minutes. (Or cut sides from peppers, discarding seeds and stems, and broil, skin sides up, on rack of a broiler pan about 2 inches from heat.) Transfer peppers to a bowl, cover, and cool. Peel and seed peppers and cut into 1-inch pieces.

Heat remaining teaspoon oil in a 12-inch nonstick skillet over moderately high heat until hot but not smoking, then sauté mushrooms with salt and pepper to taste, stirring occasionally, until browned and tender, 6 to 8 minutes. Stir into stew with bell peppers and salt and pepper to taste and gently simmer goulash 10 minutes to blend flavors.

Serve over noodles.

**Cooks' note:**
· **Goulash, like all stews, will taste even better if made 1 day ahead. Cool uncovered, then chill, covered. Reheat gently.**

each serving, including noodles, about 408 calories and 10 grams fat

## SPICY RED PORK AND BEAN CHILI

### Serves 8
Active time: 1½ hr   Start to finish: 3½ hr

*This recipe works best with ordinary chili powder, which typically includes not only ground dried chiles but other spices as well. Pure chile powder will be too strong.*

½ lb sliced bacon
1 (4-lb) boneless pork shoulder, cut into
    1-inch cubes
2 tablespoons vegetable oil
1 large white onion, chopped
1 to 2 fresh jalapeño chiles, seeded and chopped
4 large garlic cloves, minced
2 teaspoons dried oregano, crumbled
⅓ cup chili powder
1 tablespoon ground cumin
¼ teaspoon cayenne
1 (14½-oz) can beef broth
1 cup brewed coffee
1 cup water
1 (28- to 32-oz) can crushed tomatoes with purée
2 (19-oz) cans small red beans or kidney beans,
    rinsed and drained

*Accompaniments:* toasted salted pumpkin seeds
    (recipe follows), chopped red onion, fresh
    cilantro sprigs, diced avocado, lime wedges, sour
    cream, and warmed corn chips or tortilla chips

Cook bacon in a 6- to 8-quart heavy pot over moderate heat, turning, until crisp. Transfer with tongs to paper towels to drain and pour off all but 2 tablespoons fat from pot. Crumble bacon.

Pat pork dry and season with salt and pepper. Add oil to pot and heat over moderately high heat until hot but not smoking. Brown pork in about 6 batches without crowding and transfer with a slotted spoon to a plate. Add onion and jalapeños and cook over moderate heat, stirring, until softened. Add garlic, oregano, chili powder, cumin, and cayenne, then cook, stirring, 1 minute. Return pork to pot with any juices accumulated on plate and add broth, coffee, water, and tomatoes with purée.

Simmer chili, uncovered, stirring occasionally, until pork is very tender, about 2 hours. Stir in beans and bring to a simmer, stirring.

Serve chili with bacon and accompaniments.

Cooks' notes:
• Chili may be made 2 days ahead, cooled completely, then chilled, covered. Reheat before serving.
• Onion, cilantro sprigs, and lime wedges can be prepared up to 6 hours ahead and chilled in separate sealed plastic bags.

PHOTO ON PAGE 15

## TOASTED SALTED PUMPKIN SEEDS

### Makes 2 cups
Active time: 5 min   Start to finish: 20 min

*Besides serving these crunchy pumpkin seeds in our chili and chopped salad, we love to make up a batch to keep on hand as a snack.*

1 tablespoon olive oil
2 cups hulled (green) pumpkin seeds (sources on
    page 264)

Heat oil in a 12-inch nonstick skillet over moderate heat until hot but not smoking, then toast pumpkin seeds with salt and pepper to taste, stirring constantly, until seeds are puffed and beginning to pop, about 5 minutes. Transfer to a plate and cool completely.

Cooks' note:
• Toasted pumpkin seeds may be kept in an airtight container at room temperature 3 days.

## FENNEL-CRUSTED ROAST PORK

### Serves 4
Active time: 15 min   Start to finish: 1¼ hr

4 small red onions (10 oz total), each cut into
    6 wedges
3 teaspoons balsamic vinegar
2 teaspoons fennel seeds
½ teaspoon salt
1 (1-lb) boneless pork loin, trimmed
    and tied
2 cups fat-free chicken broth
1 teaspoon cornstarch

1 tablespoon water

1 teaspoon unsalted butter

*Garnish:* fresh flat-leaf parsley

Preheat oven to 425°F.

Brush onions with 2 teaspoons vinegar in a lightly oiled shallow (1-inch-deep) baking pan. Roast in middle of oven, turning over halfway through roasting and keeping wedges intact, until browned and tender, about 15 minutes. Cover to keep warm.

Reduce temperature to 400°F.

Coarsely grind fennel seeds, salt, and pepper to taste with a mortar and pestle or in an electric coffee/spice grinder, then spread on a plate. Roll pork in fennel mixture, coating all sides evenly.

Roast in a flameproof small shallow roasting pan in middle of oven until a thermometer inserted 2 inches into center of pork registers 155°F, 40 to 45 minutes. Transfer to a plate and let stand, covered, 15 minutes.

Add broth to roasting pan and deglaze by boiling over moderately high heat, scraping up brown bits, 1 minute. Transfer broth to a small saucepan and simmer until reduced to about ½ cup, 10 to 15 minutes. Add remaining teaspoon vinegar and simmer 1 minute. Stir together cornstarch and water and stir into broth. Bring to a boil, then remove from heat and stir in butter.

Serve pork with onions and sauce.

*each serving about 274 calories and 12 grams fat*

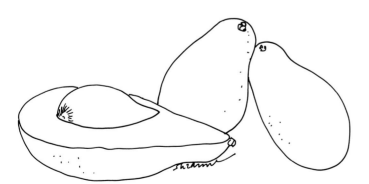

## SPICED PORK TENDERLOIN AND PINEAPPLE-AVOCADO SALSA

**Serves 6**
Active time: 10 min   Start to finish: 40 min

2½ tablespoons kosher salt

1 tablespoon ground allspice

1 tablespoon cayenne

3 (¾-lb) pork tenderloins

1 tablespoon oil

*Accompaniment:* pineapple-avocado salsa (recipe follows)

Preheat oven to 400°F.

Stir together kosher salt, allspice, and cayenne. Pat pork dry and sprinkle spice rub all over pork, pressing to adhere.

Heat oil in a 12-inch heavy skillet over moderately high heat until hot but not smoking, then brown pork, 1 tenderloin at a time, on all sides, about 1 minute each. Transfer as browned to a large roasting pan and arrange 2 inches apart.

Roast in middle of oven until an instant-read thermometer inserted diagonally 2 inches into center of each tenderloin registers 155°F, 20 to 25 minutes. Let pork stand 5 minutes before slicing.

PHOTO ON PAGE 30

## PINEAPPLE-AVOCADO SALSA

**Serves 6**
Active time: 25 min   Start to finish: 25 min

1 cup ¼-inch-dice fresh pineapple

2 plum tomatoes, seeded and cut into ¼-inch dice

1 firm-ripe California avocado, cut into ¼-inch dice

½ cup chopped sweet onion

¼ cup chopped fresh cilantro

1½ teaspoons minced fresh jalapeño chile, including seeds

3 tablespoons fresh lime juice

3 tablespoons fresh orange juice

2 tablespoons extra-virgin olive oil

Stir together all ingredients and season with salt.

## CORNMEAL- AND CUMIN-COATED PORK LOIN

*Serves 4*
Active time: 20 min   Start to finish: 1 hr

1 (1¼-lb) boneless pork loin, trimmed
2 tablespoons yellow cornmeal
1 tablespoon cumin seeds, toasted and coarsely
    ground
1½ teaspoons olive oil

Preheat oven to 350°F.

Pat pork dry and season with salt and pepper. Stir together cornmeal and cumin and transfer to a plate. Turn pork in cornmeal mixture to coat well and discard any remaining mixture.

Heat oil in a 10-inch nonstick skillet until hot but not smoking, then brown pork, turning, about 3 minutes. Transfer to a shallow baking pan and roast in middle of oven until a thermometer inserted diagonally at least 2 inches into pork registers 155°F, 30 to 45 minutes. Let stand, loosely covered, 10 minutes.

Cut pork into 12 slices (about ¼ inch thick).

each serving about 208 calories and 11 grams fat

PHOTO ON PAGE 80

## CARAWAY-CRUSTED PORK CHOPS

*Serves 2*
Active time: 10 min   Start to finish: 25 min

1 tablespoon caraway seeds
½ teaspoon black peppercorns
2 (¾-inch-thick) center-cut pork chops
2 teaspoons vegetable oil
¼ cup cider vinegar
½ cup apple juice
1 teaspoon cold unsalted butter

Finely grind caraway seeds and peppercorns in an electric coffee/spice grinder or with a mortar and pestle and spread on a small plate. Season chops with salt and dredge in spice mixture, coating completely.

Heat oil in a 10-inch nonstick skillet over moderately high heat until hot but not smoking, then sauté chops until golden brown and just cooked through, about 5 minutes on each side. Transfer to a plate. Add vinegar to

skillet and deglaze over moderately high heat, scraping up brown bits, until most of vinegar is evaporated, about 20 seconds. Add juice and simmer until reduced by half, about 3 minutes. Stir butter into sauce with salt to taste and pour over pork chops.

## FRIZZLED BLACK FOREST HAM

*Serves 8*
Active time: 5 min   Start to finish: 5 min

16 very thin slices Black Forest ham (8 oz)

Sauté ham in batches without crowding in a large nonstick skillet over moderately high heat, turning once, until lightly browned and curled, about 1 minute total.

each serving (2 slices) about 32 calories and 5 grams fat

**LAMB**

## HIBISCUS-MARINATED LEG OF LAMB

*Serves 8*
Active time: 1 hr   Start to finish: 15 hr

1 qt water
3 large garlic cloves, peeled and smashed
10 black peppercorns, coarsely cracked
1 cup dried nontoxic, organic hibiscus flowers
    (1½ oz; sources on page 264) or 20 bags Red
    Zinger tea leaves (1 box), removed from bags
¼ cup sugar
1 (6- to 8-lb) leg of lamb, with aitch bone
    (rump bone) removed by butcher
2 tablespoons olive oil
1 tablespoon red currant jelly
2 tablespoons cold unsalted butter, cut into pieces

*Special equipment:* 2 extra-large (2-gallon) sealable
    plastic bags

*Make marinade:*

Bring water to a boil with garlic and peppercorns. Add hibiscus flowers and gently simmer 5 minutes. Remove from heat and let marinade steep 30 minutes.

Pour through a fine sieve into a bowl, pressing on solids, then discard solids. Add sugar, stirring until dissolved, and chill until cold.

*Marinate lamb:*

Remove most of fat from lamb and put lamb in a double layer of sealable plastic bags with marinade. Marinate lamb, chilled, turning bag over once or twice, 12 to 24 hours.

*Roast lamb:*

Remove lamb from bag, reserving marinade, and transfer to a roasting pan just large enough to hold it. Pat lamb dry and rub with oil, then season generously with salt and pepper.

Preheat oven to 450°F. Put lamb in upper third of oven and reduce heat to 350°F. Roast until a thermometer inserted in thickest part of leg (without touching bone) registers 125°F, about 1 to 1½ hours.

Transfer lamb to a platter, cover with foil, and let stand 15 to 25 minutes (internal temperature will rise to about 135°F).

While lamb is standing, pour reserved marinade into roasting pan. Straddle pan across 2 burners and deglaze by boiling marinade, stirring and scraping up brown bits, until reduced to about 1 cup.

Add any meat juices that have accumulated on platter and whisk in jelly and salt and pepper to taste. Add butter and swirl or shake roasting pan until incorporated. Pour sauce through a fine sieve into a sauceboat to serve with lamb.

PHOTO ON PAGE 26

## GRILLED LAMB CHOPS WITH SALMORIGLIO SAUCE

**Serves 4**
Active time: 15 min   Start to finish: 15 min

1½ tablespoons finely chopped fresh oregano
1½ tablespoons finely chopped fresh thyme
2 teaspoons finely grated fresh lemon zest
1½ tablespoons fresh lemon juice
1 teaspoon kosher salt plus additional for
　　seasoning
6 tablespoons extra-virgin olive oil
4 (¾-inch-thick) shoulder-blade lamb chops

Grind herbs, zest, lemon juice, and 1 teaspoon kosher salt to a paste with a mortar and pestle. Transfer

to a bowl and add oil in a slow stream, whisking until emulsified. Season with salt and pepper.

Pat lamb dry and season with kosher salt and pepper. Heat a lightly oiled well-seasoned ridged grill pan over moderately high heat until hot but not smoking, then grill lamb, turning once, about 4 minutes on each side for medium-rare.

Serve sauce spooned over lamb.

## LAMB CHOPS WITH COARSE-GRAIN MUSTARD

**Serves 4**
Active time: 15 min   Start to finish: 15 min

4 (¾-inch-thick) lamb shoulder arm (round bone)
　　chops, trimmed (2 lb total)
¼ cup coarse-grain mustard

Prepare grill for cooking or heat a well-seasoned ridged grill pan (preferably cast-iron) over moderately high heat until hot.

Pat chops dry and season with salt and pepper. Grill until undersides are browned, about 3 minutes, then turn over and spread browned sides with mustard. Grill about 4 minutes more for medium-rare.

**Cooks' note:**
- **To prevent chops from curling while grilling, make two ¼-inch cuts in outer curved edge of each chop.**

## LEMON-GARLIC LAMB CHOPS WITH YOGURT SAUCE

**Serves 4**
Active time: 20 min   Start to finish: 45 min

*For yogurt sauce*
1 cup plain yogurt
1 garlic clove, minced
2 tablespoons chopped fresh mint
*For chops*
¼ cup fresh lemon juice
2 large garlic cloves, chopped
½ teaspoon dried oregano, crumbled
3 tablespoons olive oil
4 (½-inch-thick) shoulder lamb chops
1 tablespoon water

*Make sauce:*

Drain yogurt in a sieve lined with a double thickness of cheesecloth at room temperature 20 minutes. Stir together with garlic, fresh mint, and salt and pepper to taste.

*Prepare chops while yogurt drains:*

Stir together lemon juice, garlic, oregano, and 2 tablespoons oil in a shallow baking dish. Add lamb chops, turning to coat, and marinate 20 minutes.

Remove lamb from marinade, reserving marinade, and season with salt and pepper. Heat remaining tablespoon oil in a 12-inch nonstick skillet over moderately high heat until hot but not smoking, then sauté chops in 2 batches, without crowding, about 2 minutes on each side for medium-rare. Transfer to plates. Boil reserved marinade in skillet with water 1 minute and pour over lamb chops.

Serve chops with yogurt sauce.

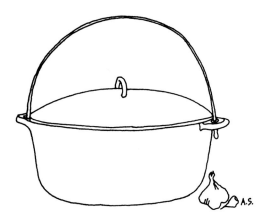

## CORIANDER- AND CHILE-RUBBED LAMB CHOPS

**Serves 6**
Active time: 25 min   Start to finish: 55 min

½ cup fresh lemon juice
2 tablespoons minced garlic
12 (1-inch-thick) boneless lamb loin chops
   (tied by butcher) or shoulder chops
¼ cup plus 1 tablespoon coriander seeds
1½ teaspoons dried hot red pepper flakes
About 6 tablespoons olive oil

Divide lemon juice and garlic between 2 sealable plastic bags and put 6 tied chops in each bag, shaking to distribute marinade. Marinate 20 minutes.

Grind coriander seeds and red pepper flakes with a mortar and pestle or in an electric coffee/spice grinder, then pour onto a plate. Pat chops dry and season well with salt. Dip both sides of each chop into spice mixture to coat.

Preheat oven to 450°F. Heat 2 tablespoons oil in a 12-inch heavy skillet over moderately high heat until hot but not smoking, then brown chops, 4 at a time, until browned on all sides (add more oil to skillet for each batch). Transfer chops to a large shallow (1-inch-deep) baking pan as browned.

When all chops are browned, roast in middle of oven 10 minutes for medium-rare. Remove string before serving chops.

Cooks' note:
• **Chops may be browned 30 minutes ahead and kept at room temperature.**

PHOTO ON PAGE 25

## LAMB KOLUMBU

### LAMB IN FENNEL-COCONUT SAUCE

**Serves 6**
Active time: 50 min   Start to finish: 2¾ hr

*For coconut spice paste*
½ cup desiccated coconut or ¾ cup freshly
   grated coconut
8 garlic cloves, finely chopped
2 tablespoons finely chopped peeled fresh ginger
1 cup water

1 tablespoon fennel seeds, finely ground

2 tablespoons ground coriander

1½ teaspoons Indian red chile powder
   (sources on page 264)

½ teaspoon turmeric

*For lamb*

⅓ cup vegetable oil

1 teaspoon cumin seeds

1 teaspoon fenugreek seeds

¼ teaspoon fennel seeds, finely ground

4 green cardamom pods

1 (3-inch) cinnamon stick

10 fresh curry leaves (sources on page 264)

1 large onion, chopped

2 plum tomatoes, chopped

1 teaspoon salt

1 (2½-lb) trimmed boneless lamb shoulder,
   cut into 1½-inch pieces

3 cups water

½ cup finely chopped fresh cilantro

*Make coconut spice paste:*

If using desiccated coconut, soak in a bowl of warm water to cover 1 hour and drain well.

Purée coconut, garlic, and ginger with ½ cup water in a blender, then blend in remaining ½ cup water, fennel, coriander, chile powder, and turmeric.

*Make lamb:*

Heat oil in a 6- to 7-quart heavy pot over moderately high heat until hot but not smoking, then cook cumin, fenugreek, fennel, cardamom pods, and cinnamon stick, stirring, until fragrant, about 30 seconds. Add curry leaves and cook, stirring, until fragrant, about 30 seconds. Add onion and cook, stirring, until softened and beginning to brown. Add tomatoes and cook, stirring occasionally, until softened, about 1 minute.

Add coconut spice paste and salt and cook, stirring occasionally, 5 minutes. Add lamb and cook, stirring occasionally, until no longer pink on outside, 2 to 3 minutes. Add water and simmer, covered, stirring occasionally, until lamb is very tender, about 1½ hours. Transfer lamb with a slotted spoon to a bowl and simmer sauce until thickened. Return lamb to pot and season with salt.

Just before serving, stir in cilantro.

**Cooks' note:**
· **Lamb may be made 1 day ahead and chilled, covered.**

## BUFFALO MEAT LOAF

**Serves 6**
Active time: 40 min   Start to finish: 2 hr

1 cup chopped onion

2 celery ribs, cut into ¼-inch dice

1 carrot, cut into ¼-inch dice

1 tablespoon chopped garlic

3 teaspoons vegetable oil

¾ cup fine fresh bread crumbs

½ cup chopped fresh flat-leaf parsley

1 large egg

2 tablespoons ketchup

1 tablespoon Worcestershire sauce

2 teaspoons salt

¼ teaspoon black pepper

1¾ lb ground buffalo (sources on page 264)

6 shallots, each cut into ⅓-inch wedges

6 plum tomatoes, each cut into 6 wedges

⅓ cup water

Preheat oven to 375°F.

Cook onion, celery, carrot, and garlic in 2 teaspoons oil in a large nonstick skillet over moderate heat until onion is softened. Transfer to a large bowl and stir in bread crumbs, parsley, egg, ketchup, Worcestershire sauce, salt, and pepper. Stir in buffalo (do not overmix) and form mixture into a 10- by 4-inch oval loaf in a large shallow metal baking pan. Toss shallots and tomatoes with remaining teaspoon oil and salt and pepper to taste, then scatter around meat loaf. Bake in middle of oven 1 hour and 10 minutes, or until a thermometer inserted 2 inches into center registers 160°F. Transfer meat loaf and vegetables to a platter and let stand 10 minutes.

While meat loaf is standing, add water to baking pan and deglaze by boiling over moderate heat, stirring and scraping up brown bits, and pour through a fine sieve into a bowl.

Serve meat loaf with shallots, tomatoes, and sauce.

each serving about 221 calories and 8 grams fat

## CREAMED CHICKEN WITH CORN AND BACON OVER POLENTA

*Serves 6*
Active time: 35 min   Start to finish: 35 min

*For creamed chicken*
6 bacon slices, cut into ½-inch pieces
1 lb skinless boneless chicken breast halves
2 cups fresh corn kernels (3 ears)
1 cup milk
2 tablespoons unsalted butter
2 tablespoons all-purpose flour
1¼ cups heavy cream
½ teaspoon black pepper
1 teaspoon kosher salt
3 large plum tomatoes, seeded and finely diced
*For polenta*
6 cups water
2½ teaspoons kosher salt
1½ cups instant polenta
½ lb Fontina cheese (preferably Italian), diced
½ cup finely grated parmesan

¼ cup chopped fresh basil

*Cook bacon and chicken:*
Cook bacon in a large heavy skillet (preferably cast-iron) over moderate heat, stirring, until crisp. Transfer with a slotted spoon to paper towels, then pour off all but about 1½ tablespoons fat from skillet.

Pat chicken dry and season with salt and pepper. Add to skillet with bacon fat and cook over moderately high heat, turning several times, until nicely crusted and just cooked through, 8 to 10 minutes. Transfer to a plate and cool. Tear chicken into bite-size pieces.

*Prepare corn and sauce while chicken cooks:*
Gently simmer corn and milk in a heavy saucepan until corn is crisp-tender, about 5 minutes. Pour mixture through a sieve into a bowl and reserve corn and milk separately.

Melt butter in same saucepan over moderately low heat. Add flour and cook roux, stirring, 3 minutes. Gradually whisk in cream, then reserved warm milk, pepper, and salt. Bring to a boil, whisking, then simmer, whisking, 3 minutes. Stir in tomatoes, chicken, and corn. Keep warm, covered, over very low heat.

*Make polenta:*
Bring water with salt to a boil in a heavy saucepan.

Gradually add polenta and cook over moderately high heat, whisking, 5 minutes. Stir in cheeses.

Divide polenta among 6 shallow bowls. Stir basil into chicken mixture and spoon over polenta. Sprinkle with bacon.

## MUSTARD-ROASTED CHICKEN LEGS ON ARUGULA

*Serves 4*
Active time: 15 min   Start to finish: 45 min

8 chicken drumsticks (2 to 2¼ lb)
⅓ cup mustard with horseradish
½ cup dry bread crumbs
2 tablespoons sesame seeds
2 tablespoons unsalted butter, melted
2 tablespoons extra-virgin olive oil
1 tablespoon cider vinegar
4 cups arugula, coarse stems discarded and
   leaves torn into pieces

Preheat oven to 450°F.
Pat drumsticks dry and season with salt and pepper. Coat drumsticks with mustard.

Combine bread crumbs and sesame seeds in a pie plate and season with salt and pepper. Coat drumsticks with crumb mixture and put in an oiled shallow (1-inch-deep) baking pan. Drizzle with butter.

Roast drumsticks, turning once, until golden brown and cooked through, 25 to 30 minutes.

Whisk together oil and vinegar until emulsified, then season with salt and pepper. Toss arugula with dressing and mound on a platter. Arrange drumsticks on top of greens.

## JUANA'S CHICKEN-STUFFED POBLANOS

*Serves 4*
Active time: 45 min   Start to finish: 1¼ hr

8 medium *poblano* chiles (1¼ lb)
1 large onion, finely chopped
½ tablespoon corn oil
¼ cup water
2 plum tomatoes, finely diced
2 cups chopped cooked chicken breast meat (½ lb)

1 teaspoon kosher salt
½ teaspoon black pepper
2½ oz Monterey Jack cheese, cut into
    ¼-inch dice (⅔ cup)

*Roast chiles:*

Lay 4 chiles on their sides on racks of gas burners and turn flames on high. (Or broil all 8 chiles on rack of a broiler pan about 2 inches from heat.) Roast chiles, turning with tongs, until skins are blistered but not blackened, 4 to 6 minutes (do not overroast because chiles may fall apart). Transfer immediately to a large sealable plastic bag, then close to allow chiles to steam. Roast remaining chiles in same manner.

*Make filling:*

Cook onion in oil in a nonstick skillet over moderately low heat, stirring, until onion begins to turn golden, about 4 minutes. Add water and cook, stirring occasionally, until water is evaporated and onion is tender, about 5 minutes. Add tomatoes and cook, stirring, until softened, about 4 minutes. Remove from heat and stir in chicken, salt, and pepper. Cool completely, then stir in cheese.

*Stuff and bake chiles:*

Preheat oven to 350°F.

Rub skins off chiles. Cut a slit lengthwise in each chile and carefully remove seeds (leave stem attached).

Stuff filling into chiles through slits, keeping chiles intact. Place chiles in a 13- by 9-inch baking dish and cover tightly with foil. Bake in middle of oven until cheese is melted, about 30 minutes.

each serving about 200 calories and 10 grams fat

**ASSORTED FOWL**

3 (1½-lb) Cornish hens
3 red bell peppers, cut into 1-inch-wide strips
3 large carrots, cut diagonally into ¾-inch pieces
6 shallots, halved
1 medium celery root (sometimes called celeriac),
    peeled and cut into 1-inch pieces
1 large boiling potato, peeled and cut into 1-inch
    pieces
1 tablespoon caraway seeds
2 tablespoons chopped fresh flat-leaf parsley
1 cup sour cream
3 tablespoons water

Preheat oven to 475°F. Heat a 17- by 11½- by 2-inch flameproof roasting pan in upper third of oven 10 minutes.

Stir together oil, paprika, cayenne, and salt in a large bowl. Rinse hens and pat dry. Remove any excess fat from opening of cavities and season cavities with salt and pepper. Tie drumsticks together if desired. Brush some of spice oil over hens. Toss vegetables and caraway seeds in remaining spice oil to coat and transfer to hot roasting pan. Roast vegetables, uncovered, 25 minutes. Stir vegetables and arrange hens, breast sides up, on top. Roast 40 minutes, then baste hens with pan juices and roast 20 minutes more, or until a thermometer inserted in fleshy part of thigh registers 170°F. Pour any juices from inside hens into pan.

Transfer hens to a cutting board and halve each lengthwise along backbone. Transfer vegetables with a slotted spoon to a platter. Sprinkle parsley over vegetables and top with hen pieces. Skim fat from pan juices and pour over hens. Stir together sour cream and water and serve on the side.

PHOTO ON PAGE 83

### PAPRIKA-ROASTED CORNISH HENS AND VEGETABLES

**Serves 6**
Active time: 30 min   Start to finish: 2 hr

¼ cup vegetable oil
1½ tablespoons sweet paprika (preferably
    Hungarian)
½ teaspoon cayenne, or to taste
2½ teaspoons salt

## ORANGE PEKING DUCK

### Serves 8
Active time: 40 min   Start to finish: 3½ days

*Ken Hom likes to dry his duck the traditional way: He hangs it in front of a fan at cool room temperature for 1 day. In keeping with U.S. food-safety standards, we've adapted his technique for the refrigerator, with excellent results. The Pekin (Long Island) duck available in the U.S. has a thicker layer of fat than the French variety, but we were still able to roast away most of the fat layer, leaving mahogany-colored crisp skin.*

*For honey syrup*

2 oranges, cut into ¼-inch-thick rounds

4 cups water

3 tablespoons honey

3 tablespoons dark (black or mushroom) soy sauce

*For duck*

1 (5½- to 6-lb) fresh Pekin duck (sometimes called Long Island duck), excess fat removed from cavity, rinsed inside and out, and patted dry

1 tablespoon Chinese five-spice powder (sources on page 264)

1 tablespoon coarse sea salt

1 teaspoon coarsely ground mixed or black peppercorns

2 small oranges, quartered

6 (¼-inch-thick) fresh ginger slices

*Make honey syrup:*

Bring honey syrup ingredients to a boil in a heavy saucepan, stirring, then simmer, stirring occasionally, 20 minutes.

*Season duck while syrup simmers:*

Fold neck skin of duck under body and fasten with a small skewer. Stir together five-spice powder, salt, and pepper, then rub inside cavity. Put duck on a rack set in a roasting pan.

*Coat and dry duck:*

Ladle hot syrup over duck (do not ladle any into cavity), turning duck occasionally to coat all over. Discard syrup in roasting pan and set duck, breast side up, on rack in pan. Prop rack up over a short edge of pan so duck is tilted (large-cavity side down) to facilitate draining of any moisture it gives off. (To prevent rack from slipping, put a piece of crumpled plastic wrap between pan and rack.) Dry duck, uncovered and chilled in refrigerator, 3 days.

*Roast duck:*

Preheat oven to 325°F. Let duck stand at room temperature 30 minutes.

Remove plastic wrap and set rack back into pan. Stuff duck with orange quarters and ginger and close cavity opening with a wooden skewer. Prick duck all over with tip of a sharp paring knife and pour 1 cup water into pan.

Roast in middle of oven 1½ hours. Increase oven temperature to 450°F and roast until skin is dark brown and very crisp and a thermometer inserted in thick part of thigh registers 170°F, 25 to 30 minutes more.

Transfer duck to a heated platter and remove cavity skewer. Let stand 30 minutes before carving.

PHOTO ON PAGE 64

## ROAST TURKEY WITH APPLES, ONIONS, FRIED SAGE LEAVES, AND APPLE CIDER GRAVY

### Serves 8
Active time: 1¼ hr   Start to finish: 3¾ hr

*Lady apples are often used decoratively, but we love them for their flavor. They're widely available in markets during the fall.*

*For turkey*

1 (12- to 14-lb) turkey (preferably kosher), feathers removed if necessary and neck and giblets (excluding liver) reserved for making stock

1 lb pearl onions (preferably red)

16 to 20 (2-inch) Lady apples (2 lb)

¾ stick (6 tablespoons) unsalted butter, melted

*For gravy*

Pan juices from roast turkey

About 4 cups turkey giblet stock (page 138)

1 cup apple cider

2 tablespoons cider vinegar

¼ cup all-purpose flour

*Accompaniment*: fried sage leaves (recipe follows) and cranberry chutney (page 138)

*Roast turkey:*

Preheat oven to 425°F.

Rinse turkey inside and out and pat dry. Season with salt and pepper inside and out. Fold neck skin under body and secure with a small skewer. Tie drumsticks together with kitchen string and secure wings to body with small skewers. Put turkey on a rack set in a large flameproof roasting pan. Roast turkey in middle of oven 30 minutes.

While turkey is roasting, blanch onions in boiling water 1 minute and rinse under cold water. Peel onions. Toss onions and apples in separate bowls with 1 tablespoon melted butter each and salt and pepper to taste.

Reduce temperature to 350°F. Brush remaining ¼ cup melted butter over turkey and roast 30 minutes more. Baste turkey and scatter onions around it, then roast 30 minutes more.

Baste turkey and add apples to roasting pan. Roast another 1 to 1½ hours, or until a thermometer inserted into fleshy part of a thigh registers 180°F.

Transfer turkey, onions, and apples to a heated platter, leaving juices in pan. Remove skewers and discard string. Let turkey stand at least 30 minutes, up to 45.

*Make gravy while turkey stands:*

Skim fat from pan juices and reserve ¼ cup fat. Pour pan juices into a 2-quart glass measure and add enough turkey giblet stock to make 4½ cups total. Set pan to straddle 2 burners. Add 1 cup stock mixture and deglaze by boiling over moderately high heat, stirring and scraping up brown bits. Add remaining 3½ cups stock mixture, cider, and vinegar and bring to a simmer. Transfer to glass measure.

Whisk together reserved fat and flour in a large heavy saucepan and cook roux over moderately low heat, whisking, 3 minutes. Add hot stock mixture in a fast stream, whisking constantly to prevent lumps, then simmer, whisking occasionally, until thickened, about 10 minutes.

Stir in any additional turkey juices from platter and season gravy with salt and pepper. Pour gravy through a fine sieve into a gravy boat.

Cooks' note:
· Onions can be blanched and peeled 2 days ahead and chilled, covered.

PHOTO ON PAGE 69

## FRIED SAGE LEAVES

*Makes about 3 cups*
Active time: 5 min   Start to finish: 10 min

About 4 cups vegetable oil
1 cup packed fresh sage leaves

Heat 1 inch of oil in a 4-quart heavy saucepan until it registers 365°F on a deep-fat thermometer. Fry sage in 4 batches, stirring, 3 to 5 seconds. Transfer with a slotted spoon to paper towels to drain, then season with salt.

Cooks' note:
· Sage can be fried 2 days ahead and kept in an airtight container at room temperature.

## CRANBERRY CHUTNEY

**Makes about 2 cups**
Active time: 10 min   Start to finish: 20 min

5 shallots (6 oz), coarsely chopped
1½ tablespoons vegetable oil
1 (12-oz) bag fresh or frozen cranberries
⅔ cup sugar
¼ cup cider vinegar
1 teaspoon minced garlic
1 teaspoon minced peeled fresh ginger
½ teaspoon salt
½ teaspoon black pepper

Cook shallots in oil in a 3-quart heavy saucepan over moderate heat, stirring occasionally, until softened. Stir in remaining ingredients. Simmer, stirring occasionally, until berries just pop, 10 to 12 minutes, then cool.

PHOTO ON PAGES 68 AND 69

## TURKEY GIBLET STOCK

**Makes about 4 cups**
Active time: 10 min   Start to finish: 1 hr

1 tablespoon vegetable oil
Neck and giblets (excluding liver) from turkey
1 celery rib, coarsely chopped
1 carrot, coarsely chopped
1 onion, quartered
4 cups water
2 cups chicken broth
1 bay leaf
1 teaspoon black peppercorns

Heat oil in a 3-quart saucepan over moderately high heat until hot but not smoking, then brown neck and giblets. Add remaining ingredients and simmer until reduced to about 4 cups, 45 minutes to 1 hour. Pour stock through a fine sieve into a bowl. Skim off and discard any fat.

Cooks' note:
· **Stock can be made 1 day ahead. Cool completely, uncovered, then chill, covered.**

## TURKEY SCALLOPINI WITH CAPERS AND LEMON

**Serves 4**
Active time: 25 min   Start to finish: 25 min

1½ lb (¼-inch-thick) sliced raw turkey cutlets
½ cup all-purpose flour
4 tablespoons olive oil
2 garlic cloves, minced
1 cup chicken broth
1 to 1½ tablespoons fresh lemon juice
2 tablespoons capers, rinsed
2 tablespoons chopped fresh flat-leaf parsley

Pat turkey dry and season with salt and pepper. Dredge half of turkey slices in flour, shaking off excess. Heat 1½ tablespoons oil in a 12-inch heavy skillet over high heat until hot but not smoking, then sauté turkey until browned on both sides and just cooked through, about 4 minutes total. Transfer to a platter and keep warm, covered. Dredge and sauté remaining turkey with another 1½ tablespoons oil in same manner.

Add remaining tablespoon oil to skillet and cook garlic over moderate heat, stirring, until fragrant, about 30 seconds. Add broth and deglaze by boiling over moderately high heat, stirring and scraping up brown bits. Boil until broth is reduced to about ¾ cup. Stir in lemon juice, capers, parsley, and salt and pepper to taste. Return turkey to skillet with any juices on platter and simmer until heated through, about 1 minute.

# BREAKFAST AND BRUNCH DISHES

## SALMON-WRAPPED POACHED EGGS

**Serves 8**
Active time: 1 hr   Start to finish: 1 hr

*When poaching eggs for a crowd, we've found the baking pan method below to be almost foolproof. Have a friend help you wrap the eggs in salmon before they get cold. If you're working on your own, you may want to simply drape the salmon over the eggs.*

*For sauce*
½ cup sour cream
2 teaspoons fresh lemon juice
¼ cup olive oil
1 tablespoon finely chopped fresh chives
½ tablespoon chopped fresh tarragon
½ teaspoon kosher salt

1 small red onion, thinly sliced
2 ripe California avocados
1 to 2 tablespoons fresh lemon juice
6 individual brioches, each cut horizontally into
    3 (½-inch-thick) rounds and lightly toasted
¼ lb sorrel or arugula, coarse stems discarded
4 teaspoons distilled white vinegar
16 large eggs
1 lb thinly sliced smoked salmon

*Garnish:* chopped fresh chives

Preheat oven to 350°F.
*Make sauce:*
Whisk together sour cream and lemon juice. Add oil in a slow stream, whisking until emulsified. (If necessary, add water, ½ tablespoon at a time, for a thick yet spoonable consistency.) Stir in chives, tarragon, kosher salt, and pepper to taste.
*Prepare brioches for serving:*

Soak onion in cold water to cover 10 minutes, then drain and pat dry.

Halve and peel avocados and cut crosswise into ¼-inch-thick slices, then sprinkle slices with lemon juice. Put 2 brioche toasts on each of 8 plates and season with salt and pepper. Arrange a few sorrel leaves on each toast, then top with avocado and onion.

*Poach eggs:*
Fill a well-buttered 17- by 11- by 2-inch flameproof baking pan with 1¼ inches water and stir in vinegar (to help whites coagulate faster). Set pan to straddle 2 burners and bring water to a simmer.

Break 1 egg into a cup and slide into water. Repeat with remaining eggs, adding them in rows so you can easily take them out in same order. Poach eggs at a bare simmer 3 to 4 minutes, or until whites are firm but yolks are still runny. Transfer eggs as cooked with a slotted spoon to kitchen towels to drain and season with salt and pepper.

Wrap each egg in a slice of salmon. Put a wrapped egg on top of each toast and drizzle sauce over salmon.

Cooks' notes:
· If you can't get individual brioches, you can use a brioche or challah loaf. Cut 16 (½-inch-thick) slices and halve them diagonally.
· Serving these eggs with runny—not fully cooked—yolks may be of concern if there is a problem with salmonella in your area.

PHOTO ON PAGE 51

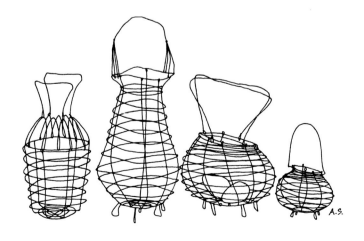

## BREAKFAST EMPANADAS

**Serves 4 (8 empanadas)**
Active time: 1 hr   Start to finish: 1¼ hr

3 cups plus 2 teaspoons vegetable oil
2 Spanish *chorizo* links (spicy dried pork
    sausage; 6 to 8 oz), cut into ½-inch pieces
1 onion, chopped
1 lb boiling potatoes such as Yukon Gold,
    peeled and cut into ½-inch cubes
2 jalapeño chiles, seeded and finely
    chopped
2 plum tomatoes, seeded and chopped
½ teaspoon ground cumin
¼ cup finely chopped fresh cilantro
⅓ cup grated *queso blanco* or Monterey Jack
8 frozen *empanada* or turnover wrappers, thawed

*Accompaniments:* bottled or homemade *salsa verde*
    and sour cream

Heat 2 teaspoons oil in a 12-inch nonstick skillet over moderately high heat until hot but not smoking, then sauté *chorizo* and onion, stirring, until onion is softened. Add potatoes with salt and pepper to taste and cook, covered, stirring occasionally, until potatoes begin to turn golden brown, about 6 minutes. Stir in jalapeños, tomatoes, and cumin and cook, uncovered, stirring occasionally, until potatoes are tender and golden brown, about 6 minutes. Transfer to a bowl and cool completely. Stir in cilantro, cheese, and salt and pepper to taste.

Roll out each *empanada* wrapper into a 6-inch round on a lightly floured surface. Put about ⅓ cup filling in center of each wrapper and form filling into a log. Moisten wrapper edges with a finger dipped in water and fold each wrapper over filling to form a half-moon. Press down around filling to force out air and seal by pressing edges together firmly with a fork.

Heat remaining 3 cups oil in a deep 12-inch skillet over moderate heat until hot but not smoking, then fry *empanadas* in 3 batches, gently turning, until golden brown, about 3 minutes. Transfer *empanadas* to paper towels to drain.

Cooks' note:
• Breakfast *empanadas* may be filled 1 day ahead and chilled in 1 layer on a lightly floured plate, covered. Reseal edges if necessary.

## FRIED EGGS OVER WARM LENTIL SALAD WITH LARDONS

**Serves 4**
Active time: 40 min   Start to finish: 45 min

*One of our food editors savored this breakfast dish in a small bistro as her first meal in Paris and has never forgotten it. We've made it easy to re-create at home. It makes a hearty breakfast, brunch, or supper dish.*

¾ cup lentils (preferably French green lentils)
6 oz thick-cut bacon, cut crosswise into
    ¼-inch-thick strips
2 leeks (white and pale green parts only),
    finely chopped
2 celery ribs, finely chopped
1 large carrot, finely chopped
2 tablespoons red-wine vinegar, or to taste
1 tablespoon finely chopped fresh tarragon
1 tablespoon olive oil
8 large eggs
1 cup baby spinach

Cover lentils with cold water by 2 inches in a saucepan, then simmer, uncovered, until just tender, about 20 minutes.

While lentils are simmering, cook bacon in a 12-inch nonstick skillet over moderate heat, stirring, until crisp, then transfer with a slotted spoon to paper towels to drain, leaving fat in skillet. Add leeks, celery, and carrot to skillet and cook, stirring, until just tender. Add vinegar and boil until most of liquid is evaporated. Remove skillet from heat and stir in tarragon, half of bacon, and salt and pepper to taste. Transfer to a bowl and keep warm, covered. Reserve skillet.

Drain lentils well in a large sieve. Stir into vegetable mixture and season with salt and pepper. Keep warm, covered.

Wipe skillet with paper towels, then add oil and heat over moderate heat until hot but not smoking. Fry eggs in batches until whites are just set but yolks are still runny and season with salt and pepper.

Divide lentil salad among 4 plates. Top salad with spinach, eggs, and remaining bacon.

Cooks' note:
• Serving eggs with runny—not fully cooked—yolks may be of concern if salmonella is a problem in your area.

## PECAN WAFFLES WITH CARAMELIZED BANANAS

*Serves 4*
Active time: 35 min   Start to finish: 35 min

1 cup all-purpose flour
½ cup pecans, toasted and finely chopped
1 teaspoon baking powder
¼ teaspoon baking soda
½ teaspoon salt
1 cup well-shaken buttermilk
1 stick unsalted butter, melted
1 large egg, lightly beaten
3 large firm-ripe bananas
¾ cup sugar

*Special equipment:* a well-seasoned or nonstick
   standard waffle iron
*Accompaniment:* warm honey

Preheat oven to 250°F and preheat waffle iron.

Whisk together flour, pecans, baking powder and soda, and salt. Stir in buttermilk, 6 tablespoons butter, and egg until smooth (batter will be thick). Spoon batter into waffle iron, using half of batter for 4 (4-inch) standard waffles and spreading batter evenly, and cook according to manufacturer's instructions. Transfer waffles to a baking sheet and keep warm, uncovered, in middle of oven. Make more waffles in same manner.

Halve bananas crosswise and then lengthwise. Roll bananas in sugar to coat. Heat remaining 2 tablespoons butter in a large nonstick skillet over moderately high heat until foam subsides, then sauté bananas, starting with cut sides down and turning once, until golden brown. Transfer bananas with a spatula to an oiled baking sheet and cool slightly.

Put 4 waffles on 4 plates and divide bananas among them. Top bananas with remaining waffles.

## SAGE BUTTERMILK BISCUITS WITH SAUSAGE AND CHEDDAR

*Serves 8*
Active time: 50 min   Start to finish: 1¼ hr

*For biscuits*
2 cups all-purpose flour
2 tablespoons finely chopped fresh sage
2 teaspoons baking powder
2 teaspoons sugar
¾ teaspoon baking soda
½ teaspoon salt
¾ stick cold unsalted butter, cut into pieces
½ cup grated sharp Cheddar (2 oz)
¾ cup well-shaken buttermilk plus additional
   for brushing

¾ lb bulk fresh pork sausage
16 thin slices sharp Cheddar (8 oz)

*Make biscuits:*
Preheat oven to 450°F.

Whisk together flour, sage, baking powder, sugar, baking soda, and salt. Blend in butter with your fingers or a pastry blender until mixture resembles coarse meal. Stir in grated cheese, then buttermilk, stirring until a dough forms. Gather dough into a ball and gently knead on a lightly floured surface 8 times. Pat dough into an 8-by 4-inch rectangle and cut into 8 (2-inch) squares.

Arrange squares about 1 inch apart on a greased baking sheet and brush tops with additional buttermilk. Bake in middle of oven until golden brown and biscuits are cooked through, about 15 minutes. Leave oven on. Transfer biscuits to a rack to cool 10 minutes.

*Cook sausage while biscuits bake:*
Cut sausage crosswise into 8 equal pieces and flatten each into a 3-inch round. Cook sausage in 2 batches in a large nonstick skillet over moderate heat, turning, until cooked through, about 8 minutes per batch. Transfer to paper towels to drain.

*Make sandwiches:*
Split biscuits, then make sandwiches, each with 1 biscuit, 1 slice cheese, 1 sausage round, and another slice of cheese. Bake sandwiches on baking sheet in middle of oven until cheese is melted, about 10 minutes.

## CHEDDAR, ONION, AND RED BELL PEPPER SOUFFLÉED OMELET

### Serves 8
Active time: 45 min   Start to finish: 2¾ hr

1 cup chopped onion
1 cup chopped red bell pepper
½ teaspoon unsalted butter
3 cups 1% milk
⅔ cup yellow cornmeal (not polenta)
4 oz extra-sharp reduced-fat Cheddar (made
   from 2% milk), coarsely grated
2 tablespoons chopped fresh flat-leaf parsley
2 large egg yolks
¼ teaspoon black pepper
1 teaspoon salt
7 large egg whites
¼ teaspoon cream of tartar

Preheat oven to 375°F.

Cook onion and bell pepper in butter in a 2-quart heavy saucepan over moderate heat, stirring frequently, until softened. Add milk and bring to a boil. Add cornmeal in a slow stream, whisking, and cook over low heat, stirring constantly, until thickened, about 5 minutes. Remove from heat and cool 5 minutes. Whisk in Cheddar, parsley, yolks, pepper, and ½ teaspoon salt.

Beat whites with cream of tartar and remaining ½ teaspoon salt in a large bowl with an electric mixer on medium speed until they just hold stiff peaks. Fold one fourth of whites into cornmeal mixture to lighten, then fold cornmeal mixture gently but thoroughly into remaining whites. Spoon mixture into a greased 3-quart casserole and smooth top.

Bake in middle of oven until puffed and golden brown, 30 to 35 minutes. Serve immediately.

each serving about 170 calories and 6 grams fat

## EGGS, CARAMELIZED ONION, AND PANCETTA ON PITAS

### Serves 4
Active time: 45 min   Start to finish: 1 hr

¼ lb sliced *pancetta* or bacon, chopped
1½ lb onions, thinly sliced
¼ cup chopped fresh flat-leaf parsley

4 (7-inch) pita pockets, halved horizontally
2 tablespoons olive oil
4 large eggs

Cook *pancetta* in a large nonstick skillet over moderate heat, stirring, until crisp, about 4 minutes. Transfer *pancetta* with a slotted spoon to paper towels to drain. Pour off all but 1 tablespoon fat from skillet, reserving remaining fat. Add onions to skillet with salt and pepper to taste and cook over moderate heat, stirring occasionally and adding some of reserved fat if onions are sticking, until golden brown, about 20 minutes. Remove from heat and stir in parsley.

Preheat oven to 400°F.

Divide pitas, cut sides up, between 2 shallow baking pans and brush with oil. Season with salt and pepper and bake in upper and lower thirds of oven until golden and slightly crisp, about 7 minutes.

Remove 1 pan of pitas from oven and set aside. Top remaining pitas with onions (about ½ cup each), covering pitas. Form a well (with sides about ½ inch high) in center of onions to hold egg. Crack an egg into each and bake in middle of oven until whites are set, about 12 minutes. If desired, reheat plain pita toasts in oven until hot. Top eggs with *pancetta* and bake until yolks are cooked to desired doneness, about 3 to 5 minutes more. Top eggs with pitas to make sandwiches and cut into wedges if desired.

Cooks' note:
· Serving the eggs with runny—not fully cooked—yolks may be of concern if salmonella is a problem in your area.

MEXICO
# HUEVOS DIVORCIADOS

FRIED EGGS ON CORN TORTILLAS WITH TWO SALSAS

*Serves 4*
Active time: 45 min   Start to finish: 45 min

*For red and green salsas*
½ lb plum tomatoes
½ lb fresh tomatillos, husks discarded and
    tomatillos rinsed
2 fresh jalapeño chiles
1 (1-inch) wedge of large white onion
2 garlic cloves
2 teaspoons salt
3 tablespoons chopped fresh cilantro
¼ to ½ cup water

4 to 8 tablespoons corn or vegetable oil
8 large eggs
8 (6- to 7-inch) corn tortillas

*Make salsas:*

Heat a *comal* (griddle) or a dry well-seasoned cast-iron skillet over moderate heat until a bead of water evaporates quickly, then roast tomatoes, tomatillos, jalapeños, and onion, turning with tongs, until charred on all sides, 10 to 15 minutes. Core roasted tomatoes. Discard stems from jalapeños and discard half of seeds from each chile.

For red salsa: Coarsely purée tomatoes, 1 jalapeño, 1 garlic clove, and 1 teaspoon salt in a blender or food processor, then transfer to a bowl.

For green salsa: Coarsely purée tomatillos, remaining jalapeño, remaining garlic clove, remaining teaspoon salt, cilantro, and ¼ cup water (add more if needed for desired consistency), then transfer to a bowl.

*Cook eggs:*

Heat 2 tablespoons oil in a small nonstick skillet over moderately low heat until hot. Gently break 2 eggs into a cup, keeping yolks intact, then pour into skillet and cook, covered, 5 minutes, or to desired doneness. Season with salt and pepper. Make more eggs in same manner, adding oil as needed.

*Fry tortillas while each serving of eggs cooks:*

Heat 2 tablespoons oil in another small nonstick

skillet over moderate heat until hot but not smoking. Stack 2 tortillas in skillet. Cook bottom tortilla 30 seconds on first side, then flip stack with tongs. While second tortilla cooks on bottom, turn top tortilla over with tongs, then flip stack again. Continue until both sides of both tortillas are cooked. Tortillas will soften and puff slightly, then deflate (do not let them become brown or crisp). Fry more tortillas in same manner, adding oil as needed.

Put tortillas on plate, overlapping slightly, and top with eggs. Spoon a different salsa over each egg.

Cooks' notes:
· Salsas keep, covered and chilled, 3 days.
· Depending on how you like your eggs, the yolks may not be fully cooked, which may be of concern if there is a problem with salmonella in your area.
· Cooking 2 tortillas stacked together helps them stay moist and pliable, as they are heated by steam trapped between the 2 layers.

SCANDINAVIA
# CURRIED HERRING

*Serves 4*
Active time: 20 min   Start to finish: 20 min

*Herring is an essential part of Scandinavian cuisine and always has a place in the breakfast smorgasbord, along with other kinds of salted and pickled fish, breads, pastries, cheeses, cereals, eggs, and potatoes. (We admit that herring for breakfast may seem a little unusual to some people. But try it on a thick slice of buttered rye—you'll be quickly converted.)*

2 (8-oz) jars herring "party snacks" in white wine
    sauce, rinsed, drained, and patted dry
⅓ cup mayonnaise
⅓ cup sour cream
1½ tablespoons coarse-grained mustard
2 teaspoons fresh lemon juice
1 teaspoon curry powder
1 teaspoon sugar

*Accompaniment:* rye bread and butter

Remove and discard skin and dark flesh from herring. Cut herring into ¼-inch pieces. Whisk together remaining ingredients and stir in herring. Season with salt and pepper.

WEST AFRICA
## BEAN FRITTERS WITH HOT SAUCE

**Makes about 40 fritters**
Active time: 45 min   Start to finish: 1 hr

*These bean fritters appear in several West African countries; they are called akara in Nigeria and Sierra Leone and akla or koosé in Ghana. Although eaten as a snack or side dish, bean fritters are also consumed as breakfast food with hot sauce as an accompaniment.*

1 cup dried black-eyed peas
*For hot sauce*
2 red bell peppers, chopped
1 medium onion, chopped
1 medium tomato, chopped
1 teaspoon minced fresh *habanero* chile
   (with seeds)
1 teaspoon salt
¼ cup vegetable or peanut oil
½ to 1 teaspoon dried shrimp (optional; sources
   on page 264), ground
*For fritters*
½ medium onion, finely chopped
¼ teaspoon minced fresh *habanero* chile
   (with seeds)
1 large egg
1 teaspoon salt
6 to 8 tablespoons water
6 to 8 cups vegetable or peanut oil

*Prepare peas:*
Soak peas in water to cover by 2 inches for 8 hours. Drain in a colander.
*Make sauce:*
Purée bell peppers, onion, tomato, chile, and salt in a food processor.

Heat oil in a 10-inch heavy skillet over moderately high heat until hot but not smoking, then cook purée over moderate heat, stirring, about 8 minutes. Stir in ground shrimp. Cook, stirring occasionally, until most of liquid is evaporated, 3 to 5 minutes more.
*Make fritters:*
Purée peas, onion, and chile in food processor until as smooth as possible and blend in egg and salt. Blend in 6 tablespoons water until smooth and fluffy, adding remaining 2 tablespoons water if necessary to form a batter just thin enough to drop from a spoon.

*Fry fritters:*
Heat 2 inches oil in a 4-quart Dutch oven or a wide 4-inch-deep heavy pot until a deep-fat thermometer registers 375°F, then gently drop batter by tablespoons into hot oil, forming 8 fritters. Fry until golden, about 1½ minutes on each side, and transfer to paper towels to drain. Make more fritters in same manner, returning oil to 375°F between batches.

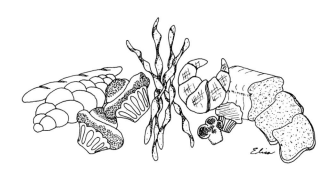

FRANCE
## PAINS AUX RAISINS

### RAISIN BRIOCHE PASTRIES

**Makes 11 buns**
Active time: 1½ hr   Start to finish: 18¼ hr

*Along with croissants and pains au chocolat, these buns are ubiquitous in the morning bread basket that arrives after you order your express or café crème in Paris. It's the pastry cream that makes them unique. We used former Gourmet editor Sally Darr's brioche recipe as the base.*

Cold brioche dough (recipe follows)
1 cup raisins
1 cup boiling-hot water
*For pastry cream*
1 cup whole milk
3 large egg yolks
⅓ cup sugar
1½ tablespoons cornstarch
½ teaspoon vanilla
½ tablespoon unsalted butter

¼ cup apricot preserves
2 tablespoons water

Make brioche dough the day before making pastry and chill.

Just before making pastry cream, soak raisins in hot

water until softened, about 10 minutes. Drain, pressing out excess liquid, and cool to room temperature.

*Make pastry cream:*

Bring whole milk to a simmer in a 1½-quart heavy saucepan. Whisk together yolks, sugar, and cornstarch in a bowl and gradually whisk in hot milk. Return mixture to pan and cook over moderately low heat, stirring with a wooden spoon, until mixture begins to boil. Simmer, stirring, until thickened and smooth, about 3 minutes. Transfer to a clean bowl and stir in vanilla and butter. Cover surface with plastic wrap and cool to room temperature.

*Make pastries:*

Roll out brioche dough on a well-floured surface into an 18- by 11-inch rectangle with a short side toward you. Spread pastry cream evenly over dough, leaving a ½-inch border at top edge. Sprinkle raisins evenly over cream. Roll up dough, starting from bottom, to make a log 11 inches long and about 3½ inches in diameter. Moisten top edge with water and press to seal closed.

Transfer log to a cutting board and cover loosely with plastic wrap. Chill until firm, about 1 hour.

Cut chilled log into 11 (1-inch-thick) rounds and arrange about 2 inches apart on 2 buttered baking sheets. Let pastries rise in a warm place, uncovered, 1 hour. (They will increase slightly in size and feel very tender to the touch.)

While pastries are rising, preheat oven to 425°F.

Bake in batches in middle of oven until tops are golden brown, 12 to 15 minutes. Transfer to a rack.

Simmer preserves and water, stirring, 1 minute. Pour through a sieve into a bowl, pressing on solids. Brush glaze onto pastries.

**Cooks' notes:**
- **Uncut log can be chilled overnight if desired.**
- **Pains aux raisins can be frozen 1 month, thawed, and reheated in a 350°F oven. However, the pastries really are best when eaten the day they are made.**

### Brioche Dough

*Makes about 1¼ lb*
Active time: 45 min   Start to finish: 15½ hr

*For starter*
1 teaspoon sugar
¼ cup warm milk or water (105°F)
1 (¼-oz) package active dry yeast (2½ teaspoons)

½ cup sifted all-purpose flour (sift before measuring)

*For dough*
¼ teaspoon salt
3 tablespoons sugar
1 tablespoon hot milk or water
3 large eggs
1½ cups sifted all-purpose flour (sift before measuring)
1½ sticks (¾ cup) unsalted butter, cut into ½-inch slices and well softened

*Special equipment:* a standing electric mixer with whisk and dough-hook attachments

*Make starter:*

Stir together sugar and warm milk in a small bowl. Sprinkle yeast over mixture and let stand until foamy, about 10 minutes. Stir flour into yeast mixture, forming a soft dough, and cut a deep X across top. Let starter rise, covered with plastic wrap, at room temperature, 1 hour.

*Make dough:*

Combine salt, sugar, and hot milk in a small bowl and stir until salt and sugar are dissolved.

Fit mixer with whisk attachment, then beat 2 eggs at medium-low speed until fluffy. Add sugar mixture and beat until combined well. With motor running, add in order, beating after each addition: ½ cup flour, remaining egg, ½ cup flour, about one fourth of butter, and remaining ½ cup flour. Beat mixture 1 minute.

Remove bowl from mixer and fit mixer with dough-hook attachment. Spread starter onto dough with a rubber spatula and return bowl to mixer. Beat dough at medium-high speed 6 minutes, or until dough is smooth and elastic. Add remaining butter and beat 1 minute, or until butter is incorporated.

Lightly butter a large bowl and scrape dough into bowl with rubber spatula. Lightly dust dough with flour to prevent a crust from forming. Cover bowl with plastic wrap and let dough rise at room temperature until more than doubled in bulk, 2 to 3 hours.

Punch down dough and lightly dust with flour.

Cover bowl with plastic wrap and chill dough, punching down after first hour, at least 12 hours.

**Cooks' note:**
- **Dough may be chilled up to 3 days. Punch down dough each day.**

ISRAEL

## TOMATO AND CUCUMBER SALAD WITH PITA BREAD AND ZA'ATAR

**Serves 6**
Active time: 20 min   Start to finish: 20 min

*A typical Israeli breakfast would include this salad (either already prepared or with the vegetables available), the pita bread, and za'atar along with fresh goat's- or cow's-milk cheeses, yogurt, hummus, hard-boiled eggs, olives, and avocados (in season).*

3 tomatoes, chopped
1 large cucumber, peeled and chopped
4 scallions, thinly sliced
¼ cup chopped fresh flat-leaf parsley
2 tablespoons fresh lemon juice, or to taste
¼ cup extra-virgin olive oil

*Accompaniments:* warm pita bread, olive oil, and za'atar (recipe follows)

Stir together tomatoes, cucumber, scallions, parsley, and salt and pepper to taste. Squeeze lemon juice over salad and stir. Drizzle oil over salad and stir.

ISRAEL

## ZA'ATAR

SESAME-THYME SEASONING

**Makes about ¼ cup**
Active time: 15 min   Start to finish: 15 min

*Variations of this seasoning are found all over the Middle East. It's used to flavor eggs and is also served with pita—dunk warm flatbread in good olive oil and then the spice dip. The kind sold dried (with dried thyme) in Middle Eastern stores just doesn't compare to za'atar made fresh.*

2 tablespoons sesame seeds, toasted
2 teaspoons ground sumac (sources on page 264)
1½ to 2 tablespoons minced fresh thyme
½ teaspoon salt

Stir together all ingredients in a small bowl.

**Cooks' note:**
• *Za'atar* keeps in an airtight container, chilled, 1 week.

CHINA

## RICE SOUP WITH PUMPKIN

**Makes about 4 cups (serving 4)**
Active time: 20 min   Start to finish: 2 hr

*This soup, known as congee or jook, is found in one form or another in many Asian countries and is eaten at all times of day. At breakfast plain congee is the norm, served with a variety of strongly flavored accompaniments to awaken the palate. Those who like oatmeal for breakfast might enjoy this with just a touch of sugar.*

½ cup long-grain white rice, rinsed well
1¼ cups (¼-inch-dice) fresh pumpkin or butternut squash
6 cups water
1 tablespoon minced peeled fresh ginger
1½ teaspoons salt, or to taste

*Accompaniments:* thinly sliced scallion, very finely julienned ginger, chopped salted peanuts, and Chinese hot oil

Combine all ingredients in a 3- to 4-quart heavy saucepan and bring to a boil, stirring occasionally. Simmer, covered, stirring occasionally, until thickened and creamy, about 1½ hours.

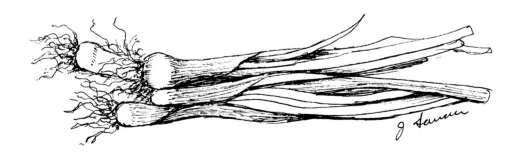

# PASTA AND GRAINS

## ARROSSEJAT DE FIDEUS AMB LLAGOSTA

### SAUTÉED PASTA WITH LOBSTER

**Serves 6**
Active time: 1½ hr   Start to finish: 2 hr

*This Catalan specialty could be described as a pasta cooked like a rice dish. Arrossejat is Catalan for "golden" and refers to the technique of sautéing noodles in oil until golden brown before simmering them in fish stock.*

*The base of our intensely flavored dish is a sofregit—onion slow-cooked with tomatoes and often garlic and herbs—the foundation for almost every sauce and stewed dish in the region's cooking.*

4 (1- to 1¼-lb) live lobsters
½ cup dry white wine
¼ teaspoon crumbled saffron
14 cups water
6 tablespoons olive oil
1 large onion, sliced
1 bay leaf
1½ lb tomatoes, peeled, seeded, and coarsely
    chopped
2 garlic cloves, chopped
1 lb angel's hair pasta nests or *fideos* (*fideus* in
    Catalan) coils, broken in half, or *capellini*,
    broken into 2-inch lengths
2 tablespoons chopped fresh flat-leaf parsley

*Prepare lobsters:*

Fill an 8-quart pot three fourths full with salted water and bring to a boil. Plunge 2 lobsters headfirst into water and boil, covered, 3 minutes. Transfer with tongs to a colander to cool. Repeat with remaining 2 lobsters in same manner.

When lobsters are cool enough to handle, remove meat from shells, catching juices in a separate bowl.

Add shells to bowl with juices. Cut meat into 1-inch pieces and chill lobster, covered.

*Make stock:*

Stir together wine and saffron and let mixture steep 10 minutes. Bring wine mixture, water, and lobster shells with juices to a boil in 8-quart pot. Boil until liquid is reduced to about 8 cups, about 1 hour. Pour stock through a cheesecloth-lined sieve into a bowl, discarding solids.

*Make sofregit:*

While stock reduces, heat 2 tablespoons oil in a heavy skillet over low heat until hot, then cook onion with bay leaf until onion is very soft and browned, about 45 minutes. Add tomatoes and garlic and cook, stirring frequently, until *sofregit* is very thick, about 15 minutes. Discard bay leaf.

*Cook pasta:*

Preheat oven to 400°F.

Heat 1 tablespoon oil in a *cassola* (glazed earthenware casserole) or an ovenproof 12-inch heavy skillet over moderately low heat until hot but not smoking, then cook pasta in 4 batches, stirring, until golden brown. Transfer pasta to a bowl as browned and add an additional tablespoon oil for each batch.

When all of pasta is browned, return to pan and stir in *sofregit* and 4 cups stock (if using a *cassola*, use 4½ cups stock; you'll need more liquid because of the dish's straight sides). Reserve remaining stock for another use. Bring pasta mixture to a simmer, then continue to simmer, covered, 4 minutes. Stir in lobster and season with salt and pepper.

Transfer pan to middle of oven and bake, uncovered, 10 minutes, or until liquid is absorbed and top of pasta is crisp. Stir in parsley.

Cooks' notes:
· **Lobster and stock may be prepared 1 day ahead, cooled completely, then chilled, covered.**
· **Leftover stock, which is wonderful for lobster bisque or as a base for a *sauce armoricaine*, keeps, frozen, 3 months.**
· ***Sofregit* can be made 1 day ahead and chilled, covered.**

PHOTO ON PAGE 23

## PASTA WITH ARTICHOKES AND PARSLEY PESTO

### Serves 2
Active time: 30 min   Start to finish: 40 min

½ lemon
2 artichokes
2 cups fresh flat-leaf parsley
¼ cup pine nuts, toasted
¼ cup freshly grated parmesan
1 garlic clove, smashed
3½ tablespoons extra-virgin olive oil
½ lb dried pasta such as *campanelle* (small, bell-shaped pasta) or small shells

Halve lemon and squeeze juice from 1 half into a bowl of water. Cut off stem of 1 artichoke and discard. Bend back outer leaves of artichoke until they snap off close to base and discard several more layers of leaves in same manner until exposed leaves are pale green at top and pale yellow at base. Cut across artichoke 1½ inches above stem end and scrape out choke with a spoon. Trim dark-green fibrous parts from base and sides of artichoke bottom and trim any remaining leaves. Put artichoke bottom in bowl of lemon water and trim remaining artichoke in same manner.

Pureé parsley, nuts, parmesan, garlic, and oil in a food processor until smooth and season with salt and pepper. Transfer pesto to a large bowl.

Boil artichokes and pasta in a large pot of salted water until tender, about 10 minutes. Reserve ½ cup of cooking water and drain artichokes and pasta in a colander. Quarter artichokes and thinly slice. Add pasta, artichokes, and 2 tablespoons reserved cooking water to pesto, tossing to coat and adding more cooking water to thin if necessary, and season with salt and pepper.

## "CONFETTI" COUSCOUS

### Serves 4
Active time: 15 min   Start to finish: 20 min

½ fennel bulb (sometimes called anise; 6 oz)
1 teaspoon olive oil
2 garlic cloves, minced
1 cup water
1 teaspoon salt

2 plum tomatoes, seeded and cut into ¼-inch dice
1½ tablespoons fresh lemon juice
1 teaspoon finely grated fresh lemon zest
¾ cup couscous
6 dried pitted prunes, cut into ⅓-inch pieces

Trim fennel stalks flush with bulb and remove any discolored areas from bulb. Cut bulb into ¼-inch dice and coarsely chop fronds.

Heat oil in a large nonstick skillet over moderately high heat until hot but not smoking, then sauté diced fennel and garlic, stirring, 1 minute. Reduce heat to low and cook, covered, until fennel is just tender, about 6 minutes. Add water and salt and bring to a boil.

Remove from heat and stir in tomatoes, lemon juice, lemon zest, couscous, and dried prunes. Cover skillet and let stand 5 minutes. Stir in fennel fronds and season with salt and pepper.

each serving about 184 calories and 2 grams fat

## STEAMED COUSCOUS WITH TOASTED PUMPKIN SEEDS

### Serves 6
Active time: 15 min   Start to finish: 50 min

*Steaming couscous may be a bit more time-consuming than the usual boiling method, but we feel the results are well worth it. Steaming makes the grains fluffier and more tender. You'll need a bowl-shaped steamer, such as a basket steamer, or you could set a metal sieve into the saucepan.*

2¼ cups couscous
1 cup water
½ cup green (hulled) pumpkin seeds (sources on page 264)
½ teaspoon fennel seeds
2 tablespoons olive oil

Soak couscous in water to cover 10 minutes, then drain. Steam couscous in a steamer (lined with cheesecloth if holes are large) set over 1 inch simmering water, tightly covered, 20 minutes.

Transfer couscous to a bowl and fluff with a fork. Pour 1 cup water over couscous and season with salt. Let stand, uncovered, 10 minutes.

While couscous stands, toast pumpkin and fennel seeds in oil in a skillet over moderate heat, stirring constantly, until pumpkin seeds are puffed and beginning to pop, 4 to 5 minutes. Season with salt.

Return couscous to steamer and steam, tightly covered, 20 minutes more. Transfer couscous to bowl and toss with pumpkin and fennel seeds.

Cooks' notes:
*   If you're using the sieve steaming method or if your steamer doesn't have a tight seal, cover pot with a kitchen towel, then with the lid.
*   After first steaming and addition of water to bowl, couscous may stand, covered and chilled, up to 1 day.

PHOTO ON PAGE 61

## FENNEL AND SAUSAGE RAGÙ OVER PASTA

### Serves 4
Active time: 25 min   Start to finish: 35 min

*This ragù is also excellent served over instant polenta.*

1 fennel bulb (sometimes called anise) with fronds
1 medium onion, chopped
1 tablespoon olive oil
1 lb sweet Italian sausage, casings discarded
½ cup dry white wine
2 cups prepared marinara sauce
1 lb rotini, *fusilli*, or other spiral pasta

Trim fennel stalks flush with bulb and remove any discolored areas from bulb. Chop and reserve 2 tablespoons fronds and chop bulb. Sauté fennel bulb and onion in oil in a 12-inch heavy skillet over moderately high heat, stirring, until beginning to brown. Add sausage and cook, stirring and breaking up lumps with a fork, until no longer pink. Add wine and simmer until reduced by about half, then add marinara sauce and simmer, stirring frequently, until vegetables are tender and sauce is thickened, about 10 minutes.

While sauce simmers, cook pasta in a pot of boiling salted water until al dente, 8 to 10 minutes. Drain and toss with sauce. Sprinkle with reserved fennel fronds.

## PASTA WITH BUTTERNUT SQUASH AND SAGE

### Serves 4
Active time: 25 min   Start to finish: 35 min

*For a savory addition, toss a little sautéed pancetta or bacon into this pasta.*

1 medium onion, chopped
2 tablespoons olive oil
1 (1-lb) butternut squash, peeled and cut into 2-inch pieces
¾ cup water
1 teaspoon chopped fresh sage
1 lb *gemelli* or *penne rigate* pasta
2 tablespoons chopped fresh flat-leaf parsley
1 cup freshly grated parmesan plus additional for sprinkling
2 tablespoons unsalted butter (optional)

Cook onion in oil in a large nonstick skillet over moderately high heat, stirring occasionally, until golden. Finely chop squash pieces in a food processor and add to onion with water and salt to taste. Simmer, covered, stirring occasionally, 15 minutes, or until squash is tender. Add sage and simmer 1 minute more.

Cook pasta in a 6-quart pot of boiling salted water until al dente. Reserve 1 cup cooking liquid and drain pasta. Return pasta to pot and add squash mixture, parsley, 1 cup parmesan, butter (if using), and plenty of pepper, stirring until butter is melted. Season with salt and add some of reserved pasta cooking liquid to moisten if necessary.

Serve sprinkled with additional parmesan.

## FETTUCCINE WITH SMOKED SALMON AND ASPARAGUS

*Serves 4*
Active time: 10 min   Start to finish: 25 min

8 to 9 oz dried egg fettuccine
1 lb asparagus, trimmed and cut diagonally
    into ½-inch pieces
1 cup heavy cream
1 tablespoon drained bottled horseradish
2 tablespoons chopped fresh dill
6 oz smoked salmon, cut into ½-inch-wide
    ribbons

Cook pasta in a large pot of boiling salted water according to package instructions. Add asparagus to pot for last 3 minutes of pasta-cooking time.

While asparagus is boiling, heat cream, horseradish, and dill in a large skillet over moderate heat just until hot, about 1 minute. Drain pasta and asparagus and add to cream mixture, tossing. Gently toss in salmon and season with salt and pepper.

Cooks' note:
• For a lighter sauce, you can replace ⅓ cup of the cream with an equal amount of the pasta-cooking water.

## TOMATO AND MOZZARELLA LASAGNE

*Serves 12*
Active time: 30 min   Start to finish: 2 hr

*For sauce*
3 onions, chopped
1 tablespoon unsalted butter
2 tablespoons olive oil
½ teaspoon dried oregano
½ teaspoon dried thyme, crumbled
6 garlic cloves, minced
3 (28- to 32-oz) cans crushed tomatoes in
    thick purée
1 cup chopped fresh flat-leaf parsley
¼ cup fresh orange juice
*For lasagne*
18 (7- by 3½-inch) sheets dry no-boil
    lasagne (1 lb)
2½ lb fresh mozzarella (smoked or plain),
    chilled and coarsely grated (6 cups)
1 cup freshly grated parmesan

*Make sauce:*

Cook onions in butter and oil with oregano, thyme, and salt and pepper to taste in a 4-quart saucepan over moderate heat, stirring, until onions are softened. Add garlic and cook, stirring, 1 minute. Add tomatoes and simmer, uncovered, stirring occasionally, until slightly thickened, about 18 minutes. Remove from heat and stir in parsley, orange juice, and salt and pepper to taste.

Preheat oven to 375°F and butter 2 (13- by 9-inch) baking dishes.

*Assemble lasagne:*

Soak lasagne sheets in hot water to cover by 1 inch until softened and flexible, about 20 minutes.

Spread 1½ cups sauce in each baking dish and top sauce in each dish with 3 drained pasta sheets, overlapping if necessary. Sprinkle 1 cup mozzarella and ¼ cup parmesan evenly in each dish. Top with 3 drained pasta sheets per dish, overlapping if necessary. Repeat layering with 1 cup mozzarella, ¼ cup parmesan, 1½ cups sauce, and 3 drained pasta sheets in each dish. Finish assembling lasagne by topping each with 1½ cups sauce. (You will have leftover sauce and mozzarella.)

Bake lasagne, covered with foil, in middle of oven 30 minutes. Remove foil and sprinkle evenly with remaining 2 cups mozzarella. Bake until bubbling and cheese is melted, about 10 minutes more.

Serve lasagne with some of remaining sauce.

Cooks' notes:
• Sauce may be made 3 days ahead and chilled, covered.
• You can make and bake lasagne 1 day ahead up to point of adding last layer of mozzarella. Cool completely, then chill, covered. Bring to room temperature before reheating with final layer of mozzarella, covered, in a 375°F oven until hot, 20 to 30 minutes.

PHOTO ON PAGE 16

## PENNE WITH YELLOW PEPPERS AND CAPERS

*Serves 4 (main course)*
Active time: 20 min   Start to finish: 40 min

2 tablespoons olive oil
3 yellow, red, or orange bell peppers, cut
    lengthwise into ¼-inch-thick strips
1 large onion, cut lengthwise into
    ¼-inch-thick slices
2 garlic cloves, minced

3 anchovy fillets, rinsed and chopped
3 tablespoons capers, rinsed and chopped
1 teaspoon white-wine vinegar
12 oz dried penne (preferably ridged)
¼ cup chopped fresh basil

*Accompaniment:* freshly grated parmesan

Heat oil in a 12-inch nonstick skillet over moderate heat until hot but not smoking, then add bell peppers, onion, garlic, and anchovy. Reduce heat to moderately low and cook, covered, stirring occasionally, until vegetables are very tender and lightly browned, 15 to 20 minutes. Stir in capers and vinegar.

Meanwhile, cook pasta in a large pot of boiling salted water until al dente. Drain, reserving ½ cup cooking water. Add pasta to pepper mixture and toss, adding enough cooking water for sauce to coat pasta. Season with salt and pepper and toss with basil.

## POTATO PIEROGI WITH CABBAGE AND BACON

### Serves 2 generously
Active time: 25 min   Start to finish: 25 min

*These turnovers are typically deep-fried, or boiled and then panfried. Instead, we used a method often employed for cooking frozen Asian dumplings and found it works well.*

4 bacon slices, chopped
1 large onion, thinly sliced
½ head cabbage, thinly sliced
2 tablespoons balsamic vinegar (optional)
2 tablespoons chopped fresh flat-leaf parsley
2 tablespoons unsalted butter
1 (12- to 16-oz) package potato pierogi
  (sources on page 264), thawed if frozen
½ cup water

Cook bacon in a large heavy skillet over moderate heat, stirring occasionally, until golden. Add onion and cook, stirring occasionally, until golden. Stir in cabbage and salt to taste and cook, covered, stirring occasionally, 10 minutes, or until cabbage is very tender and beginning to brown. Stir in vinegar and 1 tablespoon parsley.

While cabbage is cooking, heat butter in a 12-inch nonstick skillet over moderate heat until foam subsides, then cook pierogi until bottoms are golden. Turn pierogi over and add water to skillet. Simmer until water is evaporated and bottoms are golden, about 2 minutes. (If pierogi are large, cook in 2 batches, using half of butter and water for each batch.) Stir in remaining tablespoon parsley.

Serve potato pierogi over cabbage mixture.

## HERBED SPAETZLE

### Serves 2 (side dish)
Active time: 30 min   Start to finish: 30 min

*Spaetzle are much easier to make than you might think. Whether you use a spaetzlemaker (sources on page 264) or a food mill, be sure that the pot you select for boiling water is the right diameter to support the equipment properly.*

1 cup plus 2 tablespoons all-purpose flour
½ teaspoon salt
3 large eggs
⅓ cup whole milk
1 teaspoon vegetable oil
¼ cup coarsely chopped fresh dill
¼ cup coarsely chopped spinach leaves
1 tablespoon coarsely chopped fresh chives
2 tablespoons cold unsalted butter

Bring a large pot of salted water to a boil. Fill a large bowl with cold water. Stir together flour and salt. Whisk together eggs and milk, then whisk into flour until batter is smooth.

Working over boiling water, force one third of batter through a spaetzlemaker or large holes of a food mill. As dumplings float to surface, transfer them to bowl of cold water with a slotted spoon. Make 2 more batches in same manner. Drain dumplings well and toss with oil.

Pulse dill, spinach, chives, and 1 tablespoon butter in a food processor until a paste forms. Heat remaining tablespoon butter in a large nonstick skillet over moderately high heat until foam subsides, then sauté dumplings, stirring, until golden. Add herb butter and sauté, stirring, until dumplings are coated and heated through. Season with salt and pepper.

## TAGLIERINI WITH MORELS, ASPARAGUS, AND NASTURTIUMS

### Serves 8 (first course)
Active time: 1¼ hr   Start to finish: 1½ hr

¾ lb fresh *taglierini* (recipe follows) or ½ lb dried
   ⅛-inch-wide flat egg noodles
1 oz small dried morels (sources on page 264)
¾ lb thin asparagus, trimmed
⅓ cup dry white wine
3 tablespoons fresh lemon juice
¼ cup finely chopped shallots
⅓ cup heavy cream
1 cup chicken broth
1½ sticks (¾ cup) cold unsalted butter, cut
   into pieces
50 nontoxic and organic nasturtiums, halved
   if large (sources on page 264)

Prepare fresh pasta if using.

Soak dried morels in 1 cup warm water 20 minutes. Agitate morels to dislodge grit, then lift from water, squeezing liquid from mushrooms back into bowl. Reserve liquid. When grit has settled, carefully pour mushroom liquid into a small bowl, leaving sediment behind (if necessary, strain liquid through a dampened coffee filter or cheesecloth). Remove any tough stems from morels.

Cut off top 2 inches of asparagus tips and halve tips lengthwise. Cut remaining asparagus into long diagonal slices about ¼ inch thick.

Simmer wine, lemon juice, and shallots in a large heavy skillet until liquid is reduced to about 2 tablespoons. Add cream and simmer 1 minute. Add morels, mushroom soaking liquid, and broth, then simmer 5 minutes. Add butter all at once and cook sauce over moderately low heat, whisking constantly, just until creamy and butter is incorporated. (Do not let sauce get so hot that butter separates and sauce loses creamy consistency.) Remove skillet from heat and season sauce with salt and pepper. Keep warm, covered.

If using fresh *taglierini*, shake off excess flour. Cook fresh *taglierini* with asparagus in a 6-quart pot of boiling salted water until pasta is al dente, about 1 minute. (For dried pasta, follow package instructions and add asparagus during last minute of cooking.) Reserve ½ cup cooking water and drain pasta and asparagus in a colander.

Toss pasta and asparagus in a large bowl with ½ cup sauce (without morels), one third of nasturtiums, and enough reserved pasta water to keep moist. Stir remaining nasturtiums into sauce.

To serve, wind each portion of *taglierini* around a carving fork and transfer to center of a soup plate. Surround with asparagus, morels, and sauce.

Cooks' note:
· For a simpler presentation, just toss pasta and asparagus mixture with sauce and nasturtiums, adding some of pasta water if necessary.

PHOTO ON PAGE 27

## FRESH TAGLIERINI PASTA

### Makes about ¾ lb
Active time: 40 min   Start to finish: 40 min

2 cups unbleached all-purpose flour plus additional
   for kneading and rolling
3 large eggs
1 tablespoon water
1 tablespoon olive oil

*Special equipment:* a pasta machine

*Make dough:*
Pulse together all ingredients except additional flour

in a food processor until mixture just begins to form a ball. Knead dough on a work surface, incorporating additional flour as necessary, until smooth and elastic, about 8 minutes. Quarter dough and keep each piece wrapped in plastic wrap until ready to roll out.

*Roll out dough:*

Set smooth rollers of pasta machine at widest setting. Flatten 1 piece of dough into a rectangle and feed through rollers. Fold in half and feed through rollers 8 or 9 more times to continue kneading, folding in half each time and dusting with flour as necessary to prevent sticking.

*Cut pasta:*

Turn dial to next narrower setting and feed dough through rollers without folding. Continue to feed dough through, without folding, making space between rollers narrower each time until narrowest setting is reached. Halve sheet crosswise and arrange on a dry kitchen towel, letting pasta hang over edge of work surface. Roll out remaining dough in same manner.

Attach ribbon-pasta cutters to pasta machine and attach handle to ⅛-inch-wide cutter. Line a tray with a dry kitchen towel. Feed first rolled-out pasta sheet, which will have dried slightly but should still be flexible, through cutter and toss with some flour. Form pasta loosely into a nest and arrange on kitchen-towel–lined tray. Make more *taglierini* with remaining dough. Cover *taglierini* with plastic wrap until ready to use.

Cooks' notes:
- Cut pasta as soon as all sheets are rolled out—if pasta becomes too dry and brittle, *taglierini* will break. (The softer the pasta sheets are when cutting, the more flour you will need to keep the *taglierini* from sticking together before cooking.)
- If keeping for longer than an hour, chill uncooked *taglierini* (up to 24 hours).

---

**GRAINS**

---

## QUINOA-FENNEL PILAF

### Serves 8
Active time: 20 min   Start to finish: 35 min

1 cup quinoa
½ small white onion, finely chopped
1 celery rib, cut into ¼-inch dice

1 carrot, cut into ¼-inch dice
1 small fennel bulb (sometimes called anise), trimmed, cored, and cut into ¼-inch dice
1 tablespoon unsalted butter
1½ cups water

Rinse quinoa in a bowl in at least 5 changes of water, rubbing grains and letting them settle before pouring off water, until water runs clear. Drain.

Cook onion, celery, carrot, and fennel in butter in a 3-quart heavy saucepan over moderate heat, stirring occasionally, until onion is softened, 5 to 6 minutes. Add quinoa and sauté over moderately high heat, stirring, until lightly toasted, 2 to 3 minutes. Add water and salt and pepper to taste and cook over moderately low heat, covered, until quinoa is tender and liquid is absorbed, 12 to 15 minutes.

PHOTO ON PAGE 55

## BULGUR "RISOTTO" WITH SPINACH AND BACON

### Serves 2 or 3
Active time: 20 min   Start to finish: 35 min

1 medium onion, chopped
1 tablespoon olive oil
1 teaspoon minced garlic
1 cup coarse (No. 3) bulgur
2 cups chicken broth
1¾ cups water
¼ lb sliced bacon, chopped
6 cups baby spinach (4 oz), trimmed
⅓ cup freshly grated parmesan

Cook onion in oil in a 2-quart heavy saucepan over moderate heat, stirring, until softened. Add garlic and cook, stirring, 30 seconds.

Add bulgur, broth, and water and bring to a boil. Reduce heat and simmer, covered, until bulgur is tender and creamy (like risotto), about 20 minutes.

While bulgur is simmering, cook bacon in a skillet over moderate heat, stirring, until crisp, then drain on paper towels.

Stir spinach into bulgur until wilted, then stir in parmesan, half of bacon, and salt and pepper to taste.

Serve "risotto" sprinkled with remaining bacon.

## HERBED BULGUR

**Serves 4**
Active time: 10 min   Start to finish: 35 min

¾ cup bulgur
1 cup boiling-hot water
¼ cup chopped fresh dill
2 tablespoons chopped fresh tarragon
2 tablespoons thinly sliced fresh chives
1 tablespoon olive oil

Combine bulgur and boiling-hot water in a large bowl and let stand 20 minutes.

Fluff with a fork and stir in herbs, oil, and salt and pepper to taste.

## SPICY FRIED BASMATI RICE

**Serves 8**
Active time: 40 min   Start to finish: 9½ hr

3 tablespoons extra-virgin olive oil
3 tablespoons coarsely chopped garlic
1 to 2 tablespoons finely chopped seeded fresh red chile such as cayenne
2 teaspoons finely chopped peeled fresh ginger
4 cups cold cooked basmati rice (recipe follows), chilled at least 8 hours
1½ teaspoons salt
1 teaspoon freshly ground mixed or black peppercorns

¼ cup packed drained sun-dried tomatoes (packed in oil), coarsely chopped
3 tablespoons finely chopped scallion
3 tablespoons finely chopped fresh chives
3 tablespoons finely chopped fresh cilantro
3 tablespoons finely chopped fresh flat-leaf parsley

Heat a wok or 12-inch nonstick skillet over high heat until hot. Add oil, garlic, chile, and ginger, then stir-fry 15 seconds. Add cold rice, salt, and pepper, then stir-fry, pressing on rice to break up any lumps, 2 minutes. Add sun-dried tomatoes, scallion, and herbs, then stir-fry 3 minutes.

Cooks' note:
• **You could use leftover Chinese or Indian take-out rice instead of cooking rice yourself.**

PHOTO ON PAGE 64

## BASMATI RICE

**Makes 4 cups (serving 8)**
Active time: 10 min   Start to finish: 50 min

2 cups basmati rice
3 cups water

Wash rice in several changes of water, rubbing grains and letting them settle before pouring off water, until water runs clear. Drain well in a sieve.

To cook on stovetop: Bring rice and 3 cups water to

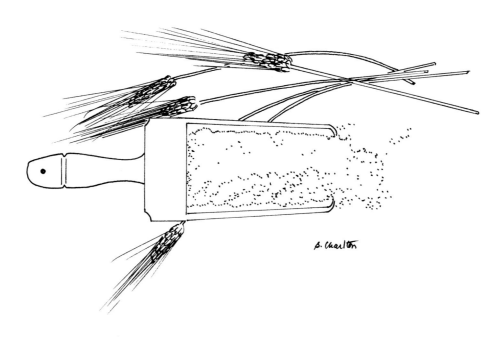

β. Charlton

a boil in a 3-quart heavy saucepan. Reduce heat to very low and cook, covered, until water is absorbed and rice is tender, 15 to 20 minutes. Remove from heat and let stand, covered, 10 minutes. Fluff gently with a fork.

To cook in microwave: Put rice and 3 cups water in a 3-quart microwave-safe dish and cook, uncovered, at high power 15 minutes, or until steam holes appear in rice. Cover dish with a microwave-safe lid or plate and cook at high 5 minutes more. Let rice stand, covered, 5 minutes. Fluff gently with a fork.

If using rice for preceding fried-rice recipe, chill, covered, 8 hours.

## CUMIN-SCENTED HERBED RICE

**Serves 4**
Active time: 15 min   Start to finish: 25 min

⅔ cup long-grain rice
½ teaspoon cumin seeds
½ tablespoon corn oil
⅔ cup fat-free chicken broth
2 scallions, thinly sliced
¼ cup chopped fresh cilantro

Wash rice in several changes of cold water in a bowl until water runs clear and drain well in a sieve.

Toast cumin seeds in oil in a 2-quart heavy saucepan over low heat, stirring occasionally, until a shade darker, 2 to 3 minutes.

Stir rice into cumin. Stir in broth and bring to a boil. Reduce heat to low and simmer gently, covered, until rice is tender, 16 to 18 minutes. Remove from heat.

Fluff rice with a fork and let stand, covered, 10 minutes. Just before serving, stir in scallions and cilantro.

each serving about 135 calories and 2 grams fat

## JASMINE RICE WITH CUMIN AND MUSTARD SEEDS

**Serves 4**
Active time: 10 min   Start to finish: 35 min

1½ cups jasmine rice
1½ teaspoons cumin seeds
4 teaspoons yellow mustard seeds
1 tablespoon olive oil

1 garlic clove, minced
2¼ cups water
3 scallions, thinly sliced

Rinse rice in a sieve until water runs clear and drain well. Cook cumin and mustard seeds in oil in a 2-quart heavy saucepan over moderate heat, stirring, until mustard seeds begin to pop, about 2 minutes. Stir in garlic and rice and cook, stirring, 1 minute. Add water and bring to a boil, uncovered. Cover rice and cook over very low heat until water is absorbed and rice is tender, about 20 minutes. Remove pan from heat and let rice stand, covered, 5 minutes. Fluff rice with a fork and stir in scallions and salt and pepper to taste.

## ELUMICHAMPAZHA SADAM

### LEMON RICE WITH PEANUTS

**Serves 6**
Active time: 20 min   Start to finish: 45 min

2 cups basmati rice
3 cups water
1 tablespoon vegetable oil
2 teaspoons black mustard seeds (sources on page 264)
1 tablespoon minced peeled fresh ginger
⅓ cup finely chopped salted roasted peanuts
½ teaspoon turmeric
3 tablespoons fresh lemon juice
1 tablespoon julienne strips of fresh lemon zest

Wash rice in several changes of water until water runs clear, then drain well. Bring rice and 3 cups water to a boil in a 3-quart heavy saucepan and cook, covered, over very low heat until water is absorbed and rice is tender, 20 to 25 minutes. Remove from heat and let stand, covered, 10 minutes. Fluff rice gently with a fork.

Heat oil in a deep 12-inch heavy skillet over moderately high heat until hot but not smoking, then cook mustard seeds, stirring, until seeds begin to pop. Add ginger and ¼ cup peanuts and cook, stirring, 2 minutes. Add turmeric, rice, and salt to taste, stirring to coat rice thoroughly. Remove from heat and stir in lemon juice. Sprinkle with remaining peanuts and zest.

PHOTO ON PAGE 12

## RICE WITH SOY-GLAZED BONITO FLAKES AND SESAME SEEDS

*Serves 4*
Active time: 15 min   Start to finish: 45 min

*We love this recipe as much for the soy-glazed bonito flakes, with their maddeningly good smoky-savory-sweet flavor, as for making such great use of leftovers.*

*For bonito-flake topping*
1 cup *katsuo bushi* (dried bonito flakes) from
    making *dashi* (page 121) or *katsuo bushi*
    fresh from package (sources on page 264)
1 tablespoon sake
¼ teaspoon sugar
1½ tablespoons soy sauce
2 tablespoons sesame seeds, toasted
*For rice*
2 cups Japanese short-grain rice (sources on
    page 264)
2 cups water

*Make topping:*

If using *katsuo bushi* flakes from package, moisten with a few drops of sake or water. Finely chop *katsuo bushi*, then cook in a dry heavy skillet over moderate heat, stirring frequently, until fragrant and mostly dry. Add sake, sugar, and soy sauce and cook over moderate heat, stirring frequently, until mixture is dry and glazed. Stir in sesame seeds and spread on a plate to cool.

*Prepare rice:*

Rinse rice in a bowl in several changes of cold water until water is almost clear; drain well. Combine rice and 2 cups water in a 3-quart heavy saucepan and let stand 10 minutes. Cover with a tight-fitting lid and bring to a boil over high heat. Cook at a rapid boil (lid will be rattling and foam may drip down outside of pan) 5 minutes, or until water is absorbed. Remove from heat and let stand, covered, 10 minutes.

Serve rice with bonito-flake topping.

Cooks' note:
• Bonito-flake topping keeps in an airtight container at room temperature 1 week.

## WILD RICE DRESSING

*Serves 8*
Active time: 30 min   Start to finish: 1¾ hr

1½ cups wild rice
6 cups 1-inch cubes country-style
    bread (½ lb)
½ lb sliced bacon, coarsely chopped
2 onions, chopped
4 celery ribs, cut crosswise into ¼-inch-
    thick slices
½ cup chopped fresh flat-leaf parsley
1 cup chicken broth

Preheat oven to 325°F.
*Prepare rice:*
Rinse rice in a sieve under cold water, then cover with cold water by 2 inches in a 4-quart pot. Simmer, covered, until tender, 50 minutes to 1 hour. Drain rice in sieve and cool 10 minutes.
*Prepare other ingredients while rice simmers:*
Toast bread in a large shallow baking pan in middle of oven until dry, about 30 minutes.
Cook bacon in a large skillet over moderate heat, stirring, until crisp and transfer with a slotted spoon to a large bowl. Cook onions in fat remaining in skillet, stirring, until softened. Add celery and cook, stirring, 1 minute.
*Assemble and bake dressing:*
Add onions and celery to bacon and stir in parsley, bread, rice, and salt and pepper to taste.
Increase temperature to 375°F.
Transfer dressing to a buttered 3- to 4-quart baking dish and drizzle chicken broth over dressing. Bake dressing, covered, 20 minutes, then uncover and bake 20 minutes more, or until bread is golden brown and dressing is heated through.

Cooks' note:
• Dressing can be assembled (but not baked) 1 day ahead and chilled, covered. Bring to room temperature before baking.

PHOTO ON PAGE 68

# VEGETABLES AND BEANS

VEGETABLES

*The first five recipes below are part of the aïoli menu on page 56, which serves 12. If making any of these recipes for another menu, reduce amounts accordingly.*

## ASSORTED DIPPING VEGETABLES

**Serves 12 (as part of aïoli menu)**
Active time: 1½ hr   Start to finish: 1¾ hr

*Feel free to add, subtract, or substitute any raw or cooked vegetables you'd like, but make sure there's a good variety of textures and colors.*

*For raw vegetables*
1 large fennel bulb (sometimes called anise)
3 Belgian endives, trimmed
12 small (not baby) carrots with tops, greens
    trimmed to 2 inches
2 lb small zucchini, halved lengthwise
2 pints red and yellow pear or cherry
    tomatoes
2 bunches radishes, trimmed
2 bunches scallions, trimmed
*For cooked vegetables*
2 lb green beans, trimmed
2 lb cauliflower, cut into florets
2 lb small turnips, peeled
1½ lb fingerling, Yukon Gold, or red-skinned
    potatoes

*Prepare raw vegetables:*
Trim fennel stalks flush with bulb, discarding stalks, and trim any discolored spots from bulb. Quarter bulb lengthwise and cut out most of cores, leaving enough to keep pieces intact. Cut quarters lengthwise into ¼-inch-thick slices.

Separate endive leaves. Wrap all raw vegetables separately in damp paper towels and chill in sealed plastic bags.

*Prepare cooked vegetables:*
Have ready a large bowl of ice and cold water. Cook beans in a large pot of boiling salted water until crisp-tender, about 4 minutes. Transfer beans to ice water with a slotted spoon to cool, then transfer to a colander to drain.

Add cauliflower to boiling water and cook until crisp-tender, about 4 minutes. Transfer to ice water to cool, then transfer to colander to drain.

Add turnips to boiling water and cook until crisp-tender, about 7 minutes. Transfer to ice water to cool, then drain in colander.

*Cook potatoes about 30 minutes before serving:*
Steam potatoes in a large steamer over boiling water, covered, until tender, 10 to 15 minutes. Serve hot or warm.

Arrange raw and cooked vegetables on a platter and serve with *aïoli* (page 158).

Cooks' notes:
· Raw vegetables may be cut and chilled 1 day ahead.
· Cooked vegetables (not including potatoes) may be prepared 1 day ahead and chilled in sealed plastic bags with paper towels to absorb excess moisture.

## ARTICHOKES

**Serves 12 (as part of aïoli menu)**
Active time: 30 min   Start to finish: 1 hr

¼ cup fresh lemon juice plus 1 lemon, halved
6 large artichokes, with stems intact

Combine 1 quart cold water and lemon juice in a large bowl. Working with 1 artichoke at a time, bend back outer leaves until they snap off close to base and discard several more layers of leaves in same manner until exposed leaves are pale green at top and pale yellow at base. Cut off leaves flush with top of base and cut a thin slice from end of stem to expose a fresh cross section. Trim dark green fibrous parts from base and stem of artichoke, being careful not to break off stem.

Rub artichoke all over with lemon halves. Quarter lengthwise and remove fuzzy center and any purple leaves. Put in bowl of lemon water.

Have ready a bowl of ice and cold water. Drain artichokes and cook in a large pot of boiling salted water until tender, about 10 minutes. Drain and transfer to ice water to cool. Drain well.

**Cooks' note:**
• Artichokes may be cooked 2 days ahead and chilled in sealed plastic bags with paper towels to absorb moisture.

## ROASTED BEETS AND ONIONS

**Serves 12 (as part of aïoli menu)**
Active time: 15 min   Start to finish: 1¼ hr

24 (1-inch) red or white boiling onions
12 beets (preferably mixed red and golden; 4 lb),
    trimmed, leaving 1 inch of stems attached

Preheat oven to 475°F.

Blanch onions in a large pot of boiling water 1 minute, then drain. Trim and peel.

Tightly wrap onions and beets in double layers of foil to make 5 packages (2 of onions and 3 of beets) and roast until tender, 30 to 40 minutes for onions and about 1 hour for beets. When beets and onions are cool enough to handle, discard foil. Slip off skins and stems from beets and cut into wedges.

**Cooks' note:**
• Beets and onions may be roasted 1 day ahead. Cool, then chill separately in sealed plastic bags.

## CLASSIC AÏOLI

**Makes about 2 cups (serving 12)**
Active time: 50 min   Start to finish: 50 min

*We found that using a blender to begin the emulsion process for aïoli is much faster than pounding by hand from start to finish, which is the traditional method. Once using the mortar, resist the impulse to add the oil quickly—it will cause the mixture to separate. All the slow stirring requires a strong arm, so you may want to recruit a friend to help. A version that can be made entirely in the blender follows— it's quicker to make and includes a whole egg or two yolks (the consistency is creamier and more mayonnaise-like).*

*Very fresh garlic is crucial to this recipe. Bulbs should have smooth, tight skin and be firm and heavy for their size.*

½ cup coarsely chopped very fresh garlic, at room
    temperature
2 teaspoons coarse sea salt or kosher salt
2 cups extra-virgin olive oil, at room temperature

*Special equipment:* a large mortar and pestle

Blend ¼ cup garlic, 1 teaspoon salt, and 2 tablespoons oil in a blender on high speed until smooth and creamy, about 2 minutes, then transfer to mortar. Add ¾ cup plus 2 tablespoons oil very slowly, 1 to 2 teaspoons at a time, stirring and mashing constantly and vigorously with pestle. This will take about 15 minutes, and mixture will become very thick and glossy. (*Aïoli* will separate if oil is added too quickly.) Transfer to a bowl. Make second batch with remaining ingredients.

PHOTO ON PAGE 56

## QUICK AÏOLI WITH EGG

**Makes about 2 cups (serving 12)**
Active time: 20 min   Start to finish: 20 min

½ cup coarsely chopped very fresh garlic, at room
    temperature
2 teaspoons coarse sea salt or kosher salt
2 cups extra-virgin olive oil, at room temperature
2 whole large eggs or 4 large egg yolks, at room
    temperature

Blend ¼ cup garlic, 1 teaspoon salt, and 2 tablespoons oil in a blender at high speed until smooth and creamy. Add 1 egg or 2 yolks and, with motor running, very slowly add ¾ cup plus 2 tablespoons oil in a thin, steady stream until *aïoli* is thick. This will take about 2 minutes. Transfer to a bowl. Make second batch with remaining ingredients.

Cooks' notes:
• The eggs will not be cooked in this recipe, which may be of concern if there is a problem with salmonella in your area.

## GRILLED ASPARAGUS

**Serves 4**
Active time: 15 min   Start to finish: 30 min

1½ lb medium asparagus (24), trimmed
2 tablespoons extra-virgin olive oil
Kosher salt

*Special equipment:* 8 (6-inch) wooden skewers, soaked in warm water 10 minutes

Prepare grill for cooking.

Divide asparagus into 4 bunches. Align each bunch in a flat row and thread 2 skewers crosswise through each bunch. Brush asparagus with oil and season with kosher salt.

Grill on an oiled rack set 5 to 6 inches over glowing coals until tender, 3 to 5 minutes on each side.

## GREEN BEANS WITH WHOLE-GRAIN MUSTARD

**Serves 4**
Active time: 15 min   Start to finish: 20 min

¾ lb *haricots verts* or other thin green beans, trimmed
2 teaspoons extra-virgin olive oil
2 teaspoons whole-grain Dijon mustard

Fill a bowl with ice water.

Cook beans in a large pot of salted boiling water just until crisp-tender, 3 to 4 minutes. Drain and transfer to ice water. Drain well and pat dry.

Heat oil in a 12-inch nonstick skillet over moderately high heat until hot but not smoking, then sauté beans with mustard and salt and pepper to taste, stirring, until heated through, about 4 minutes.

each serving about 53 calories and 3 grams fat

## BEANS PORIYAL

### DRY CURRIED BEANS

**Serves 6**
Active time: 20 min   Start to finish: 1¼ hr

*For information on specialty ingredients, see sources on page 264.*

½ cup desiccated coconut or ¾ cup finely grated fresh coconut
2 teaspoons vegetable oil
1½ teaspoons black mustard seeds
1½ teaspoons cumin seeds
1½ teaspoons picked-over split skinned *urad dal*
1½ teaspoons picked-over split skinned *chana dal*
½ teaspoon *asafetida* powder
1 fresh hot red chile such as *serrano* or Thai, halved lengthwise
4 fresh curry leaves
1½ lb green beans, trimmed and cut into ¼-inch pieces
½ cup water

If using desiccated coconut, soak in warm water to cover 1 hour and drain well in a sieve.

Heat oil in a 3-quart heavy saucepan over moderate heat until hot but not smoking, then cook mustard seeds, cumin, *dals*, asafetida, chile, and curry leaves, stirring occasionally, until mustard seeds begin to pop. Stir in beans, water, and salt to taste and simmer, covered, until beans are just tender and most of water is evaporated, 6 to 8 minutes. Stir in coconut.

Cooks' note:
• Beans may be made 6 hours ahead and chilled, covered. Undercook slightly so beans retain color when reheated.

PHOTO ON PAGE 13

## CAVALO NERO WITH CILANTRO

**Serves 6**
Active time: 30 min   Start to finish: 30 min

*Cavalo nero is a member of the kale family and is available year-round in the United States. The reason you might have trouble finding it at farm stands, specialty produce markets, or natural foods stores is because of its many aliases: Tuscan kale, black cabbage, lacinata, lacinato, dinosaur kale, flat black cabbage, thousand-headed cabbage. Its rich, sweet, almost meaty flavor will have you hooked with the first bite.*

2 lb *cavalo nero* or kale, stems and
   center ribs discarded
1 cup finely chopped white onion
1 cup chopped fresh cilantro
2 tablespoons olive oil

Cut *cavalo nero* crosswise into ¼-inch-wide strips and cook in a large pot of salted boiling water 3 minutes. Reserve ¼ cup cooking liquid and drain *cavalo nero* in a colander.

Cook onion and ½ cup cilantro in oil in a deep 12-inch heavy skillet over moderate heat, stirring, until onion is softened. Add *cavalo nero*, salt to taste, and reserved cooking liquid and simmer, stirring, until *cavalo nero* is just tender, 3 to 5 minutes. Stir in remaining ½ cup cilantro and season with salt and pepper.

PHOTO ON PAGE 72

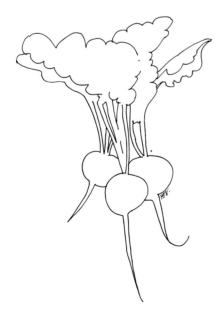

## HARICOTS VERTS WITH HOT PEPPER RELISH

**Serves 8**
Active time: 40 min   Start to finish: 40 min

1½ lb *haricots verts* or other thin green beans,
   trimmed
*For relish*
2 tablespoons olive oil
⅓ cup finely chopped shallots
3 garlic cloves, minced
3 red bell peppers, finely chopped
1 fresh *serrano* chile, seeded and finely chopped
2 tablespoons cider vinegar
½ teaspoon sugar

*Prepare haricots verts:*
Cook beans in a large saucepan of boiling salted water until crisp-tender, 2 to 3 minutes. Drain in a colander and transfer to a bowl of ice and cold water. Drain beans well and season with salt and pepper.
*Make relish:*
Heat oil in a heavy skillet over moderate heat until hot but not smoking, then cook shallots, stirring, until just softened. Add garlic and cook, stirring, 1 minute. Add bell peppers and chile and sauté over moderately high heat, stirring occasionally, until peppers are softened, about 3 minutes. Add vinegar and sugar and cook, stirring, until liquid is evaporated, about 2 minutes. Cool relish and season with salt and pepper.
Serve beans topped with relish.

Cooks' notes:
· Beans may be cooked 1 day ahead and chilled, wrapped in paper towels in a sealable plastic bag.
· Relish may be made 1 day ahead and chilled, covered.

PHOTO ON PAGE 47

## STEAMED BEETS WITH TARRAGON

**Serves 4**
Active time: 15 min   Start to finish: 25 min

1 bunch beets
2 tablespoons finely chopped shallots
2 teaspoons finely chopped fresh tarragon
1 tablespoon unsalted butter, cut into bits
1 teaspoon cider vinegar
¼ teaspoon sugar

Peel beets and halve lengthwise, then slice crosswise ⅛ inch thick. Steam beets over boiling water, covered, until tender, 10 to 12 minutes. Toss with remaining ingredients and salt and pepper to taste until butter is melted.

## PICKLED NAPA CABBAGE

**Makes about 2 cups**
Active time: 20 min   Start to finish: 3½ hr

*Pickles that refresh the palate are often the last thing eaten in a traditional Japanese meal. For information on specialty ingredients, see sources on page 264.*

¾ lb Napa cabbage, cut crosswise into ⅓-inch-
  wide strips
3 tablespoons finely chopped carrot
1½ teaspoons coarse salt
1 oz (30 grams) *kombu* (dried kelp; preferably
  left over from making *dashi*, page 121, or
  see sources), about 20 square inches
4 fresh green *shiso* leaves or ¼ cup fresh basil,
  chopped

Toss together cabbage, carrot, and salt in a bowl. Put *kombu* in a narrow straight-sided container (5 to 6 inches in diameter) and top with cabbage mixture. Cut a piece of cardboard to fit just inside container and enclose it in a sealable plastic bag. Top cabbage with plastic-covered round and stack 4 to 6 pounds of canned goods on top to weight it. Chill weighted cabbage at least 3 hours.

Discard *kombu*. Squeeze excess liquid from cabbage and toss with *shiso*.

**Cook's note:**
• Cabbage may be weighted up to 1 day.

## SPICY BROCCOLI RABE

**Serves 4**
Active time: 10 min   Start to finish: 15 min

1 cup nonfat chicken broth
1½ lb broccoli rabe, hollow stems trimmed
1 red bell pepper, cut into thin strips
½ to ¾ teaspoon dried hot red pepper flakes
3 garlic cloves, smashed

Combine all ingredients with salt and pepper to taste in a large saucepan and simmer, covered, stirring occasionally, until vegetables are just tender, about 8 minutes.

🌿 each serving about 43 calories and less than 1 gram fat

PHOTO ON PAGE 80

## SAUTÉED BROCCOLI RABE

**Serves 2**
Active time: 5 min   Start to finish: 15 min

1 lb broccoli rabe (1 bunch), hollow
  stems discarded
1 tablespoon unsalted butter
1 garlic clove, chopped

Cook broccoli rabe in a large pot of boiling salted water until just tender, about 4 minutes, and drain in a colander.

Melt butter in same pot over moderate heat, then cook garlic, stirring, until fragrant, about 30 seconds. Add broccoli rabe, tossing gently in butter to coat, and season with salt and pepper.

## CARROT AND SQUASH RIBBONS

**Serves 6**
Active time: 20 min   Start to finish: 20 min

2 medium carrots
2 medium yellow squash
2 medium zucchini
1 tablespoon olive oil

Trim vegetables and cut lengthwise into 1/16-inch-thick ribbons with a U-shaped vegetable peeler.

Have ready a bowl of ice and cold water. Cook carrots in a large pot of boiling salted water 2 minutes. Add both squashes and cook until vegetables are crisp-tender, 1 to 2 minutes. Drain vegetables and transfer to ice water, then drain in a colander.

Heat oil in a large skillet over moderate heat until hot but not smoking, then cook vegetables, tossing, until heated through. Season with salt and pepper.

PHOTO ON PAGE 34

## SEARED RAINBOW CHARD WITH LEEKS

**Serves 8**
Active time: 25 min   Start to finish: 25 min

*Rainbow chard has green leaves with stems and veins that are spectacular shades of fluorescent yellow, pink, orange, and red.*

2 (1-lb) bunches rainbow chard or red and green
   Swiss chard
3 tablespoons unsalted butter
2 tablespoons extra-virgin olive oil
2 large leeks (white and pale green parts only),
   halved lengthwise and cut crosswise into
   ¼-inch-thick slices
¾ teaspoon fine sea salt

Cut stems from chard (if leaves are large, cut out coarse portions of rib), then cut stems crosswise into ¼-inch-thick slices. Stack chard leaves and roll into cylinders. Cut cylinders crosswise to make 1-inch-thick strips of leaves.

Heat butter and oil in a 12-inch heavy skillet over moderately high heat until foam subsides, then sauté chard stems and leeks with sea salt and pepper to taste, stirring occasionally, until slightly soft, 3 to 5 minutes.

Add chard leaves and continue to sauté, stirring frequently, until wilted. (If greens begin to brown before they wilt, sprinkle with a few drops of water.)

PHOTO ON PAGE 55

## CORN AND OKRA STEW

**Serves 6 (main course)**
Active time: 45 min   Start to finish: 1¼ hr

4 ears corn, shucked and halved crosswise
3½ cups low-salt chicken broth
3½ cups water
½ lb large shrimp, shelled (reserve shells) and
   halved lengthwise
3 large garlic cloves
4 medium onions, quartered
1 fresh *poblano* chile, seeded and cut into
   1-inch pieces (sources on page 264)
2 tablespoons corn or other vegetable oil
½ teaspoon cayenne
½ teaspoon black pepper
¾ lb *andouille* sausage, sliced ¼ inch thick
1 lb okra, trimmed and sliced ½ inch thick
4 plum tomatoes, peeled and chopped
2 teaspoons kosher salt
4 scallions, thinly sliced

*Accompaniment:* white rice

Simmer corn, broth, and water in a 4- to 6-quart heavy pot, uncovered, until corn is very tender, 8 to 10 minutes. Transfer with tongs to a plate and cool.

Cut off kernels and return cobs to liquid with shrimp shells. Simmer 5 minutes, then pour broth through a sieve into a large bowl, discarding cobs and shrimp shells.

Chop garlic in a food processor. Add onions and *poblano* and pulse until chopped. Cook onion mixture in oil with cayenne and black pepper in cleaned pot over moderate heat, stirring occasionally, until onions are softened, about 8 minutes. Add sausage and cook, stirring, 2 minutes.

Add broth and bring to a simmer. Add okra, tomatoes, and salt, then simmer, partially covered, until okra is tender but not falling apart, about 30 minutes. Add corn and shrimp and cook, stirring, until shrimp are just cooked through, 2 to 3 minutes. Stir in scallions and season with salt and pepper.

## CORN ON THE COB WITH GARLIC-ANCHO BUTTER

**Serves 8**
Active time: 20 min   Start to finish: 45 min

1 dried *ancho* or *guajillo* chile (sources on page
   264), seeded and torn into pieces
½ cup warm water
¼ cup fresh cilantro
3 garlic cloves
1 tablespoon fresh lime juice
Pinch of sugar
1½ teaspoons kosher salt
1 stick (½ cup) unsalted butter, softened
8 ears corn, shucked

Soak chile in warm water in a 1-cup glass measure until softened, about 30 minutes, then drain.

Finely chop cilantro and garlic together in a food

processor. Add chile, lime juice, sugar, and salt, then process until finely chopped. Add butter and blend until smooth, then spoon into a ramekin.

Cook corn in a large pot of boiling salted water until crisp-tender, 4 to 5 minutes. Transfer with tongs to a platter and serve with butter.

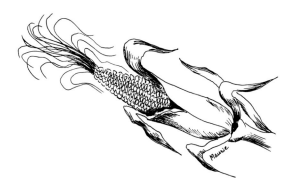

## EGGPLANT STEAKS WITH PUMPKIN, TOMATO, AND MUSHROOM RAGOUT

**Serves 6 (main course)**
Active time: 2¼ hr   Start to finish: 2¼ hr

½ lb shallots, quartered lengthwise
1 lb plum tomatoes, quartered lengthwise
    and seeded
11 tablespoons olive oil (about ¾ cup)
1½ (¾-lb) sugar pumpkins (sources on page 264)
    or butternut squash, cut into ¾-inch wedges
    and seeded
1½ cups water
1 cup dry white wine
½ lb fresh or frozen *edamame* (soybeans in the pod;
    sources on page 264) or ⅔ cup fresh or frozen
    shelled lima beans
3 large eggplants
¾ lb fresh chanterelle or shiitake mushrooms,
    trimmed (discard stems from shiitakes)
1 tablespoon minced garlic
1½ teaspoons minced fresh rosemary
1 tablespoon balsamic vinegar

*Roast shallots, tomatoes, and pumpkin:*
Preheat oven to 400°F.

Toss shallots and tomatoes with 3 tablespoons oil in a large roasting pan and season with salt. Roast until tomatoes are tender but not falling apart, about 25 minutes. Transfer tomatoes only to a large bowl.

Add pumpkins with salt to taste to shallots, tossing to coat with oil in pan. Roast until pumpkins are just tender, about 30 minutes, then add vegetable mixture to tomatoes.

Reduce oven temperature to 200°F.

Straddle roasting pan across 2 burners. Add water and ½ cup wine and deglaze by boiling over moderately high heat, stirring and scraping up any brown bits. Reserve liquid.

*Cook soybeans while vegetables roast:*
Cook soybeans in boiling salted water until just tender, about 1 minute (3 minutes for lima beans), then drain. When cool enough to handle, shell soybeans, discarding pods.

*Prepare eggplant:*
Cut 2 (2-inch-thick) crosswise slices, or "steaks," from thickest part of each eggplant and season generously with salt and pepper. (Reserve remaining eggplant for another use.) Brown 3 eggplant steaks in 3 tablespoons oil in a 12-inch nonstick skillet over moderate heat, about 5 minutes on each side.

Add ¼ cup wine to skillet and simmer, covered, turning once, until eggplant is very tender and wine is absorbed, about 5 minutes total. Transfer to a small roasting pan. (If wine is absorbed before eggplant is tender, add water, a few tablespoons at a time, and continue cooking until tender.) Repeat with remaining 3 eggplant steaks. Keep warm, uncovered, in oven.

*Make ragout:*
Heat remaining 2 tablespoons oil in skillet over moderately high heat until hot but not smoking, then sauté mushrooms with garlic, rosemary, and salt to taste, stirring, until golden and any liquid mushrooms give off is evaporated. Stir in reserved deglazing liquid and simmer until mushrooms are tender, about 10 minutes. Add roasted vegetables and soybeans and cook, stirring, until heated through. Stir in vinegar.

Serve eggplant steaks topped with vegetable ragout.

Cooks' notes:
• Shallots, tomatoes, and pumpkins can be roasted 3 hours ahead. Transfer to a bowl and keep, covered, at room temperature.
• Roasting pan may be deglazed 3 hours ahead. Transfer liquid to a bowl and chill, covered.
• Eggplant steaks can be cooked 3 hours ahead. Transfer to a baking pan and chill, covered. Reheat in a 200°F oven while preparing ragout.

PHOTO ON PAGE 61

## GREEN BEANS WITH LEMON

*Serves 8*
Active time: 20 min   Start to finish: 25 min

2½ lb *haricots verts* or other thin green beans,
    trimmed
1 tablespoon unsalted butter
½ teaspoon finely grated fresh lemon zest

Cook beans in a large pot of boiling salted water until crisp-tender, 4 to 6 minutes. Drain beans and toss with butter, zest, and salt to taste.

PHOTO ON PAGE 68

## CELERY AND FENNEL WITH BACON

*Serves 8*
Active time: 1 hr   Start to finish: 1 hr

1 bunch celery, with leaves
2 large fennel bulbs (sometimes called anise),
    with fronds
¼ lb sliced bacon, cut into ½-inch pieces
1 cup chopped shallot
1 cup chicken broth
¼ cup coarsely chopped fresh flat-leaf parsley

*Special equipment:* a Y-shaped vegetable peeler

Reserve ½ cup celery leaves. Remove strings from celery ribs with peeler, then cut celery ribs into 3- by ¼-inch sticks.

Reserve ½ cup fennel fronds. Trim fennel stalks flush with bulbs. Cut any brown spots from outer layers and quarter bulbs lengthwise. Cut out most of cores, leaving enough to hold layers together. Cut bulbs lengthwise into ¼-inch-wide slices.

Have ready 2 large bowls of ice and water. Cook celery ribs in a large pot of boiling salted water 2 minutes, then transfer with a slotted spoon to 1 bowl of ice water. Return water to a boil and cook fennel bulbs 2 minutes, then transfer to second bowl of ice water. When vegetables are cool, drain both in a colander.

Cook bacon in a 6- to 8-quart heavy pot over moderate heat until crisp, then transfer with a slotted spoon to paper towels to drain. Add shallot to bacon fat and cook, stirring, until softened. Add celery and fennel and cook, stirring, until vegetables begin to brown, about 10

minutes. Add broth and simmer, stirring frequently, until vegetables are barely tender, 12 to 15 minutes.

Coarsely chop reserved celery leaves and fennel fronds. Remove pot from heat and stir in leaves, fronds, parsley, bacon, and salt and pepper to taste.

Cooks' notes:
• Celery and fennel can be cut (but not cooked) 1 day ahead. Chill vegetables separately in large sealable plastic bags lined with damp paper towels.

PHOTO ON PAGE 77

## BRAISED ESCAROLE WITH APPLES

*Serves 2*
Active time: 25 min   Start to finish: 25 min

2 tablespoons unsalted butter
½ crisp apple such as Gala or Granny Smith, cut
    lengthwise into ⅛-inch-thick slices
1 large shallot, thinly sliced
2 garlic cloves, minced
1 head escarole, cut crosswise into ½-inch pieces
1½ tablespoons cider vinegar
1 tablespoon water
¼ cup chopped pecans, toasted

Heat 1 tablespoon butter in a large heavy skillet over moderately high heat until foam subsides, then sauté apple, stirring occasionally, until tender and slightly caramelized, about 2 minutes. Transfer apple to a dish with a slotted spoon.

Cook shallot in remaining tablespoon butter over moderate heat, stirring, until softened. Add garlic and cook, stirring, 30 seconds. Add escarole and toss over moderately high heat until it begins to wilt, about 1 minute. Add cider vinegar and water and cook, covered, until escarole is tender, about 4 minutes. Stir in apple, pecans, and salt and pepper to taste and cook until just heated through.

## SAUTÉED FENNEL AND CARROTS

*Serves 4*
Active time: 10 min   Start to finish: 25 min

1 fennel bulb (sometimes called anise; 1 lb)
2 carrots, halved crosswise
1 tablespoon olive oil

¼ cup dry white wine
¼ cup water
1 tablespoon sugar

Trim fennel stalks flush with bulb and cut bulb lengthwise into ¼-inch-thick strips, discarding core. Cut carrots into ¼-inch-thick sticks.

Heat oil in a large nonstick skillet over moderately high heat until hot but not smoking, then sauté fennel and carrots with salt to taste, stirring occasionally, until they begin to brown. Add wine, water, and sugar and simmer, covered, 5 minutes. Boil, uncovered, stirring occasionally, until liquid is evaporated and vegetables are tender. Season with salt and pepper.

## MUSHROOM BUDÍN

**Serves 6 (main course)**
Active time: 3 hr   Start to finish: 4 hr

*In Spanish, budín (pudding) refers to a pie, or layered casserole. In Deborah Madison's rendition—a wonderful vegetarian substitute for the capon in her Christmas menu, page 71—she bakes toasted corn tortillas and mushrooms in fresh-made chile colorado. Colorado in this case is Spanish for "ruddy," or "red"—as in red chile.*

1 cup finely chopped onion
2 large garlic cloves, minced
1 fresh jalapeño chile, seeded and minced
1 teaspoon dried *epazote* (sources on page 264)
    or oregano, crumbled
¼ cup chopped fresh cilantro
¼ cup vegetable oil
2 lb mushrooms, cut into ¼-inch-thick slices
2 teaspoons kosher salt
12 (6-inch) corn tortillas
¾ cup coarsely grated Monterey Jack cheese (3 oz)
¾ cup crumbled soft, mild goat cheese (3 oz)
2¼ cups *chile colorado* (page 166), cooled
1½ cups sour cream

*Garnish:* fresh cilantro leaves, sliced white onion, thinly sliced radish

Cook onion, garlic, chile, *epazote*, and cilantro in 2 tablespoons oil in a 5- to 6-quart heavy pot over moderate heat, stirring, 2 minutes. Stir in mushrooms and salt and cook, covered, 10 minutes. Remove lid and cook until mushrooms are tender, about 3 minutes more (there will be liquid from mushrooms).

Lightly brush tortillas with remaining 2 tablespoons oil and heat a well-seasoned cast-iron skillet over moderate heat. Lightly toast tortillas 30 seconds on each side. Wrap tortillas, stacking them, in a kitchen towel as toasted. Cut tortillas in half and return them to towel.

Preheat oven to 375°F and lightly oil a 10- by 8- by 2-inch ceramic or glass baking dish.

Toss cheeses together in a bowl.

Spread ⅓ cup *chile colorado* evenly in bottom of baking dish. Begin layering by arranging 5 tortillas halves over sauce in dish in 1 layer (slightly overlapping if necessary). Top with ⅓ cup sauce, one fourth (about ¾ cup) of mushroom mixture with liquid, and ¼ cup cheese. Dab 2 tablespoons sour cream over cheese. Repeat layering 3 more times.

Top with remaining 4 tortilla halves and remaining sauce. Dab with 3 tablespoons sour cream and use a rubber spatula to swirl it into the sauce, creating a marbled effect. Sprinkle top with remaining ½ cup cheese and bake, uncovered, in middle of oven, until heated through, about 20 minutes.

Whisk together remaining sour cream with a little water to loosen it, then serve on the side for drizzling over *budín.*

## CHILE COLORADO

### RED CHILE SAUCE

***Makes about 2½ cups***
Active time: 1 hr   Start to finish: 1 hr

2 oz whole dried New Mexico chiles (6)
    (sources on page 264)
1 oz whole dried *guajillo* chiles (6)
    (sources on page 264)
4 cups boiling-hot water
3 tablespoons finely chopped white onion
3 garlic cloves, minced
1½ teaspoons ground cumin
¾ teaspoon dried oregano, crumbled
2 tablespoons vegetable oil
1 tablespoon all-purpose flour
1 tablespoon kosher salt, or to taste
2 teaspoons Sherry vinegar, or to taste
1 teaspoon sugar, or to taste

Rinse chiles and split open, discarding stems, seeds, and ribs.

Heat a well-seasoned cast-iron skillet over moderate heat, then toast chiles, skin sides up, in batches, about 30 seconds (be careful not to burn them, or sauce will be bitter). Transfer chiles as toasted to a heatproof bowl and pour boiling water over them. Cover bowl and soak chiles, stirring occasionally, until softened, about 15 minutes.

Purée chiles with three fourths of soaking liquid, reserving remainder, in a blender until smooth (use caution when blending hot liquids). Pour purée through a coarse sieve into a bowl, pressing on solids, and discard solids. Whisk reserved soaking liquid into chile mixture.

Cook onion, garlic, cumin, and oregano in oil in a large heavy saucepan over moderately low heat, stirring, 2 minutes. Add flour and cook, stirring, 2 minutes. Whisk in chile mixture and simmer, partially covered, whisking occasionally, until reduced to about 2½ cups, about 30 minutes. Season with salt, vinegar, and sugar.

Cooks' note:
• Sauce may be made 1 week ahead, then cooled completely and chilled, covered.

## KALE WITH SAUTÉED APPLE AND ONION

***Serves 2***
Active time: 15 min   Start to finish: 15 min

1 Granny Smith apple
2 tablespoons olive oil
1 medium onion, cut into ¼-inch wedges
¼ teaspoon curry powder
1 lb kale, tough stems and ribs removed and
    leaves coarsely chopped
½ cup water

Peel, quarter, and core Granny Smith apple, then cut into ¼-inch-thick wedges.

Heat oil in a 5-quart pot over moderately high heat until hot but not smoking, then sauté onion, stirring occasionally, until golden. Add apple and curry powder and sauté, stirring, until apple is almost tender, about 2 minutes.

Add kale and water and cook, covered, stirring occasionally, until kale is tender and most of liquid is evaporated, about 5 minutes. Season with salt.

## SAUTÉED MUSTARD GREENS WITH GARLIC

***Serves 6***
Active time: 20 min   Start to finish: 20 min

*If using young, small mustard greens, simply stir-fry as directed, omitting the water and additional cooking time.*

3 large garlic cloves, minced
½ teaspoon salt
¼ cup olive oil
1½ lb mustard greens (2 bunches), stems and center
    ribs discarded and leaves halved
½ cup water

Mash garlic to a paste with salt. Heat oil in a 5-quart pot over moderately high heat until hot, then sauté garlic paste until fragrant. Add half of greens and toss with tongs to coat with oil, adding remaining half as greens wilt. Add water and cook, covered, stirring occasionally, 5 minutes. Continue to cook, uncovered, until greens are just tender and most of liquid is evaporated. Season with additional salt.

## ROAST PARSNIPS

### Serves 2
Active time: 10 min   Start to finish: 40 min

1 lb parsnips, peeled, then cut diagonally into
¼-inch-thick slices
1 tablespoon vegetable oil

Preheat oven to 450°F.

Toss parsnips with oil and salt to taste in a shallow (1-inch-deep) baking pan and roast in middle of oven, turning over halfway through cooking, until golden and tender, 30 to 35 minutes total.

## CURRIED TRIO OF PEAS

### Serves 4
Active time: 15 min   Start to finish: 15 min

*Served over rice, these peas—in their velvety, spicy sauce—could be a vegetarian main course. Or serve them over a piece of simply prepared fish or lamb.*

2 shallots, finely chopped
3 tablespoons unsalted butter
1½ teaspoons curry powder
½ teaspoon ground cumin
¾ cup chicken broth
½ lb sugar snap peas, trimmed
½ lb snow peas, trimmed
1 cup frozen green peas (5 oz), thawed

Cook shallots in butter in a 2-quart heavy saucepan over moderate heat, stirring, until softened. Add spices and cook, stirring, 1 minute. Add broth and bring to a simmer. Stir in all peas and simmer, covered, stirring occasionally, until tender, about 5 minutes. Season with salt and pepper.

## SUGAR SNAPS WITH FLOWERING PEA SHOOTS, PEAS, AND BABY ONIONS

### Serves 8
Active time: 40 min   Start to finish: 40 min

10 oz pearl onions, root ends trimmed and
cut with an X
2 bunches scallions (white parts only)
1 lb sugar snap peas, trimmed
1 lb fresh peas in pods, shelled (1 cup)
¼ lb pea shoots (preferably flowering; sources on
page 264), cut into 3-inch lengths
1 tablespoon unsalted butter, softened

Boil pearl onions in salted water 15 minutes and drain in a colander. Rinse under cold water, then peel.

Cook scallions and sugar snaps in a large pot of boiling salted water 1 minute. Add shelled peas and pearl onions and cook 1 minute more, or until all vegetables are crisp-tender. Drain and toss with pea shoots, butter, and salt and pepper to taste in a large bowl.

Cooks' note:
· Bear in mind you should only eat the flowering shoots of the garden pea, *Pisum sativum.* Don't try to cook with the flowering shoots of sweet peas from your flower garden—they're poisonous.

PHOTO ON PAGE 29

## PARMESAN ROASTED POTATOES

### Serves 8
Active time: 30 min   Start to finish: 2½ hr

½ cup finely grated parmesan (1½ oz)
½ cup all-purpose flour
1 teaspoon salt
¼ teaspoon black pepper
8 large boiling potatoes (3½ lb), peeled and
quartered lengthwise
1 stick (½ cup) unsalted butter, melted

Preheat oven to 350°F.

Sprinkle cheese on wax paper or foil and dry 1 hour. Transfer to a large sealable bag with flour, salt, and pepper, then shake to mix.

Rinse potatoes and drain in a colander. Add potatoes to flour mixture, tightly sealing bag, and shake to coat well.

Pour butter into a large shallow baking pan. Lift potatoes from bag and arrange in 1 layer in butter. Roast in middle or lower third of oven, turning twice, until browned and crisp, about 1¼ hours.

PHOTO ON PAGE 77

## ESCALIVADA

### ROASTED PEPPERS, ONION, AND EGGPLANT

***Serves 6***
Active time: 25 min   Start to finish: 1½ hr

*Served hot, at room temperature, or chilled, this versatile vegetable mélange shows up frequently on Catalan menus. We love to use Unió (sources on page 264), a fragrant, peppery oil made from the region's arbequina olives, both for cooking this dish and for drizzling over it.*

3 large red bell peppers
3 small Italian eggplants (1 lb total), halved
   lengthwise
About 2½ tablespoons extra-virgin olive oil
1 large sweet onion, halved through root end
   and cut into ½-inch wedges
Sea salt

Preheat oven to 400°F.

Place whole peppers in one third of an oiled, large 1-inch-deep baking pan. Brush cut sides of eggplants with ½ tablespoon oil and arrange next to peppers in pan. Toss onion with 1 tablespoon oil and spread in remaining third of pan.

Roast vegetables, turning peppers occasionally, until skins of peppers blister on all sides, about 40 minutes. Transfer peppers to a bowl, cover, and let steam 10 minutes. Continue roasting eggplants and onion until tender and browned, 20 to 30 minutes more, and keep warm, covered.

Peel peppers and cut into ½-inch-thick strips, discarding stems and seeds. Season vegetables with sea salt and pepper.

Serve eggplants topped with peppers and onion. Drizzle with remaining oil and season with sea salt.

PHOTO ON PAGE 20

## LOW-FAT MASHED POTATOES

***Serves 6***
Active time: 10 min   Start to finish: 35 min

2½ lb Yukon Gold potatoes (about 5 large),
   peeled and quartered
¼ cup nonfat sour cream
Pinch of freshly grated nutmeg

Cover potatoes with salted cold water and boil until tender, about 20 minutes. Reserve 1¼ cups cooking liquid and drain potatoes. Return potatoes to pot and mash with reserved cooking liquid and sour cream. Season with nutmeg and salt and pepper.

🍃 each serving about 125 calories and less than 1 gram fat

## POTATO-GREEN CHILE GRATIN

***Serves 6***
Active time: 45 min   Start to finish: 2 hr

*If you are making the Santa Fe Christmas Dinner (page 71) and your oven is large enough, you can cook the gratin and the capon at the same time. Put the capon in the middle of the oven and the gratin in the lower third.*

6 fresh green Anaheim or *poblano* chiles (¾ lb)
2 cups heavy cream or half-and-half
1 large garlic clove
2½ lb russet (baking) potatoes (5)

*Special equipment:* a *mandoline* or other manual
   slicer

Roast and peel chiles (procedure in herbed ricotta recipe, page 91).

Preheat oven to 375°F.

Bring heavy cream with garlic just to a simmer and remove from heat. Peel potatoes and cut crosswise into ⅛-inch-thick slices using *mandoline*.

Arrange one fourth of potatoes evenly in bottom of a well-buttered 2-quart shallow baking dish, overlapping slightly, and sprinkle with salt to taste and one fourth of chiles. Make 3 more layers in same manner. Remove garlic from cream and pour cream over potatoes.

Cover dish with foil and bake in lower third of oven 45 minutes. Remove foil and bake until gratin is golden brown on top and bubbling, about 30 minutes more. Cool slightly before serving.

Cooks' note:
• **Gratin can be baked 1 day ahead, then cooled completely before being chilled, covered. Bring to room temperature before reheating, covered, in a 350°F oven.**

PHOTO ON PAGE 72

## POTATOES WITH VINEGAR AND SEA SALT

*Serves 8*
Active time: 10 min   Start to finish: 20 min

*We liked fleur de sel or Malden flaked sea salt best in this recipe, though other types work fine. If using coarse sea salt instead of flaked or fine, crush it lightly.*

3 lb small (1½-inch) boiling potatoes
2½ tablespoons tarragon vinegar or cider vinegar
Flaked or fine sea salt to taste
1½ tablespoons extra-virgin olive oil

Cover potatoes with salted cold water by 1 inch in a 4-quart pot and simmer until just tender, about 10 minutes. (They will continue to cook after draining; do not overcook or they will break apart.)

Drain potatoes and rinse under cold water. While potatoes are still warm, gently toss with vinegar and salt. Cool potatoes to room temperature, stirring occasionally, and gently toss with oil.

PHOTO ON PAGE 47

## GOAT-CHEESE SCALLOPED POTATOES WITH CHIVE BLOSSOMS

*Serves 8*
Active time: 40 min   Start to finish: 2 hr

3 lb yellow-fleshed boiling potatoes
2 shallots, chopped
2 tablespoons unsalted butter
1 cup whole milk
1 cup heavy cream
8 oz soft mild goat cheese
1½ to 2 teaspoons kosher salt
1 teaspoon black pepper

*Garnish:* fresh chives (preferably flowering; sources on page 264) snipped with scissors

Preheat oven to 350°F.
Peel potatoes and cut into ⅛-inch-thick slices with a manual slicer or sharp thin knife. Keep slices in a large bowl of cold water while making sauce.

Cook shallots in butter in a small skillet over moderately low heat, stirring, until softened. Transfer to a blender and purée with milk, cream, cheese, kosher salt to taste, and pepper.

Drain potatoes in a large colander and pat dry. Arrange in a buttered 3-quart shallow baking dish in 3 layers, pouring some of sauce over each layer (use all of sauce) and putting best potato slices on top layer.

Bake, covered with foil, in lower third of oven. Remove foil after 45 minutes and continue to bake until potatoes are tender, 30 to 45 minutes more. If desired, briefly broil potatoes until top is golden.

Cooks' note:
• Dish may be assembled 1 day ahead and chilled, covered. Bring to room temperature before baking.

PHOTO ON PAGE 29

## RUTABAGA AND CARROT PURÉE

*Serves 8*
Active time: 15 min   Start to finish: 50 min

2 rutabagas (2½ lb total), peeled and cut into 1-inch pieces
5 carrots, cut into 1-inch pieces
3 tablespoons unsalted butter
3 tablespoons packed light brown sugar
1 teaspoon kosher salt

Cook rutabagas and carrots in boiling salted water to cover by 1 inch in a large pot until tender, about 30 minutes. Transfer vegetables with a slotted spoon to a food processor and purée with butter, brown sugar, and salt until very smooth. If necessary, transfer purée back to pot and reheat.

Cooks' note:
• Purée keeps, covered and chilled, 3 days.

PHOTO ON PAGE 68

# SALADS

## Amanida amb Espàrrec i Pernil

### Asparagus and Serrano Ham Salad
### with Toasted Almonds

**Serves 6**
Active time: 15 min   Start to finish: 15 min

*A Catalan composed salad, or amanida, may be made of almost anything, though ham, sausage, or anchovies are often included. Traditionally, ingredients are added to the final presentation individually rather than mixed together.*

2 lb thin asparagus, trimmed and peeled
½ cup extra-virgin olive oil
3 tablespoons finely chopped blanched almonds
2 tablespoons coarse dry bread crumbs
⅛ teaspoon ground cumin
3 tablespoons Sherry vinegar
1 medium head escarole, cut into ¼-inch-thick
   strips (6 cups)
½ lb sliced *serrano* ham or prosciutto

Have ready a large bowl of ice and cold water. Cook asparagus in boiling salted water until crisp-tender, 2 to 3 minutes. Drain, then refresh in ice water. Drain again and pat dry.

Heat 1 tablespoon oil in a small skillet over moderate heat until hot but not smoking, then cook almonds, bread crumbs, and cumin, stirring frequently, until toasted, 3 to 4 minutes. Cool. Add remaining oil to vinegar in a slow stream, whisking until emulsified. Season with salt and pepper.

Toss escarole with half of dressing and mound on plates. Arrange ham around escarole and top salad with asparagus. Drizzle asparagus with remaining dressing. Sprinkle salad with almond-and-crumb mixture.

PHOTO ON PAGE 22

## Lobster, Corn, and Potato Salad
## with Tarragon

**Serves 4**
Active time: 50 min   Start to finish: 1½ hr

4 (1½-lb) live lobsters or 1½ lb cooked fresh
   lobster meat
1 lb small red potatoes
3 ears corn
*For vinaigrette*
2½ tablespoons fresh lemon juice
1½ to 2 tablespoons chopped fresh tarragon
½ teaspoon Dijon mustard
½ teaspoon salt
¼ cup extra-virgin olive oil

2 cups grape or cherry tomatoes, halved
1 cup coarsely chopped frisée (French curly endive)
⅓ cup sliced scallion

*Prepare lobster, potatoes, and corn:*

Plunge 2 live lobsters headfirst into an 8-quart pot of boiling salted water. Cover and cook lobsters over moderately high heat 9 minutes from time they enter water, then transfer with tongs to sink to cool. Return water to a boil and cook remaining 2 lobsters in same manner. Leave water boiling in pot.

Simmer potatoes in lobster cooking water until just tender, 15 to 20 minutes. Transfer with a slotted spoon to a colander, reserving boiling water in pot.

Boil corn in same water until crisp-tender, about 3 minutes, then drain.

When lobsters are cool, remove meat from claws, joints, and tails, reserving shells for another use. Cut meat into 1-inch pieces. Cut potatoes into ¾-inch pieces, and cut corn from cobs.

*Make vinaigrette:*

Whisk together lemon juice, tarragon, mustard, and salt until combined, then add oil in a thin stream, whisking until emulsified.

*Assemble salad:*

Just before serving, toss together lobster, potatoes, corn, vinaigrette, tomatoes, frisée, and scallion in a large bowl and season with salt and pepper.

**Cooks' note:**
· **Lobster may be cooked 1 day ahead and chilled, covered.**

PHOTO ON PAGE 82

## GRILLED-SHRIMP GREEK SALAD

*Serves 4 (main course)*
Active time: 40 min    Start to finish: 40 min

4 tablespoons fresh lemon juice
4 tablespoons olive oil plus additional
  for brushing
1 tablespoon finely chopped fresh oregano
1 garlic clove, minced
1 pint cherry tomatoes, halved
½ English cucumber, cut into ½-inch pieces
½ small red onion, thinly sliced
1 lb large shrimp (20 to 24), shelled and deveined
2 (8-inch) pita loaves (preferably pocketless)
1 yellow bell pepper, sides cut off and remainder
  discarded
6 oz feta, cut into ½-inch cubes

*Special equipment:* 6 (8-inch) bamboo skewers,
  soaked in warm water 15 minutes

Prepare grill for cooking.
*Make dressing:*
Whisk together 2 tablespoons lemon juice, 3 tablespoons oil, half of oregano, half of garlic, and salt and pepper to taste in a large bowl.

Gently stir tomatoes, cucumber, and onion into dressing and let stand at room temperature.
*Marinate shrimp:*
Whisk together remaining 2 tablespoons lemon juice and remaining oregano and garlic in a large bowl. Stir in shrimp until well coated and marinate at room temperature 10 minutes.

*Grill pitas and bell pepper while shrimp marinates:*
Lightly brush pitas and bell pepper on both sides with some oil and season with salt and pepper. Grill pitas on an oiled rack set 5 to 6 inches over glowing coals until browned and slightly crisp, about 2 minutes on each side, then transfer to a rack to cool (pitas will continue to crisp as they cool).

Grill bell pepper until just softened, about 1½ minutes on each side.
*Grill shrimp:*
Add remaining tablespoon oil to shrimp and toss to coat. Thread 4 shrimp lengthwise, each facing in same direction (so shrimp will lay flat), on each skewer without crowding. Season shrimp with salt and pepper.

Grill shrimp until just cooked through, about 2 minutes on each side.

Break pitas into bite-size pieces and coarsely chop bell pepper. Remove shrimp from skewers and gently stir into tomato mixture with pitas, bell pepper, feta, and salt and pepper to taste.

## PANFRIED TOFU ON SESAME WATERCRESS WITH SOY-ORANGE DRESSING

*Serves 2*
Active time: 15 min    Start to finish: 25 min

¾ lb extra-firm tofu, cut into ½-inch-thick slices
1½ tablespoons vegetable oil
1½ bunches watercress, tough stems discarded
1 tablespoon sesame seeds, toasted
2 teaspoons grated peeled fresh ginger
1 large garlic clove, minced
¼ cup fresh orange juice
2 tablespoons soy sauce
2 teaspoons Asian sesame oil (sources on page 264)

Pat tofu dry. Heat 1 tablespoon vegetable oil in a 12-inch nonstick skillet over moderately high heat until hot but not smoking, then sauté tofu until golden brown, about 3 minutes on each side. Transfer to a plate.

Heat remaining ½ tablespoon vegetable oil in skillet over moderate heat until hot but not smoking, then cook watercress, turning with tongs, until just wilted. Stir in sesame seeds. Transfer watercress to a platter and arrange tofu on top.

Simmer remaining ingredients in skillet 1 minute and drizzle sauce over tofu.

## ARUGULA-CHICORY SALAD WITH PINE NUTS AND GOAT-CHEESE TOASTS

**Serves 4**
Active time: 25 min   Start to finish: 25 min

*For vinaigrette*
1 teaspoon red-wine vinegar
1 teaspoon fresh lemon juice
½ teaspoon Dijon mustard
3 tablespoons olive oil

½ lb arugula, tough stems discarded
½ head chicory (white and pale-green parts only),
    torn into pieces (2 cups)
¼ cup pine nuts, toasted
¾ cup cherry tomatoes, halved
6 oz soft mild goat cheese
8 (⅓-inch-thick) diagonal baguette slices

Preheat broiler.
*Make vinaigrette:*
Whisk together vinegar, lemon juice, mustard, and salt and pepper to taste and add oil in a slow stream, whisking.
*Make salad:*
Toss arugula, chicory, pine nuts, and tomatoes in a large bowl with just enough vinaigrette to coat, then divide among 4 plates.
Spread goat cheese on baguette slices and broil on a baking sheet 6 inches from heat until cheese is softened and edges of bread are golden, about 2 minutes.
Arrange toasts on salads and drizzle any remaining vinaigrette over cheese.

b. Charlton

## ARUGULA, ROQUEFORT, AND ROASTED-SQUASH SALAD

**Serves 4**
Active time: 25 min   Start to finish: 1 hr

1 (1¼-lb) butternut squash, peeled, halved, and
    seeds reserved
1 tablespoon light brown sugar
½ teaspoon salt
⅛ teaspoon cayenne
2 tablespoons unsalted butter, melted
⅓ cup walnut oil or extra-virgin olive oil
2 tablespoons fresh lemon juice
1½ oz Roquefort or Cabrales (Spanish blue cheese)
2 bunches arugula (½ lb)

Preheat oven to 350°F.
Cut squash into 2-inch-long pieces, about ¼ inch thick. Rinse squash seeds and pat dry. Toss together seeds, brown sugar, salt, cayenne, and 1 tablespoon butter. Toast seeds in 1 layer in a nonstick shallow baking pan in middle of oven until golden, about 10 minutes, then cool. Toss squash with remaining tablespoon butter and salt and pepper to taste in baking pan and roast, covered with foil, until just tender, about 20 minutes.
Whisk together oil, lemon juice, and salt and pepper to taste in a large bowl. Crumble cheese into bowl, then add arugula. Gently toss in warm squash and sprinkle with toasted seeds.

## ROSAURA'S FESTIVE SALAD

**Serves 12**
Active time: 2 hr   Start to finish: 2 hr

*We adapted this gorgeous salad from a recipe that Mexican chef María Dolores Torres Yzábal contributed to* México, The Beautiful Cookbook.

*For vinaigrette*
1 tablespoon soy sauce
⅓ cup cider vinegar
1 teaspoon chicken bouillon granules
1½ tablespoons chopped fresh tarragon or
    1½ teaspoons dried
1 teaspoon dried oregano, crumbled
1 tablespoon chopped fresh chives
⅔ cup safflower oil

1 cup vegetable oil

2 cups (⅓-inch) cubes firm white sandwich bread

2 bunches spinach (1½ lb), stems discarded and leaves cut crosswise into ½-inch strips

1½ lb red cabbage, finely shredded

½ medium *jícama* (¾ lb), cut into very fine julienne

3 medium raw beets, peeled and cut into very fine julienne

1 medium red onion, halved lengthwise, very thinly sliced lengthwise, and soaked in cold water 20 minutes

½ cup chopped candied citron or candied pineapple (4 oz)

¾ cup puffed amaranth seeds (optional; sources on page 264)

*Make vinaigrette:*

Stir together soy sauce, vinegar, and chicken bouillon granules. Add herbs, then add safflower oil in a slow stream, whisking constantly.

*Make salad:*

Heat vegetable oil in a heavy skillet and fry bread cubes in 2 batches, stirring occasionally, until golden, about 2 minutes.

Combine vegetables, candied citron, and three fourths of croutons and amaranth seeds in a large bowl and toss well with vinaigrette. Sprinkle with remaining croutons and amaranth seeds.

Cooks' notes:
· We used a Japanese slicer (sources on page 264), set at ¹⁄₁₆ inch, to shred the cabbage and slice the onion, *jícama,* and beets. We cut the *jícama* and beet slices by hand.
· The vegetables and vinaigrette may be prepared 1 day ahead and chilled separately in plastic bags. The croutons are best the day they are made.

PHOTO ON PAGE 18

## MANGO JÍCAMA CHOPPED SALAD

*Serves 8*
Active time: 1 hr   Start to finish: 1 hr

*For dressing*
¼ cup fresh lime juice
2 tablespoons honey
1 tablespoon Sherry vinegar or red-wine vinegar
1 teaspoon minced garlic
¼ cup olive oil

2 cups chopped peeled *jícama* (1 lb)

2 mangoes, pitted, peeled, and coarsely chopped

½ lb Napa cabbage, sliced crosswise (3 cups)

1 head romaine (1½ lb), torn into bite-size pieces

½ seedless cucumber, cut into 2- by ¼-inch sticks

*Accompaniment:* 1 cup toasted salted pumpkin seeds (page 124)

*Make dressing:*

Whisk together lime juice, honey, vinegar, and garlic. Add oil in a slow stream, whisking until emulsified. Season with salt and pepper.

*Make salad:*

Toss together *jícama*, mangoes, cabbage, romaine, and cucumber with dressing to taste.

Serve salad sprinkled with pumpkin seeds.

Cooks' notes:
· **Dressing may be made 1 day ahead and chilled, covered.**
· **You can prepare salad ingredients 1 day ahead and keep in separate sealed plastic bags, chilled.**

PHOTO ON PAGE 15

## BOSTON LETTUCE WITH CHIVES AND BUTTER DRESSING

*Serves 4*
Active time: 15 min   Start to finish: 15 min

*This dressing has a light, silky texture that keeps it from weighing down the delicate lettuce. The salad needs to be eaten immediately, before the dressing cools.*

3 tablespoons thinly sliced fresh chives
1 head Boston lettuce, larger leaves torn into pieces
½ stick (¼ cup) unsalted butter, cut into slices
1 garlic clove, finely chopped
4 teaspoons fresh lemon juice

Sprinkle chives over lettuce in a large bowl.

Heat butter and garlic in a small heavy saucepan over moderate heat, stirring occasionally, until garlic is golden and butter has a slightly nutty aroma (there will be golden-brown bits of milk solids on bottom of pan), about 5 minutes. Remove from heat and add lemon juice and salt and pepper to taste.

Toss salad with dressing and serve immediately.

## SHREDDED COLLARD GREENS WITH WALNUTS AND PICKLED APPLES

*Serves 6*
Active time: 30 min   Start to finish: 1½ hr

*For pickled apples*
2 red apples such as Gala or Ida Red
½ cup cider vinegar
1 cup water
½ cup sugar
1 teaspoon salt
1 teaspoon pickling spice

½ cup walnut halves (3 oz)
¼ cup olive oil
1 bunch collard greens (1 lb)
½ teaspoon kosher salt

*Make pickled apples:*
Quarter and core apples, then cut each quarter lengthwise into ⅛-inch-thick slices. Boil vinegar, water, sugar, salt, and pickling spice in a saucepan, stirring, until sugar is dissolved. Add apples and return to a boil. Transfer to a heatproof bowl and cool. Chill, uncovered, until cold, about 1 hour.

*Prepare nuts while apples chill:*
Toast walnuts in oil in a small skillet over moderate heat, stirring occasionally, until a shade darker. Cool nuts in oil. Transfer nuts to a cutting board with a slotted spoon, reserving oil. Coarsely chop 1 tablespoon nuts and finely chop remaining nuts.

*Prepare collard greens:*
Halve each collard leaf lengthwise with kitchen shears or a sharp knife, cutting out and discarding center ribs. Stack leaves and cut crosswise into ¼-inch-wide strips. Transfer to a large bowl.

*Just before serving:*
Transfer all nuts and oil from skillet to collards and toss with ½ teaspoon salt and pepper to taste. Add apples, discarding pickling liquid and spices, and toss.

Cooks' notes:
· Apples may be pickled 3 days ahead and kept chilled, covered.
· Nuts may be toasted and chopped 1 day ahead and kept in the oil in an airtight container at room temperature.

PHOTO ON PAGE 60

## GREEN SALAD WITH MUSTARD-HERB VINAIGRETTE

*Serves 4*
Active time: 20 min   Start to finish: 20 min

1 teaspoon white-wine vinegar
1½ teaspoons Dijon mustard
1 tablespoon fat-free chicken broth
1 tablespoon extra-virgin olive oil
2 tablespoons finely chopped mixed fresh herbs such as chives, tarragon, and parsley
1 head Boston lettuce (½ lb), leaves separated and torn into bite-size pieces

Whisk together vinegar, mustard, and broth in a large bowl, then add oil in a stream, whisking until emulsified. Season with salt and pepper and whisk in mixed herbs.

Add lettuce and toss with vinaigrette.

each serving about 43 calories and 4 grams fat

## HEARTS OF ROMAINE WITH ROASTED PEPPERS AND CABRALES DRESSING

*Serves 8*
Active time: 30 min   Start to finish: 30 min

*For roasted peppers*
2 fresh *poblano* chiles (sources on page 264)
2 red bell peppers
*For dressing*
3 oz Cabrales (Spanish blue cheese) or other blue cheese, grated
2 tablespoons chopped fresh oregano
2 tablespoons chopped fresh chives
⅓ cup fresh lime juice
½ cup extra-virgin olive oil

3 hearts of romaine, separated into leaves

*Roast peppers:*
Lay chiles and bell peppers on their sides on racks of gas burners and turn flame on high. (Or broil on rack of a broiler pan about 2 inches from heat.) Roast, turning with tongs, until skins are blackened, 5 to 8 minutes.

Transfer to a bowl, then cover and let steam 10 minutes. Peel, seed, and cut into thin strips.

*Make dressing:*

Whisk together dressing ingredients in a large bowl.

*Arrange salad:*

Dip each romaine leaf in dressing to coat, shaking off excess, and arrange on a platter. Toss pepper strips in remaining dressing and scatter over romaine.

**Cooks' notes:**
- Peppers can be roasted 1 day ahead and chilled, covered.
- You can make dressing 1 day ahead and chill, covered. Bring to room temperature before using.

## Frisée, Watercress, and Mint Salad

**Serves 6**
Active time: 20 min   Start to finish: 20 min

1 bunch frisée (French curly endive; 8 oz), trimmed
2 bunches watercress, tough stems discarded
⅓ cup fresh mint, torn into small pieces
3 scallions, thinly sliced
3 to 4 tablespoons extra-virgin olive oil
1 tablespoon aged red-wine vinegar or lemon juice, or to taste
½ cup pine nuts, toasted and salted

Toss together frisée, watercress, mint, and scallions. Drizzle with just enough oil to coat, tossing. Add vinegar and salt to taste and toss again. Sprinkle with nuts.

PHOTO ON PAGE 72

### VEGETABLE SALADS

## Haricot Vert, Edamame, and Purple-Potato Salad

**Serves 16**
Active time: 45 min   Start to finish: 1 hr

1 lb frozen or fresh *edamame* (soybeans in the pod; sources on page 264) or 2½ lb fresh fava beans in the pod, shelled
3 lb small boiling potatoes (preferably purple or red fingerling)
3 lb *haricots verts* or other thin green beans

¼ cup minced shallot
¼ cup chopped fresh mint
¼ to ⅓ cup extra-virgin olive oil

Have ready a large bowl of ice and cold water. Boil *edamame* in a large pot of boiling salted water until crisp-tender, 1 to 3 minutes. Transfer with a slotted spoon to ice water. Shell *edamame* (if using fava beans, peel off tough outer skins).

Bring potatoes to a boil in cold salted water to cover by 1½ inches and cook at a bare simmer until almost tender, 15 to 20 minutes. (Potatoes will continue to cook after being removed from water. Be careful not to over-cook or potatoes will break apart when sliced.) Transfer with a slotted spoon to ice water to cool. Drain well.

While potatoes are cooking, trim *haricots verts* and halve diagonally crosswise. Cook in 2 batches in a large pot of boiling salted water until just tender, 3 to 4 minutes. Transfer to ice water to cool. Drain well.

Just before serving, cut potatoes into ⅓-inch-thick slices and toss all ingredients together in a large bowl with salt and pepper to taste.

**Cooks' note:**
- Vegetables may be cooked 1 day ahead and chilled separately in sealable plastic bags. Do not slice potatoes until just before serving.

PHOTO ON PAGE 36

## Chopped Greek Salad

**Serves 4**
Active time: 15 min   Start to finish: 15 min

½ small green bell pepper, chopped
¼ English cucumber, chopped
½ small red onion, sliced
1 cup cherry tomatoes, halved
⅓ cup Kalamata or other brine-cured black olives, rinsed
2 teaspoons finely chopped fresh oregano
2 teaspoons fresh lemon juice
2 tablespoons extra-virgin olive oil
1 (6-oz) piece feta, quartered

Toss together all ingredients except feta, then season with salt and pepper. Put feta on 4 serving plates and top with salad.

## ROASTED-BEET SALAD

**Serves 4**
Active time: 25 min   Start to finish: 1½ hr

½ lb mixed red and candy-striped baby or
   medium beets, stems trimmed to 1 inch
1 tablespoon minced shallot
1 tablespoon fresh lemon juice
3 tablespoons fresh orange juice
1 teaspoon finely grated fresh orange zest
½ teaspoon Dijon mustard
1 tablespoon extra-virgin olive oil
1 head Bibb or butterhead lettuce (6 oz),
   leaves separated

Preheat oven to 400°F.

Rinse beets. Wrap colors separately in foil and roast
in middle of oven until tender, 45 minutes to 1 hour,
then cool. Peel beets and halve lengthwise. If using
medium beets, cut each half crosswise into ¼-inch-thick
slices, keeping colors separate.

Whisk together shallot, juices, zest, and mustard.
Whisk in oil until emulsified and season with salt and
pepper. Drizzle lettuce with three fourths of dressing.
Sprinkle with beets and drizzle with remaining dressing.

each serving about 61 calories and 4 grams fat

## SAVOY CABBAGE, CARROT, AND APPLE SALAD

**Serves 6**
Active time: 45 min   Start to finish: 1½ hr

3 tablespoons apple juice
2 tablespoons fresh lemon juice
1 tablespoon olive oil
½ teaspoon caraway seeds, lightly crushed
½ head Savoy cabbage, cored and very thinly
   sliced (4 cups)
2 large carrots, very thinly julienned (2 cups)
1 Granny Smith apple, quartered, cored, and
   sliced crosswise ⅛ inch thick

*Garnish:* fresh flat-leaf parsley leaves

Whisk together juices, oil, and caraway seeds in
a large bowl. Season with salt and pepper and toss
with cabbage, carrots, and apple. Let stand at room
temperature, tossing occasionally, 40 minutes to allow
flavors to blend and cabbage to wilt.

Cooks' notes:
• Use a *mandoline* or other manual slicer as an easy and fast
  way to slice cabbage and julienne carrots.
• Salad may be made 1 day ahead. Place plastic wrap directly on surface of salad, then cover bowl and chill. Season
  again before serving.

each serving about 63 calories and 3 grams fat

## ROASTED CHAYOTE AND RED PEPPER SALAD WITH TANGERINE DRESSING

**Serves 4**
Active time: 35 min   Start to finish: 1¼ hr

*For dressing*
2 scallions, chopped
1 fresh *serrano* chile, seeded and finely
   chopped
5 tablespoons fresh tangerine juice
2 teaspoons olive oil
1 teaspoon Sherry vinegar

2 medium chayotes (1 lb total), peeled, halved
   lengthwise, and seeded
2 medium red bell peppers (¾ lb), quartered
2 heads Bibb lettuce, torn into small pieces

Preheat oven to 450°F.
*Make dressing:*
Whisk together scallions, chile, juice, oil, and vinegar in a large bowl and season with salt and pepper.
*Make salad:*
Cut chayote halves lengthwise into ¼-inch-thick
slices and arrange in 1 layer in two thirds of a lightly
oiled shallow baking pan. Put bell pepper quarters, skin
sides up, in other third of pan. Roast in middle of oven,
uncovered, until chayote is browned in spots and bell
pepper skins are blistered, about 30 minutes. Immediately add chayote to dressing and toss to coat.

Transfer hot bell peppers to a small bowl. Cover
and let stand 10 minutes, then peel. Cut bell peppers
into ¼-inch-thick strips and add to chayote with any
pepper juices accumulated in bowl. Add lettuce and toss
to coat.

each serving about 82 calories and 4 grams fat

## ROASTED-CAULIFLOWER, WATERCRESS, AND RADICCHIO SALAD

**Serves 2**
Active time: 20 min   Start to finish: 25 min

½ large head cauliflower, cut into ¾-inch florets (about 4 cups)
4 tablespoons olive oil
¼ cup chopped walnuts
1 to 1½ tablespoons fresh lemon juice (to taste)
½ teaspoon Dijon mustard
2 cups small watercress sprigs
1 cup shredded radicchio

Preheat oven to 425°F.

Toss cauliflower with 2 tablespoons oil in a shallow baking pan and season with salt. Roast in middle of oven, stirring occasionally, until cauliflower is tender and begins to brown, about 15 minutes.

Meanwhile, cook nuts in remaining 2 tablespoons oil in a small skillet over moderately low heat, stirring occasionally, until fragrant and a shade darker, about 5 minutes. Cool slightly in skillet.

Stir together lemon juice and mustard in a large bowl. Add nuts with any oil from skillet, roasted cauliflower, watercress, radicchio, and salt and pepper to taste, then toss to coat.

## VELLARIKKAI THAKKALI VENGAYA PACHADI

### CUCUMBER, TOMATO, AND ONION YOGURT SALAD

**Makes about 3 cups**
Active time: 15 min   Start to finish: 15 min

*Pachadi is the southern version of North Indian raita. You can substitute plain low-fat yogurt for the whole-milk yogurt here, but drain it in a sieve overnight first. For information on specialty ingredients, see sources on page 264.*

1 English cucumber, peeled, seeded, and cut into ½-inch cubes
2 plum tomatoes, seeded and cut into ½-inch cubes
1 onion, finely chopped
2 cups plain whole-milk yogurt
2 teaspoons vegetable oil
1 teaspoon black mustard seeds
1 teaspoon cumin seeds
1 teaspoon picked-over split skinned *urad dal*
1 tablespoon finely chopped fresh cilantro

Stir together cucumber, plum tomatoes, onion, and yogurt. Heat oil in a small heavy skillet over moderate heat until hot but not smoking, then cook mustard seeds, cumin, and *urad dal*, stirring, until mustard seeds begin to pop. Pour oil mixture over vegetables and stir until combined. Stir in cilantro and salt to taste.

Cooks' note:
* You can make *pachadi* 6 hours ahead and chill, covered.

PHOTO ON PAGE 12

## CORN, TOMATO, AND SCALLION SALAD

**Serves 8**
Active time: 20 min   Start to finish: 20 min

4 ears fresh corn, shucked
2 tablespoons extra-virgin olive oil
2 garlic cloves, minced
1½ tablespoons balsamic vinegar
1 lb cherry tomatoes, halved
½ cup coarsely chopped scallion greens

Cut corn kernels from ears, discarding cobs. Heat oil in a large heavy skillet over moderately high heat until hot but not smoking, then sauté corn with salt and pepper to taste, stirring, until tender, about 4 minutes.

Add garlic and sauté, stirring, 1 minute. Add vinegar and cook, stirring, until most is evaporated, about 1 minute. Add tomatoes and cook, gently stirring, 1 minute. Remove skillet from heat and stir in scallions.

Transfer vegetables to a large plate to cool and season with salt and pepper.

**Cooks' note:**
• Salad can be made 1 day ahead and chilled, covered.

PHOTO ON PAGE 47

## SUGAR SNAP PEA AND CUCUMBER SALAD

**Serves 8**
Active time: 30 min   Start to finish: 30 min

1 lb sugar snap peas, trimmed
2 tablespoons chopped walnuts, toasted
1 tablespoon fat-free chicken broth or water
1 tablespoon walnut oil
1½ teaspoons fresh lemon juice
⅛ teaspoon cayenne
1 tablespoon chopped fresh dill
1 English cucumber, halved lengthwise and cut crosswise into ¼-inch-thick slices

Have ready a bowl of ice and cold water. Cook peas in a large saucepan of boiling salted water until bright green and crisp-tender, about 2 minutes. Drain and immediately transfer to ice water. When cold, drain well and pat dry.

Mash walnuts to a paste with a mortar and pestle and whisk in broth, oil, lemon juice, cayenne, and dill until blended. Season with salt and pepper. Toss walnut

mixture with peas and cucumber until vegetables are well coated.

each serving about 59 calories and 3 grams fat

## POTATO, RED PEPPER, AND FENNEL SALAD

**Makes about 6 cups**
Active time: 10 min   Start to finish: 30 min

1½ lb small (1½-inch) red potatoes
½ fennel bulb (sometimes called anise)
3 tablespoons white-wine vinegar
¼ cup extra-virgin olive oil
1 large red bell pepper, cut into ½-inch pieces

Simmer potatoes in salted cold water to cover by 1 inch in a saucepan until tender, 20 to 25 minutes. Drain and rinse under cold water. When cool enough to handle, cut each potato into eighths.

While potatoes are cooking, trim fennel stalks flush with bulb, discarding stalks, and chop enough fronds to measure 2 tablespoons. Core fennel bulb and cut into ½-inch pieces.

Whisk together vinegar, oil, and salt and pepper to taste in a large bowl. Add warm potatoes, fennel bulb and fronds, and bell pepper, then toss well. Season with salt and pepper.

## FINGERLING-POTATO SALAD WITH GREEN CHILE—CILANTRO SALSA

**Serves 8**
Active time: 15 min   Start to finish: 45 min

4 lb fingerling potatoes
4 tablespoons cider vinegar
3 fresh jalapeño chiles, seeds and ribs removed from 2 of them
2 cups fresh cilantro sprigs, coarsely chopped
1½ shallots, coarsely chopped
1 garlic clove, coarsely chopped
¼ cup extra-virgin olive oil

Cover potatoes with salted cold water by 1 inch, then simmer until just tender, 10 to 15 minutes. (Potatoes will continue to cook after draining; do not overcook.)

Drain potatoes and rinse under cold water until slightly cooled. Halve lengthwise and while still warm gently toss with 1 tablespoon vinegar. Cool potatoes to room temperature, then season with salt and pepper.

While potatoes cook, coarsely chop jalapeños and pulse in a food processor with cilantro, shallots, garlic, oil, and remaining 3 tablespoons vinegar until finely chopped. Toss potatoes with salsa.

**Cooks' note:**
- We cool the potatoes before tossing them with the salsa so the herbs won't discolor.

PHOTO ON PAGE 40

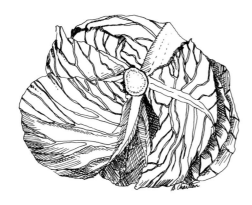

## RADICCHIO, RED CABBAGE, AND TOMATOES WITH ORANGE VINAIGRETTE

*Serves 8*
Active time: 20 min   Start to finish: 20 min

1 small red onion, thinly sliced
1 tablespoon plus 1 teaspoon Dijon mustard
2 teaspoons finely grated fresh orange zest
4½ tablespoons fresh orange juice
⅓ cup olive oil
2 heads radicchio (¾ lb total), cored and coarsely chopped
½ small head red cabbage, cored and coarsely chopped
2 pints cherry tomatoes, halved
½ teaspoon sugar, or to taste

Soak onion in cold water to cover 15 minutes.

Whisk together mustard, zest, juice, and salt and pepper to taste. Add oil in a slow stream, whisking.

Drain onion well and toss together with radicchio, cabbage, tomatoes, and enough dressing to coat. Toss salad with sugar and salt and pepper to taste.

PHOTO ON PAGE 40

## VEGETABLE SALAD WITH CURRY-SOY VINAIGRETTE

*Serves 8*
Active time: 50 min   Start to finish: 50 min

*For vinaigrette*
2 tablespoons light soy sauce
2 teaspoons Dijon mustard
2 teaspoons Madras curry powder (sources on page 264)
1 teaspoon fine sea salt
1 teaspoon freshly ground mixed peppercorns
½ cup extra-virgin olive oil
*For salad*
1 lb tomatoes
½ cup finely chopped shallots
1 bunch broccoli, cut into 1½-inch florets
½ head cauliflower, cut into 1½-inch florets
½ lb celery root (sometimes called celeriac), peeled and cut into ¼-inch-thick slices, then slices cut into 3- by 1-inch rectangles
½ lb turnips, peeled and cut into ¼-inch-thick rounds, then rounds halved
½ lb *haricots verts*, trimmed
3 tablespoons finely chopped fresh chives
3 tablespoons finely chopped fresh cilantro

*Make vinaigrette:*
Whisk together vinaigrette ingredients.
*Make salad:*
Blanch and peel tomatoes. Seed and cut into 1-inch pieces. Wrap shallots in a kitchen towel, then twist and squeeze to remove as much liquid as possible.

Cook broccoli, cauliflower, celery root, turnips, and *haricots verts* in a large pot of boiling salted water until crisp-tender, about 5 minutes, then drain well.

Toss warm vegetables with tomatoes, shallots, chives, cilantro, and vinaigrette.

**Cooks' note:**
- Vinaigrette may be made 8 hours ahead and chilled, covered. Bring to room temperature before using.

PHOTO ON PAGE 64

## ORANGE, RADISH, AND OLIVE SALAD

**Serves 4**
Active time: 20 min   Start to finish: 35 min

5 navel oranges
1 tablespoon fresh lemon juice
1 tablespoon extra-virgin olive oil
1 teaspoon honey
⅛ teaspoon cinnamon
⅛ teaspoon cayenne
8 radishes, trimmed and cut into thin wedges
12 oil-cured black olives, pitted and chopped

Cut peel and white pith from 4 oranges with a sharp knife. Halve oranges lengthwise, then cut crosswise into ¼-inch-thick slices. Squeeze enough juice from remaining orange to measure 3 tablespoons.

Whisk together orange and lemon juices, oil, honey, cinnamon, and cayenne until emulsified. Season with salt and pepper. Add orange slices, radishes, and olives and gently toss. Let stand at room temperature 15 minutes before serving.

### GRAIN SALADS

## VEGETABLE BULGUR SALAD

**Serves 8**
Active time: 1 hr   Start to finish: 1 hr 20 min

¾ cup bulgur
1 cup boiling-hot water
¼ cup extra-virgin olive oil
1½ lb small yellow squash, sliced
     ½ inch thick
1 small red onion, chopped
1 lb Asian eggplant or small Italian eggplant,
     halved lengthwise and cut crosswise into
     ½-inch-thick slices
½ cup cherry tomatoes, halved
1 English cucumber, quartered lengthwise and
     cut crosswise into ½-inch-thick slices
2 cups baby spinach, coarse stems discarded
½ cup fresh basil
2 tablespoons tomato, caper, and olive vinaigrette
     (page 116)

Combine bulgur and boiling-hot water in a bowl and let stand, covered, 20 minutes. Fluff with a fork and season with salt and pepper. Cool slightly.

While bulgur stands, heat 1 tablespoon oil in a 12-inch nonstick skillet over moderately high heat until hot but not smoking, then sauté squash and onion with salt and pepper to taste, stirring, until tender, about 5 minutes. Transfer cooked vegetables with a slotted spoon to a large plate to cool.

Add remaining 3 tablespoons oil to skillet and heat over moderately high heat until hot but not smoking, then sauté eggplant with salt and pepper to taste (add more oil, 1 tablespoon at a time, if necessary), stirring, until golden brown and tender, about 6 minutes. Transfer eggplant with slotted spoon to plate to cool.

Gently toss cooked vegetables with bulgur, tomatoes, cucumber, spinach, basil, vinaigrette, and salt and pepper to taste.

PHOTO ON PAGE 49

## QUINOA AND GRILLED-PEPPER SALAD

**Serves 6**
Active time: 15 min   Start to finish: 35 min

1¼ cups quinoa
3 yellow and/or orange bell peppers, quartered
2 teaspoons extra-virgin olive oil
1 teaspoon fresh lime juice
1 teaspoon soy sauce
½ teaspoon ground cumin
¼ cup chopped fresh cilantro
3 scallions, chopped

Prepare grill for cooking.

Wash quinoa in at least 5 changes of water, rubbing grains and letting them settle before pouring off water, until water runs clear, then drain in a large sieve. Add quinoa to a saucepan of boiling salted water and cook

10 minutes. Drain in sieve and rinse under cold water.

Set sieve over a saucepan with 1½ inches boiling water (sieve should not touch water) and steam quinoa, covered with a kitchen towel and lid, until fluffy and dry, about 10 minutes. (Check water level in pan occasionally, adding water if necessary.) Spread quinoa on a baking sheet to cool.

While quinoa is cooking, grill bell peppers on a well-oiled rack set 5 to 6 inches over glowing coals until slightly softened, about 4 minutes on each side. Cut bell peppers crosswise into thin strips.

Whisk together oil, lime juice, soy sauce, and cumin in a large bowl and stir in quinoa, bell peppers, cilantro, scallions, and salt and pepper to taste.

each serving about 166 calories and 4 grams fat

PHOTO ON PAGE 81

## RICE AND LENTIL SALAD WITH ORANGE AND DRIED CHERRIES

### Serves 6
Active time: 20 min   Start to finish: 35 min

1½ cups water
1 cup long-grain rice
½ teaspoon salt
½ cup French green lentils (sources on page 264)
¼ cup finely chopped shallot
2 tablespoons red-wine vinegar
1 tablespoon fresh lemon juice
1 orange
⅓ cup dried cherries, chopped, or currants
¼ cup olive oil
⅓ cup chopped fresh flat-leaf parsley

Boil water, rice, and salt in a 1½-quart heavy saucepan, uncovered and undisturbed, until steam holes appear and surface looks dry, about 8 minutes. Reduce heat to very low and cook, covered and undisturbed, 15 minutes more.

While rice cooks, simmer French green lentils in water to cover by 2 inches 18 to 20 minutes, or until just tender, then drain.

Stir together shallot, vinegar, and lemon juice. Finely grate zest from orange and cut away remaining peel and pith. Cut sections free from membranes and cut sections into ½-inch pieces. Toss warm rice with lentils,

shallot mixture, orange, zest, cherries, oil, and parsley and season with salt and pepper. Serve warm or at room temperature.

## WILD RICE SALAD

### Serves 12
Active time: 25 min   Start to finish: 1¼ hr

1 lb wild rice
*For vinaigrette*
¼ cup fresh orange juice
3 tablespoons chopped shallot
3 tablespoons balsamic vinegar
2 teaspoons Dijon mustard
1 teaspoon minced garlic
½ cup extra-virgin olive oil

1 cup long-grain white rice
1½ cups water
2 cups hickory nuts or chopped pecans, toasted
1¼ cups chopped fresh flat-leaf parsley
¾ cup dried apricots, thinly sliced
¾ cup dried cranberries

Rinse wild rice in a sieve under cold water, then combine with cold water to cover by 2 inches in a 5-quart pot. Simmer, covered, until tender, 45 minutes to 1 hour.

*Make vinaigrette while wild rice simmers:*
Whisk together juice, shallot, vinegar, mustard, and garlic. Gradually whisk in oil until emulsified and season with salt and pepper.

*Cook white rice:*
After wild rice has been simmering 20 minutes, boil white rice and 1½ cups water in a 1½-quart heavy saucepan, uncovered and undisturbed, until steam holes appear on surface, 8 minutes. Reduce heat to very low and cook, covered and undisturbed, 15 minutes more. Remove from heat and let stand, covered, 5 minutes.

*Assemble salad:*
Rinse cooked wild rice in a sieve under cold water and drain. Stir together rices, vinaigrette, nuts, parsley, dried fruit, and salt and pepper to taste. Serve at room temperature.

Cooks' note:
• Salad keeps, covered and chilled, 3 days.

PHOTO ON PAGE 16

# DESSERTS

CAKES

## GINGER-PECAN ROULADE WITH HONEY-GLAZED PECANS

**Serves 8**
Active time: 1¼ hr   Start to finish: 2½ hr

*This cake is actually better when prepared ahead and chilled overnight—it allows the flavors to fully develop and the cake layer to absorb more of the cream. Top the roulade with more cream, pecans, and crystallized ginger just before serving.*

*For cake layer*
½ stick (¼ cup) unsalted butter, melted, plus
   additional for brushing pan
¾ cup pecans, toasted and cooled
¼ cup cake flour (not self-rising) plus additional
   for dusting
1 tablespoon unsweetened cocoa powder plus
   additional for dusting
1½ teaspoons ground ginger
1 teaspoon ground cinnamon
½ teaspoon ground cloves
½ teaspoon salt
5 large eggs, separated
⅓ cup packed dark brown sugar
⅓ cup unsulfured molasses
*For filling and topping*
1¼ cups heavy cream
1 tablespoon granulated sugar plus additional
   for sprinkling
½ cup chopped crystallized ginger (sources on
   page 264)
Honey-glazed pecans (recipe follows)

*Make cake layer:*
Preheat oven to 350°F. Line bottom and sides of a 15- by 10- by 1-inch jelly-roll pan with foil, dull side up,
and brush with melted butter. Dust pan with flour, knocking out excess.

Finely grind pecans with cake flour, cocoa, spices, and salt in a food processor. Beat together yolks, brown sugar, and molasses with an electric mixer at high speed until mixture is very thick and pale brown and forms a ribbon when beater is lifted, about 2 minutes with a standing model and 5 minutes with a hand-held.

Fold in pecan mixture gently but thoroughly. Transfer 1 cup batter to another bowl and fold in ¼ cup melted butter, then fold butter mixture into remaining batter gently but thoroughly.

Beat whites with cleaned beaters in another bowl until they just hold soft peaks (do not overbeat). Stir one fourth of whites into batter to lighten, then fold in remaining whites gently but thoroughly.

Spread batter evenly in pan and bake in middle of oven until set and firm to the touch, about 12 minutes. Cool in pan on a rack and cover with plastic wrap.

*Make filling:*
Beat cream with sugar until it just holds stiff peaks, then fold in 6 tablespoons crystallized ginger.

*Assemble roulade:*
Put an 18-inch length of foil on a work surface and sprinkle with some sugar. Invert cake onto foil sheet and gently peel off foil from top. Spoon three fourths of whipped cream over cake, leaving a ½-inch border around edges.

Beginning with a short side and using foil as an aid, roll up cake, jelly-roll fashion, and transfer, seam side down, to a platter.

Just before serving, spoon remaining whipped cream on top of *roulade* and sprinkle with honey-glazed pecans and remaining crystallized ginger.

Cooks' notes:
• Cake layer can be made 2 days ahead and kept, wrapped well in plastic wrap, at room temperature.
• Roulade may be filled and rolled 1 day ahead, then chilled, covered.

PHOTO ON PAGE 66

## HONEY-GLAZED PECANS

**Makes about 1 cup**
Active time: 10 min   Start to finish: 1 hr

⅓ cup honey, warmed
1 cup pecans
1 tablespoon sugar

Preheat oven to 350°F.

Stir together honey and pecans, tossing to coat well. Spread pecans in 1 layer in a shallow baking pan and sprinkle with sugar. Bake in middle of oven 15 minutes, then stir and bake 5 minutes more.

Transfer while still warm to a sheet of parchment paper or foil and, working quickly, separate pecans with a fork. Cool completely (about 1 hour) and remove nuts from parchment, breaking up any large pieces.

**Cooks' note:**
· Pecans keep, layered between parchment or wax paper in an airtight container, at room temperature 3 days.

## ALMOND CORNMEAL CAKE WITH PEACH AND BERRY COMPOTE

**Serves 6**
Active time: 20 min   Start to finish: 2½ hr

¾ cup yellow cornmeal
¼ cup all-purpose flour
¾ teaspoon baking powder
½ teaspoon salt
⅔ cup whole blanched almonds
¾ cup sugar
1¼ sticks (½ cup plus 2 tablespoons) unsalted
   butter, softened
3 large eggs
¾ teaspoon vanilla

*Accompaniment:* peach and berry compote (recipe
   follows)

Preheat oven to 325°F and butter an 8½- by 4½- by 3-inch loaf pan. Put a 24- by 3½-inch strip of wax paper lengthwise down center of pan (to facilitate unmolding), leaving an overhang on each end.

Whisk together cornmeal, flour, baking powder, and salt. Finely grind almonds with ¼ cup sugar in a food processor and stir into cornmeal mixture.

Beat butter and remaining ½ cup sugar in a large bowl with an electric mixer at medium speed until combined well. Beat in eggs 1 at a time until just blended, then beat in vanilla. (Note: mixture will look curdled.) Add cornmeal mixture, stirring and folding until just combined.

Transfer batter to loaf pan, smoothing top, and bake in middle of oven until a tester comes out clean, about 1 hour. Cool cake in pan on a rack 5 minutes. Loosen edges with a knife, then use strip to carefully lift cake from pan onto rack.

PHOTO ON PAGE 53

JEANNE

## PEACH AND BERRY COMPOTE

**Serves 6**
Active time: 20 min   Start to finish: 2 hr

3 large peaches (1½ lb)
1 cup sweet dessert wine such as Muscat de
   Beaumes-de-Venise
3 tablespoons sugar, or to taste
2 cups blueberries (¾ lb)
2 cups raspberries (½ lb)

Blanch and peel peaches. Cut into ¼-inch-thick wedges. Simmer peaches, wine, and sugar in a 3-quart saucepan, stirring occasionally, 2 minutes, then remove from heat. Immediately transfer mixture to a bowl and add berries, tossing to combine. Cool compote completely. Serve compote chilled or at room temperature.

## ROASTED ORANGE CAKES

***Serves 8 to 10***
Active time: 45 min   Start to finish: 2 hr

*Chef Mary Sue Milliken has been making these cakes since she was 16 years old. This is her grown up version.*

⅓ cup golden raisins
⅓ cup dark rum
8 to 10 large navel oranges
1½ cups cake flour (not self-rising)
⅛ teaspoon baking soda
1 teaspoon baking powder
½ teaspoon salt
1 stick (½ cup) unsalted butter, softened
1 cup sugar
2 large eggs
¾ teaspoon vanilla
½ teaspoon finely grated fresh orange zest
¾ cup well-shaken buttermilk

*Accompaniment:* superpremium vanilla ice cream

Preheat oven to 450°F.

Simmer raisins and dark rum in a small saucepan, stirring occasionally, until rum is absorbed, about 5 minutes.

Cut a very thin slice off bottom of each orange so it will stand without rolling. Cut a ¾-inch-thick slice off top of each, removing any flesh from tops and reserving them. Remove as much flesh as possible from orange with a sharp knife and a spoon (reserving flesh for another use if desired), leaving an empty shell.

Sift together flour, baking soda and powder, and salt. Beat butter and sugar in a large bowl with an electric mixer until light and fluffy. Add eggs 1 at a time, beating well after each addition, then beat in vanilla and zest. Alternately fold in flour mixture and buttermilk in batches, beginning and ending with flour mixture. Fold in raisins.

Fill orange shells two-thirds full with batter and put tops in place. Wrap oranges individually in foil and arrange on a baking sheet. Bake in middle of oven 50 minutes.

Transfer oranges in foil to a rack. Remove foil when cool enough to handle, then cool oranges on racks at least 15 minutes. Serve warm or at room temperature.

PHOTO ON PAGE 55

## DATE, DRIED-CHERRY, AND CHOCOLATE TORTE

***Serves 6 to 10***
Active time: 30 min   Start to finish: 2½ hr

1 cup Deglet Noor or Medjool dates (6 oz),
    pitted and each cut into 6 pieces
½ cup Black Sphinx or Medjool dates (3 oz),
    pitted and each cut into 6 pieces
1 cup dried cherries (preferably tart; 6 oz)
1 teaspoon baking soda
1 cup boiling water
¼ cup brandy
1⅓ cups all-purpose flour
¼ cup unsweetened cocoa powder (not
    Dutch-process)
½ teaspoon salt
1½ sticks (¾ cup) unsalted butter, softened
¾ cup sugar
2 large eggs at room temperature
1 teaspoon vanilla
¾ teaspoon finely grated fresh orange zest
6 oz fine-quality bittersweet chocolate
    (not unsweetened), coarsely chopped
¾ cup pecans (4½ oz), finely chopped

*Garnish:* confectioners sugar
*Accompaniment:* brandied whipped cream
    (page 213)

Preheat oven to 375°F.

Combine dates, cherries, and baking soda in a heat-proof bowl, then stir in boiling water and brandy. Whisk together flour, cocoa, and salt in a separate bowl.

Beat together butter and sugar until pale and fluffy. Add eggs 1 at a time, beating until just combined. Beat in vanilla and zest. Add half of flour mixture and beat at low speed until just combined. Add date mixture with liquid and beat at low speed until just combined. Add remaining flour mixture and beat until just combined. Stir in chocolate and pecans.

Pour batter into a generously buttered 24-cm (9-inch) springform pan, smoothing top. Bake in middle of oven until center is slightly rounded and top of torte is cracked (edges will be dark brown), about 55 minutes. Let torte stand 5 minutes in pan on a rack. Run a sharp small knife around side of pan to loosen, then remove side. Cool torte on rack.

Cooks' note:
· Torte may be made 2 days ahead and kept in an airtight container at room temperature.

PHOTO ON PAGE 73

## BLUEBERRY-ALMOND COFFEECAKE

*Serves 8*
Active time: 25 min   Start to finish: 1½ hr

2 cups all-purpose flour
2 teaspoons baking powder
¾ teaspoon salt
1 stick (½ cup) unsalted butter, softened
1¼ cups plus 3 tablespoons sugar
2 whole large eggs
1 teaspoon vanilla or ¼ teaspoon almond extract
½ cup milk
2½ cups blueberries (15 oz)
½ large egg white
1 cup sliced almonds

Preheat oven to 350°F and butter a 2- to 2½-quart (2¼-inches-deep) ceramic or glass baking dish.

Sift together flour, baking powder, and salt. Beat together butter and 1¼ cups sugar with an electric mixer until light and fluffy. Beat in whole eggs 1 at a time, then vanilla. Alternately add flour mixture and milk in batches, beginning and ending with flour mixture and beating at low speed after each addition until just incorporated. Fold in berries. Spoon batter into baking dish, spreading evenly.

Lightly beat egg white with a fork and add remaining 3 tablespoons sugar and almonds, stirring to coat.

Spoon topping over batter and bake in middle of oven until golden brown and a tester inserted in center comes out clean, 50 minutes to 1 hour. Cool in pan on a rack 10 minutes.

Cooks' note:
· Coffeecake can be made 1 day ahead and kept, covered, at room temperature. Reheat, covered, in a 350°F oven.

## LIME SUGAR COOKIES

*Makes about 36 cookies*
Active time: 1 hr   Start to finish: 5¼ hr

¾ stick (6 tablespoons) unsalted butter, softened
2 tablespoons cold vegetable shortening
1 cup granulated sugar
½ cup lime sugar (page 190)
1 large egg
1 teaspoon vanilla
1¼ cups all-purpose flour
1 teaspoon baking powder
½ teaspoon salt

Beat together butter, shortening, granulated sugar, and 2 tablespoons lime sugar with an electric mixer until light and fluffy. Beat in egg and vanilla. Sift flour, baking powder, and salt together over egg mixture, then beat at low speed until just combined.

Form dough into a 10-inch log (2 inches in diameter) on wax paper, then wrap in wax paper. Chill dough until firm, at least 4 hours.

Preheat oven to 375°F.

Remove wax paper and cut log into ¼-inch-thick rounds. Bake cookies ½ inch apart on ungreased baking sheets in batches in middle of oven 10 to 12 minutes, or until pale golden. Immediately transfer with a metal spatula to a rack set over a sheet of wax paper and sprinkle tops with remaining lime sugar. Cool cookies.

Cooks' notes:
· Dough can be made 2 days ahead and chilled, wrapped well in plastic wrap.
· Cookies keep in an airtight container at cool room temperature 2 days.

PHOTO ON PAGE 49

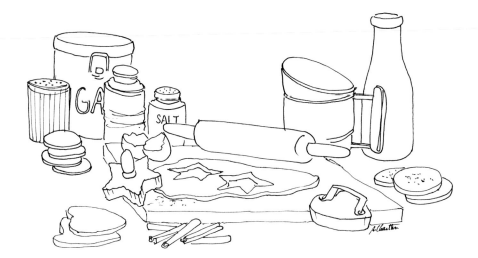

## LIME SUGAR

**Makes about 3 cups**
Active time: 45 min   Start to finish: 45 min

*This sugar is also great to have on hand for sprinkling on cut fruit or to add a boost to iced tea.*

6 limes
2¼ cups sugar

Remove zest from limes in strips with a vegetable peeler and cut away any white pith from zest (pith imparts a bitter flavor). Chop lime zest (about ½ cup), then grind in a food processor with sugar until mixture is pale green with bits of zest still visible.

Cooks' notes:
• Lime sugar may be made 3 days ahead and kept, chilled, in an airtight container.
• The sugar becomes aerated in the food processor; do not pack when measuring.

## HUNGARIAN CHOCOLATE MOUSSE CAKE BARS

**Makes 30 bars**
Active time: 2 hr   Start to finish: 5 hr

*For cake layers*
3 oz fine-quality bittersweet chocolate
   (not unsweetened), chopped
1 stick (½ cup) unsalted butter, softened
¾ cup sugar
6 large eggs, separated
⅓ cup cake flour (not self-rising)

⅓ cup unsweetened cocoa powder
¼ teaspoon salt
¼ teaspoon cream of tartar
⅔ cup apricot jam, melted and strained
*For chocolate glaze*
⅓ cup heavy cream
4 oz fine-quality bittersweet chocolate
   (not unsweetened), finely chopped
*For chocolate mousse filling*
3 cups heavy cream
12 oz fine-quality bittersweet chocolate
   (not unsweetened), finely chopped
*For whipped-cream filling*
1 teaspoon unflavored gelatin (less than 1 envelope)
2 tablespoons cold water
1 cup heavy cream
2 tablespoons confectioners sugar
1 teaspoon vanilla

*Make cake layers:*
Preheat oven to 350°F and butter 2 (15- by 10- by 1-inch) baking pans. Line bottom and sides of each pan with a large sheet of wax paper and butter paper. Dust pans with flour, knocking out excess.

Melt chocolate in a double boiler or a small metal bowl set over a small saucepan of barely simmering water, stirring occasionally. Remove from heat. Beat together butter and ½ cup sugar in a large bowl with an electric mixer until light and fluffy and beat in yolks 1 at a time, beating well after each addition. Beat in chocolate. Sift in flour, cocoa, and salt and beat at low speed until combined well.

Beat egg whites with cream of tartar in another

bowl with clean beaters until they hold soft peaks, then add remaining ¼ cup sugar, beating until whites just hold stiff peaks. Stir one fourth of whites into batter to lighten and gently fold in remaining whites.

Divide batter between pans (about 2¼ cups per pan) and carefully spread evenly. (Layers will be thin.) Bake in upper and lower thirds of oven, switching position of pans halfway through baking, until cake is set and firm to touch, 14 to 18 minutes total. Cool layers in pans on racks 10 minutes before inverting racks over pans and flipping layers onto them. Remove wax paper carefully and discard. Spread jam evenly over 1 warm layer and cool layers completely. Transfer jam-coated layer to a baking sheet or tray lined with a sheet of parchment or wax paper.

*Make chocolate glaze:*

Bring cream just to a boil and slowly pour over chocolate in a bowl. Stir until smooth, then pour over plain cake layer, spreading to coat top evenly. Let stand in a cool place until set, about 1 hour.

*Make chocolate mousse filling:*

Bring cream just to a boil and slowly pour over chocolate in a large metal bowl. Stir until smooth and set bowl in an ice bath. Stir occasionally until cold. Remove from ice bath and beat with electric mixer until mousse just holds soft peaks. (If mousse becomes grainy, melt over a saucepan of barely simmering water and repeat chilling and whipping.) Quickly spread evenly over jam layer (mousse will stiffen as it stands) and chill while making whipped-cream filling.

*Make whipped-cream filling:*

Sprinkle gelatin over water in a small metal bowl and let soften 1 minute. Put bowl over a small saucepan of boiling water and heat, stirring occasionally, until gelatin is dissolved. Remove pan from heat but keep bowl on pan.

Beat cream, confectioners sugar, and vanilla with electric mixer until it holds a soft shape and beat in warm gelatin mixture. Continue beating until cream just holds stiff peaks, then spread evenly over top of mousse-coated layer.

*Assemble cake:*

Cut glazed layer lengthwise into thirds and crosswise into tenths and reassemble bars on top of cream filling. Chill cake, uncovered, until glaze is firm, about 1 hour, then cover with plastic wrap and chill until ready to serve. Just before serving, cut cake with a large knife, wiping it off with a hot damp cloth between cuts.

Cooks' note:
• **Cake can be kept, covered and chilled, up to 3 days.**

PHOTO ON PAGE 19

## CHEWY CARAMEL PECAN BARS

*Serves 8*
Active time: 50 min   Start to finish: 1½ hr

1 stick (½ cup) unsalted butter, softened
1¼ cups packed dark brown sugar
1½ tablespoons vanilla
2 large eggs
1¼ cups all-purpose flour
½ teaspoon salt
½ teaspoon baking powder
½ cup granulated sugar
½ cup light corn syrup
¼ cup water
⅓ cup heavy cream
2¼ cups pecans, toasted

Preheat oven to 350°F and butter and flour a 13- by 9- by 2-inch baking pan, knocking out excess.

Beat together butter and brown sugar in a large bowl with an electric mixer until light and fluffy. Beat in 1 tablespoon vanilla and eggs. Sift in flour with salt and baking powder and beat until just blended.

Spoon batter into pan, spreading evenly, and bake in middle of oven until it pulls away slightly from sides of pan and a tester inserted in center comes out with crumbs adhering, 20 to 30 minutes. Cool base completely in pan on a rack.

Bring granulated sugar, corn syrup, a pinch of salt, and water to a boil in a 2-quart heavy saucepan over moderate heat, stirring constantly until sugar is dissolved. Continue to boil mixture, without stirring, until it turns a golden caramel. Remove from heat and carefully add cream and remaining ½ tablespoon vanilla (mixture will bubble up and steam). Return pan to moderate heat and cook, stirring until smooth. Stir in pecans and immediately pour mixture over base, tilting baking pan and spreading evenly. Cool mixture completely in pan on rack and cut into bars.

Cooks' note:
• **Bars can be made 2 days ahead and kept, covered, at cool room temperature.**

PHOTO ON PAGE 15

## TEULES DE TARONJA

### CANDIED-ORANGE WAFERS

**Makes 12 to 14 cookies**
Active time: 1 hr   Start to finish: 1 hr

*These crisp cookies are shaped like the terra-cotta roof tiles, teules (tejas in Castilian Spanish), that top village houses—old and new—throughout Spain. Almonds are a common ingredient in Catalan cookies, but we took another cue from the Moors and added candied orange.*

½ stick (4 tablespoons) unsalted butter, softened
½ cup sugar
¼ cup minced candied orange zest (recipe follows)
½ teaspoon vanilla
2 large egg whites
¼ cup all-purpose flour

*Special equipment:* Silpat or Exopat nonstick pad
(sources on page 264)

Preheat oven to 400°F.

Beat together butter, sugar, zest, and vanilla with an electric mixer at high speed until light and fluffy. Beat in egg whites at low speed. (Mixture will look curdled.) Whisk in flour just until incorporated.

Drop 4 rounded tablespoons of batter about 3 inches apart on a baking sheet lined with nonstick pad. Spread batter evenly into 4½- to 5-inch circles with back of a spoon dipped in cold water. Bake cookies in middle of oven, turning sheet 180 degrees halfway through baking, until golden brown, about 10 minutes total.

Cool cookies 30 seconds on baking sheet (to facilitate removal), then carefully remove cookies with a thin metal spatula and immediately drape over a rolling pin to create a curved shape. (If cookies become too brittle to drape over rolling pin, return to oven a few seconds to soften.) When cool, transfer to an airtight container. Make more cookies in same manner, cooling and cleaning nonstick pad and baking sheet between batches.

Cooks' note:
• Handle these cookies carefully, as they are fragile. Cookies keep in an airtight container 5 days.

## CANDIED ORANGE ZEST

**Makes about 1½ cups**
Active time: 30 min   Start to finish: 2½ hr

*You can sometimes find candied orange peel in stores, but it is typically thicker, chewier, and more moist than candied zest. It will also never have the intense citrusy flavor of candied zest you make yourself.*

3 large navel oranges
2 cups water
1 cup sugar

Remove zest from oranges in long ½-inch-wide strips with a vegetable peeler and remove any white pith from zest. Julienne zest diagonally and transfer to a small saucepan. Cover zest with cold water and bring to a boil, then drain and repeat. Drain again and pat dry.

Bring water with sugar to a boil in a small heavy saucepan over moderate heat, stirring until sugar is dissolved. Add zest and simmer, stirring occasionally, until translucent and tender, about 25 minutes.

Cool zest in syrup, then drain, discarding syrup. Set a rack over a baking sheet to catch drips and arrange zest on rack, separating strips with a fork. Dry 1 hour.

Cooks' notes:
• Zest may be candied up to a week ahead and kept in an airtight container.
• Leftover zest makes a great addition to rice pudding, pound cake, or ice cream.

## BERRY SQUARES

**Makes 36**
Active time: 20 min   Start to finish: 1½ hr

*For base and topping*
2 cups old-fashioned rolled oats
¾ cup all-purpose flour
¾ cup packed light brown sugar
1½ teaspoons finely grated fresh orange zest
¼ teaspoon baking soda
¼ teaspoon salt
1¼ sticks (½ cup plus 2 tablespoons) unsalted
   butter, melted
*For filling*
3 cups raspberries or blueberries (¾ lb)
⅓ cup granulated sugar
2 tablespoons fresh orange juice
1 tablespoon cornstarch

Preheat oven to 350°F.

Line a 9-inch square metal baking pan with a 12-inch-long sheet of foil, pressing it into bottom and up sides. Butter foil.

*Make base and topping:*

Blend together oats, flour, brown sugar, zest, baking soda, and salt with your fingertips until well combined. Stir in butter. Reserve ¾ cup of mixture for topping; transfer remainder to baking pan, pressing it firmly in bottom to form an even layer. Bake in middle of oven until golden, 12 to 15 minutes.

*Make filling while base bakes:*

Stir together berries, sugar, juice, and cornstarch in a small saucepan, then bring to a boil over moderate heat. Cook, stirring, until thick and no longer cloudy, about 5 minutes, and remove from heat.

*Assemble and bake squares:*

Spoon filling onto oat base, leaving a ½-inch border around edge. Crumble reserved oat mixture on top.

Bake in middle of oven until golden and bubbly, 30 to 35 minutes. Cool completely in pan on a rack. Holding 2 ends of foil, lift from pan and put on a cutting board. Cut into 1½-inch squares.

## OAT BISCUITS WITH TRIPLE-CRÈME CHEESE AND GRAPES

**Makes about 50 biscuits**
Active time: 20 min   Start to finish: 4 hr

*These oat biscuits—similar to shortbread cookies—are wonderful with seasonal grapes and a good-quality triple-crème cheese. Triple-crème is a soft, creamy cow's-milk cheese (with at least 75 percent milk fat) that has a luscious, mild flavor. Because of its natural sweetness, it's perfect with dessert; Pierre Robert, Explorateur, Le Chevrot, or Chaource are all excellent choices. We suggest serving 1 to 2 ounces of cheese per person.*

2 cups old-fashioned rolled oats
2 cups whole-wheat flour
2 sticks (1 cup) cold unsalted butter,
   cut into pieces
⅓ cup packed dark brown sugar
1¾ teaspoons baking powder
1½ teaspoons salt
½ cup whole milk

*Accompaniments:* seasonal grapes and triple-crème
   cheese

Coarsely chop oats in a food processor and transfer to a large bowl. Pulse together flour, butter, brown sugar, baking powder, and salt in processor until mixture resembles coarse meal. Add milk and blend until mixture just forms a dough. Add to oats and knead until just incorporated.

Halve dough and pat each half into a 5- by 3-inch rectangle. Chill, wrapped well in plastic wrap, until firm, about 3 hours.

Preheat oven to 350°F.

Cut 1 rectangle crosswise into scant ¼-inch-thick slices and bake on an ungreased large baking sheet in middle of oven until undersides are a shade darker, about 20 minutes. Transfer to a rack to cool and make more biscuits with remaining dough.

**Cooks' note:**
· Oat biscuits are best eaten the same day they're baked, but they can be made 3 days ahead and kept in an airtight container at room temperature.

PHOTO ON PAGE 61

## APPLE CRUMB TARTS

### Serves 20
Active time: 20 min   Start to finish: 1½ hr

*For shortbread crusts*
1¾ sticks (¾ cup plus 2 tablespoons) unsalted
   butter, cut into 1-tablespoon pieces
2½ cups all-purpose flour
⅔ cup packed light brown sugar
½ teaspoon salt
*For filling*
4 lb Gala or Golden Delicious apples
3 tablespoons all-purpose flour
3 tablespoons fresh lemon juice
1¼ cups granulated sugar
1½ cups homemade fine dry bread crumbs
1 stick (½ cup) unsalted butter, melted

Preheat oven to 350°F and grease 2 (9-inch) tart pans with removable bottoms.

*Make shortbread crusts:*

Pulse butter, flour, brown sugar, and salt in a food processor until mixture begins to form small lumps. Divide between tart pans and press onto bottoms and up sides. Bake in middle of oven until pale golden, about 20 minutes. Leave oven on.

*Prepare filling while crusts bake:*

Peel, quarter, and core apples. Cut quarters crosswise into ⅛-inch-thick slices and toss with flour, lemon juice, and 1 cup sugar. Toss fine dry bread crumbs with melted butter.

*Assemble and bake tarts:*

Remove tart pans from oven and divide apple mixture between crusts, gently shaking pans to settle apples. Sprinkle crumbs evenly over tarts and sprinkle remaining ¼ cup sugar over crumbs.

Bake tarts in middle of oven, placing a sheet of foil on rack below to catch any drips, until apples are tender and crumbs are golden brown, about 1 hour.

Cooks' note:
· **Tarts may be made 1 day ahead and chilled, covered.
Bring to room temperature before serving.**

PHOTO ON PAGE 19

## LAVENDER CRÈME-CARAMEL TART

### Serves 8
Active time: 1 hr   Start to finish: 3½ hr

*If you're short on time, you can make the crème caramel on its own—it's still delicious.*

*For crème caramel*
1½ cups sugar
1½ cups heavy cream
1½ cups whole milk
3 tablespoons dried nontoxic and organic lavender
   flowers (sources on page 264)
⅛ teaspoon salt
3 large eggs
3 large egg yolks
*For pastry crust*
1 cup all-purpose flour
2½ tablespoons sugar
⅛ teaspoon salt
5 tablespoons unsalted butter, slightly softened
1½ to 2 tablespoons ice water

*Special equipment:* a 10-inch glass pie plate (1 to
   1½ inches deep), 9½-inch plate or cardboard
   round, and 10- to 14-inch flat serving plate with
   a slight lip
*Garnish:* fresh nontoxic and organic violets
   (sources on page 264)

*Make crème caramel:*
Preheat oven to 350°F.

Cook 1 cup sugar in a dry large nonstick skillet over moderate heat, swirling and shaking pan (to help sugar melt evenly), until sugar is melted and caramel is deep golden. Immediately pour caramel into pie plate, tilting to coat bottom and sides evenly.

Bring cream, milk, lavender, salt, and remaining ½ cup sugar to a simmer and remove from heat. Let stand 15 minutes, then reheat. Pour through a fine sieve into a bowl, discarding lavender. Whisk whole eggs and yolks together in a bowl and slowly whisk in hot cream mixture. Pour custard over caramel.

Bake custard in a water bath in middle of oven until set but still trembling slightly (custard will continue to set as it cools), 40 to 45 minutes. Remove pie plate from water and cool crème caramel on a rack. Chill, loosely covered with plastic wrap, at least 2 hours.

*Make pastry crust:*

Blend together flour, sugar, salt, and butter with your fingertips or a pastry blender until mixture resembles coarse meal. Drizzle 1½ tablespoons ice water over mixture and toss with a fork until incorporated. Test mixture by gently squeezing a small handful: When it has proper texture, it should hold together without crumbling apart. If necessary, add remaining ½ tablespoon water. (If you overwork mixture or add too much water, pastry will be tough.) Turn mixture out onto a work surface and divide into 4 portions. Smear each portion once in a forward motion to help distribute fat. Gather dough together and form it into a disk.

Chill dough, wrapped in plastic wrap, until firm, at least 1 hour.

Preheat oven to 350°F.

Roll out dough on a lightly floured surface into a 10½-inch round and slide onto a baking sheet. Trim dough to a 9½-inch round (use 9½-inch plate turned upside down as a guide). Prick round all over with a fork and chill 30 minutes. Bake in middle of oven until golden, 20 to 25 minutes, and cool completely on baking sheet on a rack.

*Assemble tart just before serving:*

Run a thin knife around edge of crème caramel and rotate pie plate back and forth to make sure crème caramel is loosened. Slide crust on top of crème caramel, centering it carefully, and invert serving plate on top of crust. Invert tart onto serving plate (caramel will run to edge of plate).

Cooks' notes:
- If you substitute fresh lavender for the dried, use the same amount (fresh lavender is actually stronger than dried).
- You can make crème caramel and crust 1 day ahead, but don't assemble until just before serving. Chill crème caramel and keep crust, covered with plastic wrap, at room temperature.

PHOTO ON PAGE 28

## PEAR AND DRIED-CHERRY TART

**Serves 8**
Active time: 1¼ hr   Start to finish: 4 hr

*For filling*
8 firm-ripe Bosc or Bartlett pears
1½ cups dried tart cherries
½ cup packed light brown sugar
1 teaspoon finely chopped fresh rosemary
2 tablespoons fresh lemon juice
1 tablespoon cornstarch

Frozen-Butter Pastry Dough (page 196)
1 large egg, lightly beaten

*Special equipment:* a 2-inch leaf-shaped cookie cutter

*Make filling:*

Peel pears and cut into ½-inch pieces. Cook pears, cherries, brown sugar, and rosemary in a 4- to 5-quart heavy pot over moderate heat, stirring, until pears are tender, about 20 minutes.

Stir together lemon juice and cornstarch in a small cup and stir into pear mixture. Cook, stirring, 1 minute, or until thickened. Transfer filling to a bowl and cool completely.

*Prepare shell while filling cooks and cools:*

Roll out larger disk of pastry dough into a 13-inch round on a lightly floured surface, keeping remaining disk chilled, and fit into a 10-inch round tart pan (1 inch deep) with a removable fluted rim. Roll rolling pin over top of pan to trim dough flush with rim, then lightly prick bottom all over with a fork. Chill shell 30 minutes.

Preheat oven to 425°F and place a large baking sheet in middle of oven.

Roll out remaining dough into a 12-inch round on a lightly floured surface and with leaf-shaped cutter cut out as many leaves as possible.

*Fill and bake tart:*

Spoon filling into tart shell, smoothing top, and decorate with pastry leaves. Brush leaves and pastry rim with some beaten egg.

Bake tart on preheated baking sheet in middle of oven until pastry leaves are golden, about 50 minutes. (If pastry rim gets too brown, tent rim with foil.)

Cool tart in pan on a rack at least 1 hour.

Cooks' notes:
- Filling may be made 3 days ahead and chilled, covered. Bring to room temperature before proceeding.
- Tart may be made 1 day ahead and kept, covered, at room temperature.

PHOTO ON PAGE 66

## FROZEN-BUTTER PASTRY DOUGH

**Makes enough dough for a 10-inch tart with a partial top crust**
Active time: 15 min   Start to finish: 1¼ hr

2⅔ cups cake flour (not self-rising)
4½ tablespoons sugar
¾ teaspoon salt
2¼ sticks (1 cup plus 2 tablespoons) unsalted
   butter, frozen
9 to 12 tablespoons ice water

Sift together cake flour, sugar, and salt into a chilled large metal bowl. Set a grater in flour mixture and coarsely grate in frozen butter, gently lifting flour and tossing to coat butter.

Drizzle 9 tablespoons ice water evenly over flour mixture and gently stir with a fork until incorporated.

Test mixture by gently squeezing a small handful: When it has proper texture, it should hold together without crumbling apart. If necessary, add more ice water, 1 tablespoon at a time, stirring until just incorporated and testing again. (If you overwork mixture or add too much water, pastry will be tough.)

Turn out onto a lightly floured surface and with floured heel of your hand smear dough twice with a forward motion to help distribute fat.

Gather mixture together to form a dough. (Dough will not be smooth.) Form one third of dough into a disk, then form remaining dough into a larger disk.

Chill dough, disks wrapped separately in plastic wrap, 1 hour and up to 1 day.

## MANGO TART

**Serves 8**
Active time: 35 min   Start to finish: 1 hr

1 frozen puff pastry sheet (from a 17¼-oz package),
   thawed
1 large egg, lightly beaten
¼ cup sugar
½ cup sour cream
⅓ cup whipped cream cheese
1 teaspoon finely grated fresh lime zest
2 large mangoes, peeled

*Garnish:* finely julienned blanched lime zest

*Prepare pastry:*
Preheat oven to 400°F.

Unfold pastry sheet on a greased baking sheet, then turn over (to prevent creases from splitting during baking). Trim edges with a sharp knife. Brush pastry lightly with egg (do not allow to drip down sides). Create a ¾-inch border all around by lightly scoring a line parallel to each edge of pastry (do not cut all the way through). Prick inner rectangle evenly with a fork, then sprinkle with 1 tablespoon sugar.

Bake in lower third of oven 15 minutes, or until puffed and golden brown. Transfer to a rack and cool to room temperature.

*Make cream and cut mangoes while pastry bakes and cools:*
Whisk together sour cream, cream cheese, remaining 3 tablespoons sugar, and zest.

Thinly slice mangoes lengthwise with a *mandoline* or other manual slicer or a sharp knife (be very careful because peeled mango is quite slippery), then halve wide slices lengthwise.

*Assemble tart just before serving:*
Spread cream over inner rectangle of pastry and top with mangoes, folding decoratively.

**Cooks' note:**
· Trimming edges of pastry dough allows layers to separate so pastry rises evenly.

PHOTO ON PAGE 43

## PLUM TARTS

**Makes 2 tarts (serving 12)**
Active time: 1 hr   Start to finish: 3 hr

*We love these tarts made with Italian prune plums—small oval plums that turn up at the market from late August until mid-October. These meaty plums have a rich purple-red color and hold their shape well when baked.*

*For pastry dough*
3 cups all-purpose flour
2¼ sticks (1 cup plus 2 tablespoons) cold unsalted
   butter, cut into ½-inch pieces
½ cup sugar
1 teaspoon salt
1 teaspoon finely grated fresh lemon zest
4 large egg yolks

*For filling*
1 cup sugar
3 tablespoons cornstarch
3¾ lb small plums (preferably prune plums), halved
    and pitted
1 tablespoon fresh lemon juice

*Accompaniment:* crème fraîche or lightly sweetened
    sour cream

*Make dough:*
Combine flour, butter, sugar, salt, and zest in a food
processor and pulse until most of mixture resembles
coarse meal with remainder in small (roughly pea-size)
lumps. Add yolks and process just until incorporated
and mixture begins to clump.

Turn mixture out onto a work surface and divide
into 4 portions. Smear each portion once with heel of
your hand in a forward motion to help distribute fat.
Gather together 2 portions of dough and form into a
ball; make another ball with other 2 portions.

Pat out balls of dough with floured fingertips into
2 (9-inch) tart pans with removable bottoms, in even
¼-inch layers on bottoms and up sides (about ⅛ inch
above rim). Chill 30 minutes, or until firm.

*Make filling while shells chill:*
Stir together sugar and cornstarch in a large bowl.
Add plums and lemon juice and toss to coat. Let stand,
stirring occasionally, 30 minutes, or until juicy.

*Assemble and bake tarts:*
Preheat oven to 425°F.

Arrange plum halves, skin sides down, in tart shells,
overlapping in a rosette pattern. Halve any remaining
plums lengthwise and randomly tuck in between plum
halves in tarts. Pour all juices from bowl over plums.

Bake tarts in middle of oven 15 minutes, then
reduce temperature to 375°F. Cover tarts loosely with
foil and bake until plums are tender and juices are bubbling and slightly thickened, 40 to 50 minutes more.
Brush warm juices in tart over plums. (Juices will continue to thicken as tarts cool.) Cool tarts completely in
pans on a rack.

**Cooks' notes:**
- Tart shells can be made 1 day ahead and chilled, covered.
- Plums may stand, coated with sugar, cornstarch, and
  lemon juice and chilled, covered, 1 day. Stir well before
  proceeding.

PHOTO ON PAGE 56

## LIME ICE ON WATERMELON

***Serves 8***
Active time: 40 min   Start to finish: 7 hr

1¼ cups lime sugar (not packed; page 190)
1½ cups granulated sugar
2¼ cups water
4 whole star anise (optional)
1¾ cups fresh lime juice (10 limes)
½ chilled watermelon, cut into slices or wedges

Boil sugars, water, and star anise, stirring, until sugars are dissolved. Pour syrup through a fine sieve into a
bowl, discarding solids. Cool syrup.

Stir in lime juice. Freeze in a 13- by 9- by 2-inch
glass dish, stirring occasionally with a fork, until liquid
is frozen and granular, about 6 hours.

Serve lime ice on watermelon.

**Cooks' note:**
- **Lime ice may be made 2 days ahead and kept frozen,
  covered.**

PHOTO ON PAGE 49

JEANNE

## GRAPPA SEMIFREDDO WITH ESPRESSO SAUCE

**Serves 6**
Active time: 45 min   Start to finish: 2¾ hr

*For semifreddo*
3 large egg yolks
½ cup sugar
⅓ cup fine-quality grappa
2 large egg whites at room temperature
1 cup heavy cream
*For espresso sauce*
1 cup sugar
⅔ cup boiling water
4 teaspoons instant espresso powder
¼ teaspoon fresh lemon juice

6 teaspoons fine-quality grappa, chilled

*Special equipment:* 6 tall (2½-inch high;
   ½-cup capacity) metal *baba au rhum*
   molds (sources on page 264) or
   6 (½-cup) ramekins
*Garnish:* mocha coffee beans

*Make semifreddo:*
Have ready a large bowl of ice and cold water.
Beat together yolks, sugar, and ⅓ cup grappa with an electric mixer in a metal bowl set over a saucepan of simmering water until thick and pale and an instant-read thermometer registers 170°F, about 10 minutes. Put bowl in ice bath and beat mixture until cold.
Beat whites with a pinch of salt in another bowl with cleaned beaters until they just hold stiff peaks. Beat cream in a separate bowl until it holds soft peaks. Whisk one third of whites into yolk mixture to lighten and fold in remaining whites and then cream, gently but thoroughly. Spoon into molds and freeze, covered with plastic wrap, until firm, about 2 hours.
*Make espresso sauce while semifreddo freezes:*
Cook sugar in a 2-quart heavy saucepan over moderately low heat, stirring slowly with a fork, until melted and pale golden. Cook caramel without stirring, swirling pan, until deep golden. Remove from heat.
Stir together boiling water, espresso powder, and lemon juice. Carefully add to caramel (mixture will bubble up and vigorously steam), then cook sauce over moderately low heat, stirring, until caramel is dissolved and sauce is smooth.
*Unmold semifreddo:*
Dip molds in hot water 5 seconds, then run a small thin knife around edges and invert onto plates. Spoon a teaspoon of chilled grappa on top of each and drizzle plates with warm or room-temperature espresso sauce.

Cooks' notes:
· If egg safety is a problem in your area, use pasteurized egg whites in the carton for the *semifreddo*.
· *Semifreddo* may be made 1 week ahead and kept frozen. Let soften 30 minutes in refrigerator before unmolding.
· You can make espresso sauce 3 days ahead and chill, covered. Reheat to warm before serving.

PHOTO ON PAGE 35

## GELAT DE CREMA CATALANA I XERÈS AMB MEL I FIGUES

### SHERRY CREMA CATALANA ICE CREAM WITH HONEYED FIGS

**Serves 6**
Active time: 15 min   Start to finish: 5½ hr

*For ice cream*
3 cups half-and-half
4-inch strip fresh lemon zest
4-inch strip fresh orange zest
½ cinnamon stick
8 large egg yolks
½ cup sugar
¼ cup Amontillado Sherry
*For figs*
12 soft (moist) dried Calimyrna figs (10 oz), tough
   stems removed and figs halved lengthwise
1 cup Amontillado Sherry
1 cup fresh orange juice
6 tablespoons honey

*Garnish:* candied orange zest (page 192)

*Make ice cream:*

Bring half-and-half with lemon and orange zests and cinnamon stick just to a boil over moderate heat. Remove from heat and let stand, covered, 25 minutes, then reheat to a simmer. Discard zests and stick.

Whisk together yolks, sugar, and Sherry in a large bowl until smooth. Gradually add in hot milk mixture, whisking.

Transfer custard to cleaned saucepan and cook over moderately low heat, stirring constantly, until thickened enough to coat back of a wooden spoon and an instant-read thermometer registers 170°F.

Pour custard through a fine sieve into a bowl and cover surface with wax paper to prevent a skin from forming. Chill until thoroughly cold, about 3 hours. Freeze in an ice-cream maker. Transfer to an airtight container and freeze until firm.

*Prepare figs:*

Bring figs, Sherry, juice, and honey to a boil, covered, in a small saucepan. Simmer, covered, just until figs are tender, about 40 minutes, then uncover and simmer until liquid is reduced to about 1 cup, about 8 minutes. Cool figs in syrup.

Serve ice cream with honeyed figs and syrup.

**Cooks' notes:**
- Ice cream can be made 3 days ahead.
- You can also prepare figs 3 days ahead and chill, covered.

PHOTO ON PAGE 21

## BLUE MARTINI ICE POPS

**Makes 5 (⅓-cup) ice pops**
Active time: 25 min   Start to finish: 1 day

*Gins that emphasize fruit botanicals, such as Tanqueray No. Ten, work best in this recipe.*

1½ cups water
¼ cup sugar
6 strips fresh lemon zest (½ lemon)
3 tablespoons gin
2 tablespoons dry vermouth
1 tablespoon blue Curaçao

*Special equipment:* 5 (⅓-cup) ice pop molds (sources on page 264) and 5 wooden sticks

Simmer water, sugar, and zest in a small saucepan, stirring, until sugar is dissolved. Cool syrup, then stir in gin, vermouth, and Curaçao. Discard zest. Pour into molds and freeze at least 24 hours. Add sticks when mixture is slushy, about 1 hour.

## MIDORI MELON ICE POPS

**Makes 6 (⅓-cup) ice pops**
Active time: 15 min   Start to finish: 1 day

4 cups (½-inch pieces) peeled ripe honeydew melon (1 whole)
5 tablespoons Midori (melon liqueur)
3 tablespoons vodka
1½ tablespoons superfine granulated sugar

*Special equipment:* 6 (⅓-cup) ice pop molds (sources on page 264) and 6 wooden sticks

Blend all ingredients in a blender until smooth. Pour melon purée into a sieve lined with a double thickness of cheesecloth set over a bowl and let drain, undisturbed, 30 minutes. Discard solids in sieve. Pour liquid into molds and freeze at least 24 hours. Add sticks when mixture is slushy, about 1 hour.

## PIÑA COLADA ICE POPS

**Makes 8 (⅓-cup) ice pops**
Active time: 15 min   Start to finish: 1 day

*For ice pops without alcohol, use pineapple juice instead of rum.*

3 cups (½-inch) cubes peeled fresh pineapple (1 whole )
½ cup Malibu (coconut) rum
½ cup well-stirred canned cream of coconut

*Special equipment:* 8 (⅓-cup) ice pop molds (sources on page 264) and 8 wooden sticks

Blend all ingredients in a blender until smooth, then force through a fine sieve into a large glass measuring cup. Pour liquid into molds and add sticks. Freeze at least 24 hours.

## APPLE BROWN BETTY

*Serves 6*
Active time: 30 min   Start to finish: 1½ hr

3 tablespoons unsalted butter
¾ teaspoon cinnamon
⅛ teaspoon salt
3 tablespoons packed light brown sugar
3 cups coarse fresh bread crumbs (preferably
   from a baguette)
4 large crisp apples such as Granny Smith
   or Gala
1¼ cups water
¾ cup nonfat vanilla frozen yogurt

Preheat oven to 375°F.

Melt butter in a nonstick skillet and remove from heat. Stir in cinnamon, salt, and 1 tablespoon brown sugar, then stir in bread crumbs. Sprinkle one third of crumbs over bottom of a 1-quart shallow baking dish.

Peel and coarsely chop 2 apples. Cook with water and remaining 2 tablespoons brown sugar in a 1½-quart saucepan, covered, over moderate heat, stirring occasionally, 10 minutes. Purée apples with cooking liquid in a blender (use caution when blending hot liquids).

Peel remaining 2 apples and cut into ¼-inch-thick wedges. Arrange wedges over crumbs, then pour hot purée over wedges. Sprinkle with remaining crumbs.

Bake in middle of oven until top is golden brown and apples are tender, about 40 minutes. Cool on a rack 10 minutes and serve with frozen yogurt.

each serving, including yogurt, about 176 calories and 6 grams fat

## MIXED-BERRY COMPOTE

*Makes about 3 cups*
Active time: 5 min   Start to finish: 5 min

3 tablespoons unsalted butter
¼ cup packed light brown sugar
2 tablespoons fresh lemon juice
3 cups mixed berries (¾ lb) such as raspberries,
   blackberries, and blueberries

Melt butter in a skillet over moderate heat. Stir in brown sugar and lemon juice until sugar is dissolved. Add berries and cook, tossing gently (try to keep most of them from breaking up), until berries are warm and juices begin to be released, 2 to 3 minutes.

Serve warm or at room temperature.

## APRICOT PHYLLO NAPOLEONS

*Serves 4*
Active time: 30 min   Start to finish: 8½ hr

1 cup nonfat yogurt
4 (17- by 12-inch) phyllo sheets
1 teaspoon unsalted butter, melted
1 teaspoon vegetable oil
6 teaspoons granulated sugar
1 vanilla bean, halved lengthwise
¼ cup low-fat sour cream
1 tablespoon plus 1 teaspoon packed light
   brown sugar
6 fresh apricots (1 lb), pitted and each cut
   into 6 wedges
¼ cup water

Drain yogurt in a cheesecloth-lined sieve or colander set over a bowl, covered and chilled, 8 hours.

Preheat oven to 350°F.

Put stack of phyllo on a work surface and cover stack with 2 overlapping sheets of plastic wrap and then a damp kitchen towel.

Stir together butter and oil. Arrange 1 phyllo sheet on a large parchment-paper-lined baking sheet, then spread with one fourth of butter mixture using a dampened pastry brush.

Sprinkle with 1 teaspoon granulated sugar. Top with 3 more layers in same manner as first with remaining phyllo and butter mixture and 3 teaspoons granulated sugar. Cut stack into 12 rectangles (2 lengthwise cuts, 3 crosswise) and bake in middle of oven until crisp and golden brown, about 10 minutes. Cool in pan on a rack.

Scrape seeds from vanilla bean into a bowl using a small sharp knife. Stir in drained yogurt, sour cream, and 1 tablespoon brown sugar.

Heat a large nonstick skillet over moderately high heat. Add apricots and sprinkle with remaining 2 teaspoons granulated sugar. Gently toss until apricots are warm and tender, 2 to 3 minutes. Transfer apricots to a bowl with a slotted spoon. Add water and remaining teaspoon brown sugar to skillet and deglaze by boiling over moderately high heat, stirring and scraping up brown bits, until reduced by about half. Toss apricots in warm syrup.

Place 1 phyllo rectangle on a plate and top with 3 apricot pieces and 1 generous tablespoon yogurt mixture. Make 2 more layers with phyllo squares, apricots, and yogurt mixture. Make 3 more napoleons in same manner.

🥄 each serving about 192 calories and 5 grams fat

## MIXED-BERRY PAVLOVAS

### Serves 16
Active time: 30 min   Start to finish: 2 hr

13 large egg whites
¼ teaspoon salt
2½ cups superfine granulated sugar
1½ tablespoons cornstarch
1½ tablespoons distilled white vinegar
2 lb strawberries, halved or quartered if large
3 tablespoons fresh lime juice
¼ cup plus 1½ tablespoons granulated sugar
1 lb blackberries
2½ cups heavy cream
2 teaspoons vanilla

*Special equipment:* a standing electric mixer

*Make meringues:*
Preheat oven to 250°F and line 2 large baking sheets with parchment paper.

Swirl whites in a metal bowl set over a saucepan of simmering water until barely warm to the touch. Beat whites with salt with an electric mixer until they hold soft peaks. Beat in 2 cups superfine sugar and continue beating until mixture holds stiff, glossy peaks (see cooks' note, below). Stir together remaining ½ cup superfine sugar and cornstarch. Beat into meringue, then beat in vinegar.

Spoon 8 mounds of meringue (each about 2 inches high and approximately ⅔ cup) 1 inch apart on each baking sheet. Divide any remaining meringue among mounds. Bake in upper and lower thirds of oven, switching position of sheets halfway through baking,

until crisp but still soft inside, 1 to 1¼ hours total. If meringues are still not crisp after 1¼ hours, turn off oven and cool in oven 1 hour. Transfer from parchment to racks to cool. (Meringues may stick if cooled completely on paper.)

*Assemble pavlovas:*
Just before serving, toss strawberries with lime juice and ¼ cup granulated sugar and let stand, tossing occasionally until sugar is dissolved, about 10 minutes. Add blackberries and toss to coat.

Beat cream with vanilla and remaining 1½ tablespoons granulated sugar with cleaned beaters. Tap meringues gently with back of a spoon to create indentations, then mound whipped cream and berries onto each.

Cooks' note:
· Beating the egg whites in this recipe is easiest using a standing mixer with a 5-quart bowl. If you use one with a 4½-quart bowl, occasionally remove the bowl from the mixer and stir the whites to avoid overbeating any parts.

PHOTO ON PAGE 37

## CANTALOUPE AND GRAPE COMPOTE

### Serves 4
Active time: 15 min   Start to finish: 2¼ hr

1 ripe cantaloupe (1½ lb), halved
   and seeded
1 cup dry white wine
⅓ cup sugar
⅓ cup water
1 strip fresh lime zest
1 to 2 tablespoons fresh lime juice
2 cups seedless green grapes, halved
   lengthwise

Scoop cantaloupe into balls with a melon-ball cutter and reserve rinds.

Bring wine, sugar, water, and lime zest to a boil in a small saucepan, stirring until sugar is dissolved. Squeeze juice from rinds into wine mixture. Boil, skimming froth, until reduced to about 1 cup, 15 to 20 minutes. Remove from heat. Discard zest and stir in lime juice.

Combine grapes, melon balls, and warm syrup in a bowl and chill, covered, stirring occasionally, 2 hours.

🥄 each serving about 196 calories and less than 1 gram fat

## POACHED PEARS WITH SPICED CARAMEL SAUCE

**Serves 6**
Active time: 30 min   Start to finish: 4½ hr

*Poaching time for pears will vary, depending on their firmness.*

*For poached pears*
4 juice oranges
1 lemon, halved
8 cups water
2 cups granulated sugar
6 firm-ripe Anjou pears
*For caramel*
½ cup granulated sugar
¼ cup packed light brown sugar
1½ cups heavy cream
1 whole clove
5 cardamom pods
¼ teaspoon fennel seeds
¼ teaspoon black peppercorns
2 (3-inch) cinnamon sticks

3 tablespoons chopped toasted almonds or hazelnuts

*Poach pears:*
Remove zest of oranges in strips with a vegetable peeler and cut away any white pith from strips. Squeeze juice from oranges and lemon into a 6-quart pot and add lemon halves, water, granulated sugar, and zest. Peel pears, leaving stems attached, and add to pot.

Simmer pears 15 to 25 minutes, or until just tender, and cool in liquid. (Poached pears will continue to cook a bit as they cool.)

*Make caramel:*
Put granulated sugar in a 2-quart heavy saucepan and crumble brown sugar over. Melt sugars, undisturbed, over moderate heat until granulated sugar is mostly melted. Continue to cook, stirring occasionally with a fork, until a deep golden caramel. Carefully add cream (mixture will bubble up and caramel will harden slightly) and stir in clove, cardamom, fennel, peppercorns, and cinnamon sticks. Simmer, stirring, until caramel is dissolved and sauce is reduced to about 1½ cups, about 10 minutes. Pour sauce through a sieve into a 2-cup measure and cool to just warm.

*Assemble dessert:*
Drain pears and pat dry. Serve drizzled with sauce and sprinkled with chopped nuts.

Cooks' notes:
• **You can poach pears 2 days ahead and chill, covered, in poaching liquid. Bring pears to room temperature before serving.**
• **Sauce may be made 2 days ahead and chilled, covered. Reheat to warm before serving.**

PHOTO ON PAGE 25

## BROILED PEACHES WITH CRÈME FRAÎCHE

**Serves 4**
Active time: 10 min   Start to finish: 20 min

4 firm-ripe peaches, halved and pitted
3 tablespoons sugar

*Accompaniment:* crème fraîche or sour cream

Preheat broiler.

Line a small shallow baking pan with foil and arrange peaches cut sides up. Sprinkle peaches evenly with sugar and let stand 10 minutes. Broil 4 to 5 inches from heat until sugar is golden brown and peaches are tender, 6 to 8 minutes. Serve warm.

## CITRUS SALAD WITH STAR ANISE

**Serves 4**
Active time: 10 min   Start to finish: 1¼ hr

¼ cup water
¼ cup sugar
4 whole star anise or 1 teaspoon anise seeds

3 assorted grapefruits such as white, pink, and ruby
2 navel oranges

Simmer water with sugar and anise in a small saucepan over moderate heat, stirring occasionally, 1 minute. Cool slightly.

Cut peel and white pith from grapefruits and oranges with a sharp knife. Working over a bowl, cut grapefruit and orange sections free from membranes. Pour off juice released during cutting from bowl and reserve. Stir syrup into fruit and chill, covered, 1 hour. Stir in reserved juice to taste.

Cooks' note:
• **Salad can be made 1 day ahead and chilled, covered.**

each serving about 135 calories and less than 1 gram fat

PHOTO ON PAGE 80

## GRAPEFRUIT WITH GOLDEN RAISIN RUM SYRUP

### Serves 4
Active time: 20 min   Start to finish: 8½ hr

3 tablespoons sugar
3 tablespoons water
¼ cup golden raisins
¼ cup dark rum
3 red, pink, or white grapefruit
1 tablespoon sliced almonds, toasted

Bring sugar and water to a boil in a very small saucepan, stirring until sugar is dissolved, then boil 1 minute. Stir together raisins, rum, and sugar syrup in a small bowl and let raisins plump, covered, at room temperature overnight.

Cut peel from grapefruit, including all white pith, with a sharp knife and cut sections free from membranes. Put sections in a serving bowl and pour rum-raisin syrup over them.

Serve sprinkled with almonds.

Cooks' note:
• **Grapefruit may be combined with rum-raisin syrup 1 day ahead and chilled, covered. Sprinkle with almonds just before serving.**

each serving about 164 calories and 1 gram fat

## PEACHES IN GINGER SYRUP

### Serves 8
Active time: 20 min   Start to finish: 40 min

¾ cup dry white wine
¾ cup water
¾ cup sugar
1 (2-inch) piece fresh ginger, coarsely grated
2 lb peaches (8)
2 tablespoons fresh lemon juice

Simmer white wine, water, sugar, and ginger, stirring occasionally, until reduced to about ¾ cup, about 15 minutes.

While syrup is simmering, slice peaches and toss with lemon juice.

Pour hot syrup through a fine sieve onto peaches, discarding ginger, then stir. Let stand 20 minutes.

Cooks' note:
• **Peaches can stand in syrup, covered, up to 2 hours at room temperature.**

PHOTO ON PAGE 51

## PEACH SOUP

### Serves 4 (dessert)
Active time: 20 min   Start to finish: 1½ hr

2½ cups water
¾ cup sugar
1 bag peach tea
¼ teaspoon finely grated fresh lime zest
1 large white peach, peeled and cut into
   ¼-inch dice
1 large yellow peach, peeled and cut into
   ¼-inch dice
1 pint peach sorbet or ice cream

Simmer water and sugar, stirring until sugar is dissolved. Remove from heat and stir in tea bag and zest. Steep 5 minutes, then discard tea bag. Chill until cold.

Stir peaches into chilled syrup and serve with scoops of sorbet.

Cooks' note:
• **Syrup can be made 3 days ahead and chilled, covered.**

## CARAMELIZED PLUMS WITH LEMON-GINGERSNAP YOGURT

**Serves 4**
Active time: 15 min   Start to finish: 15 min

¼ cup coarsely crushed gingersnaps
8 oz lemon yogurt
3 to 4 tablespoons sugar
4 plums, halved

Preheat broiler.

Sprinkle gingersnaps over yogurt in a bowl and fold once only (for a marbled effect).

Put sugar in a small dish and dip cut side of each plum half in sugar to coat well. Broil plums, cut sides up, in a lightly oiled shallow (1-inch-deep) baking pan 3 inches from heat until sugar is golden, 2 to 3 minutes.

Serve plums with yogurt.

Cooks' note:
• To coarsely crush the gingersnaps, place them in a sealed plastic bag and crush them with a rolling pin.

## TROPICAL-FRUIT SPLITS WITH RUM SAUCE AND CHILE-MACADAMIA BRITTLE

**Serves 8**
Active time: 1 hr   Start to finish: 1¼ hr

*For sauce*
⅔ cup dark rum
¼ cup boiling-hot water
1 teaspoon vanilla
2 cups sugar
1 tablespoon unsalted butter
*For grilled fruit*
1 firm-ripe mango, peeled
1 papaya, peeled, halved, and seeded
½ fresh pineapple, peeled and cored
12 small ripe finger bananas or 6 small regular
   bananas
1 tablespoon chili powder

Chile-macadamia brittle (recipe follows)
3 pints premium vanilla ice cream

*Garnish:* toasted fresh coconut shavings or toasted
   sweetened flaked coconut

*Make sauce:*

Stir together rum, boiling-hot water, and vanilla. Cook sugar in a 3-quart heavy saucepan over moderately low heat, stirring slowly with a fork, until melted and pale golden. Cook caramel without stirring, swirling pan, until deep golden. Remove pan from heat and carefully stir in rum mixture (caramel will harden and steam vigorously). (Pan is removed from the flame to prevent alcohol from igniting. If it does ignite, simply allow flames to burn out on their own.) Simmer sauce until smooth. Remove pan from heat and when bubbling subsides stir in butter. Cool to room temperature.

*Grill fruit:*

Prepare grill for cooking.

Standing mango upright, cut 1 lengthwise slice from each broad side of mango (be careful because peeled mango is slippery) and discard pit. Cut each papaya half lengthwise into thirds. Standing pineapple upright, cut lengthwise into ½-inch-thick slices. Halve bananas lengthwise. Sprinkle all fruit lightly on 1 side with chili powder.

Grill fruit on a well-oiled rack set 5 to 6 inches over glowing coals until grill marks form, about 1 minute. Turn fruit over and grill 1 minute more. Transfer to a cutting board and slice into decorative pieces.

Coarsely chop three fourths of brittle, reserving remainder for garnish.

Put 3 scoops ice cream into each of 8 dishes and top with grilled fruit and sauce. Sprinkle splits with chopped brittle.

Cooks' note:
• Rum sauce may be made 2 days ahead and chilled, covered. If sauce is too thick, bring to room temperature.

PHOTO ON PAGE 41

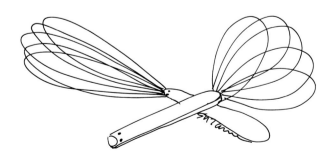

## CHILE-MACADAMIA BRITTLE

**Serves 8**
Active time: 20 min   Start to finish: 35 min

½ cup coarsely chopped salted macadamia
   nuts (2 oz)
1 cup sugar
½ cup water
1 teaspoon dried hot red pepper flakes

Preheat oven to 250°F. Lightly oil a large sheet of foil on a baking sheet, then warm in oven.

Shake nuts in a coarse sieve to remove any nut powder (this will create a clearer brittle).

Cook sugar and water in a deep 2-quart heavy saucepan over moderately low heat, stirring slowly with a fork, until melted and pale golden. Cook caramel without stirring, swirling pan, until golden. Immediately stir in red pepper flakes and nuts and cook, stirring, until nuts are golden, about 1 minute. Quickly pour onto foil, tilting baking sheet to spread brittle evenly before it hardens. (If caramel hardens too fast, put in a 400°F oven until warm enough to spread, 1 to 2 minutes.)

Cool brittle on baking sheet on a rack until completely hardened, then break into large pieces.

**Cooks' note:**
- **Brittle may be made 3 days ahead and kept in an airtight container at cool room temperature.**

## CARAMELIZED FIGS WITH RASPBERRY COULIS AND YOGURT

**Serves 4**
Active time: 10 min   Start to finish: 15 min

1 (10-oz) package frozen raspberries in syrup,
   thawed
8 fresh figs, trimmed and halved lengthwise
½ tablespoon sugar
½ cup low-fat vanilla yogurt, stirred

Preheat broiler.

Force raspberries through a fine sieve into a bowl to remove seeds.

Sprinkle cut side of figs with sugar and put, sugared sides up, in a flameproof baking dish. Broil about 4 inches from heat until tops are bubbling and lightly browned, 3 to 5 minutes.

Spoon 1½ tablespoons raspberry *coulis* onto each of 4 dessert plates. Spoon a heaping tablespoon of yogurt in center of each, then arrange 4 fig halves on top.

**Cooks' note:**
- **Leftover raspberry *coulis* makes a great topping for ice cream or sorbet and is also delicious stirred into club soda.**

each serving about 121 calories and less than 1 gram fat

## JELLIED QUINCES AND MANCHEGO CHEESE

**Serves 8**
Active time: 30 min   Start to finish: 10½ hr

1 qt apple juice
2 cups sugar
2 tablespoons fresh lemon juice
1 (1-inch) piece fresh ginger, peeled and sliced
½ teaspoon whole white peppercorns
8 small quinces, peeled

*Accompaniment:* Manchego cheese wedges (¾ lb)
   at room temperature

Bring all ingredients except quinces to a boil in a 4-quart heavy pot, stirring until sugar is dissolved. Add quinces and simmer, partially covered, turning occasionally, until tender when pierced near core with a fork (core will remain hard), about 1½ hours.

Transfer quinces with a slotted spoon to a pie plate or baking dish. Pour cooking juices through a sieve into a 2-cup measure. (If you have more than 1½ cups juice, boil until syrupy and reduced.) Pour juices over quinces, then cool, spooning syrup over quinces several times. Chill, spooning syrup over quinces occasionally, at least 8 hours. (Syrup will gel and coat quinces as it chills.)

Cut quinces in half lengthwise and serve with some jelly and cheese.

**Cooks' note:**
- **Jellied quinces can be prepared 3 days ahead and chilled, covered.**

PHOTO ON PAGE 78

## STRAWBERRY-DAIQUIRI SLUSH WITH HONEYDEW MELON

**Serves 6**
Active time: 15 min   Start to finish: 15 min

1 (12-oz) package frozen unsweetened strawberries
⅓ cup light corn syrup
¼ to ⅓ cup white rum
2 tablespoons fresh lime juice
½ ripe honeydew melon, seeded and cut into
   ½-inch cubes

*Garnish:* lime slices

Purée frozen strawberries, corn syrup, rum to taste, and lime juice in a blender until slushy. Spoon into 6 (8-oz) wineglasses or other stemmed shallow glasses and top with melon.

## WARM FRUIT COMPOTE WITH LEMON VERBENA AND CRÈME FRAÎCHE

**Serves 8**
Active time: 15 min   Start to finish: 20 min

*The thing Ken Hom likes most about this dessert is the contrast of the warm, sweet fruit and the cold, tangy crème fraîche.*

1 vanilla bean, halved lengthwise
1 cup sugar
2 cups water
½ cup fresh lemon verbena or mint
24 small whole (Mediterranean) dried apricots
   (6 oz; sources on page 264)
1½ lb firm apples such as Gala, Empire, or
   Golden Delicious
2 tablespoons unsalted butter

*Accompaniment:* crème fraîche

Scrape seeds from vanilla bean into a 5- to 6-quart wide saucepan (a wide pan minimizes breakage of apples) and add pod, sugar, water, and lemon verbena. Simmer, stirring until sugar is dissolved, 10 minutes. Add apricots and a pinch of salt and simmer, partially covered, until tender, about 10 minutes.

While apricots simmer, peel and core apples and cut each into eighths. Add apples to syrup and simmer, uncovered, until just tender, 5 to 7 minutes. Remove from heat and stir in butter until melted.

Cooks' note:
• Compote can be made 1 day ahead and chilled, covered. Reheat before serving.

PHOTO ON PAGE 65

---

**CONFECTIONS**

## CANDIED GRAPEFRUIT PEEL

**Makes about 45 strips**
Active time: 45 min   Start to finish: 6 hr

2 small grapefruits
1 cup granulated sugar
½ cup water
1 cup superfine granulated sugar

With peel still on fruit, quarter peel lengthwise then remove, keeping pieces of peel intact. Reserve fruit for another use. Diagonally cut pieces of peel into ⅓-inch-wide strips.

Put peel in a 3-quart saucepan filled with cold water and bring slowly to a boil over moderate heat. Boil 1 minute and drain. Repeat procedure 4 times to remove bitterness.

Have ready a lightly oiled large rack set in a shallow baking pan.

Bring regular granulated sugar and water to a boil in a large heavy skillet, stirring until sugar is dissolved. Add peel and boil, stirring, until most of syrup is absorbed, about 10 minutes.

Turn out peel onto rack, separating pieces. Dry candied peel, uncovered, at room temperature until only slightly sticky, 4 to 8 hours. Toss, a few pieces at a time, in superfine sugar, shaking off excess.

Cooks' notes:
• If sugar syrup begins to crystallize on peel, turn out of skillet immediately. Peel will still be good but will have a different appearance and won't need a sugar coating.
• Candied peel keeps in an airtight container at room temperature 1 week or chilled 1 month. If chilled peel becomes too moist, pat dry and reroll in sugar.

PHOTO ON PAGE 75

Pour *ganache* into a plastic-wrap–lined 8-inch square baking pan and chill, uncovered, until firm, about 4 hours.

Invert *ganache* onto a work surface and remove plastic wrap. Cut *ganache* into 64 squares and roll each piece between your palms to form a ball. When all balls are formed, roll in coconut to cover completely, then chill truffles, covered, until ready to serve.

Cooks' note:
- Truffles keep, covered and chilled, 1 week.

PHOTO ON PAGE 75

## CHOCOLATE STAR ANISE TRUFFLES

*Makes 40 truffles*
Active time: 45 min   Start to finish: 5 hr

½ cup heavy cream
1½ tablespoons crushed star anise (about 8
   whole star anise)
8 oz fine-quality bittersweet chocolate
   (not unsweetened)
1 tablespoon Cognac
1½ cups unsweetened cocoa powder

Bring cream to a boil with star anise in a small heavy saucepan, then remove from heat and let stand 15 minutes.

Finely grind bittersweet chocolate in a food processor and transfer to a bowl.

Return cream to a simmer, then remove from heat and stir in Cognac. Pour cream mixture through a fine sieve onto chocolate and whisk until chocolate is melted and *ganache* is smooth. Pour *ganache* into an 8- by 4-inch loaf pan lined with plastic wrap, smoothing top, and chill, uncovered, until firm, about 4 hours.

Loosen edges of *ganache* with a sharp small knife and invert onto a cutting surface. Remove plastic wrap and cut *ganache* into 40 squares.

Dust your palms with cocoa and roll each piece of *ganache* between them to form a ball. Drop ball into cocoa bowl and turn to cover completely. Lift truffle with a fork and transfer to a plate. Chill truffles, covered, until ready to serve.

Cooks' note:
- Truffles keep, covered and chilled, 1 week.

PHOTO ON PAGE 75

## COCONUT MACADAMIA TRUFFLES

*Makes 64 truffles*
Active time: 1 hr   Start to finish: 5 hr

8 oz Lindt white chocolate
1 cup salted dry-roasted macadamia nuts (5 oz)
¼ cup heavy cream
2 tablespoons dark rum
1½ cups finely shredded unsweetened desiccated
   coconut

Finely grind white chocolate in a food processor and transfer to a bowl. Pulse nuts in food processor until finely ground (be careful not to grind to a paste).

Bring heavy cream to a simmer in a medium skillet. Remove from heat and stir in rum. Whisk in white chocolate until melted and *ganache* is smooth. Stir in nuts.

207

## CRANBERRY COGNAC TRIFLE

### Serves 8 to 12
Active time: 2½ hr   Start to finish: 13 hr

*This impressive dessert is the sum of many parts that can each be made several days in advance. Assemble the trifle the day before serving to allow the cake to absorb the custard and the flavors to fully develop.*

*For cake layers*
12 large egg yolks
2¼ cups sugar
6 tablespoons whole milk
1½ teaspoons vanilla
1½ cups all-purpose flour
¾ teaspoon salt
6 large egg whites
*For assembling trifle*
Cranberry jam (recipe follows)
Cognac syrup (page 209)
Rich custard (page 209)
*For cream topping*
1⅓ cups chilled heavy cream
¼ cup confectioners sugar
2 tablespoons Cognac or other brandy
¼ teaspoon vanilla

*Garnish:* sugared cranberries and mint leaves
(procedure on page 210)
*Special equipment:* 3 (15- by 10- by ½-inch) baking
pans and a 3½-quart straight-sided glass trifle or
soufflé dish

*Make cake layers:*
Preheat oven to 350°F and butter pans. Line bottom of each pan with wax or parchment paper and butter paper. Dust pans with flour, knocking out excess.

Whisk together yolks, 1½ cups sugar, milk, and vanilla in a large bowl until combined well, then whisk in flour and salt until smooth. (Batter will be thick.)

Beat whites with an electric mixer until they hold soft peaks. With mixer at low speed, gradually beat in remaining ¾ cup sugar. Increase speed to high and beat until whites hold stiff, glossy peaks. Fold about one third of whites into batter to lighten, then fold in remaining whites gently but thoroughly.

Divide batter among pans and spread evenly. Rap pans against a work surface to release any air bubbles. Bake, 1 pan at a time, in middle of oven until cake is pale golden and beginning to shrink around edges, 10 to 11 minutes per pan. Cool cake layers completely in pans on racks.

*Assemble trifle:*
Loosen edges of 1 cake layer with a knife. Place a sheet of wax or parchment paper on top of layer and invert onto a rack. Carefully peel paper from cake. Place a new sheet of wax or parchment paper on inverted cake and reinvert onto work surface, peeling off paper that is now on top. Repeat with remaining 2 layers.

With long side of layers toward you, halve layers vertically with a serrated knife. Spread 1 half of each layer (3 of 6 halves) with cranberry jam, then top with remaining plain halves.

Cut each "sandwich" crosswise into 10 (7½- by ¾-inch) strips. Arrange 1 strip vertically in trifle dish with a cut side against glass, then trim strip flush with top of dish. Using trimmed piece as a guide, cut remaining strips to fit dish, reserving trimmings. Brush strips on all sides with Cognac syrup and fit strips tightly all around

edge of dish. (If your trifle dish is slightly smaller on bottom than on top, cut a few strips in half diagonally to fill any gaps.)

Brush trimmings with syrup and arrange one fourth of them in 1 layer in bottom of dish. Pour in 1 cup custard. Repeat layering of trimmings and custard to fill dish, ending with custard. (You may have a small amount of custard left over.) Brush top of strips around edge with syrup. Cover trifle with plastic wrap and chill at least 8 hours.

*Make topping:*

Beat chilled heavy cream with confectioners sugar, Cognac, and vanilla with an electric mixer until it holds soft peaks. Remove plastic wrap from trifle and mound cream on top.

**Cooks' notes:**
- Resist the temptation to bake more than 1 cake layer at a time; layers will bake extremely unevenly.
- Cake layers can be baked 2 days ahead of assembling and chilled, wrapped well, or frozen up to 1 month.
- Trifle can be assembled (before topping with cream) up to 1 day ahead and chilled, covered.

PHOTO ON PAGE 79

## CRANBERRY JAM

*Makes about 2 cups*
Active time: 15 min   Start to finish: 1 hr

1 vanilla bean, halved lengthwise
1 (12-oz) bag fresh or unthawed frozen cranberries
    (3½ cups)
1½ cups sugar
½ cup fresh orange juice
½ cup water

*Special equipment:* a food mill fitted with fine disk

Scrape vanilla seeds from pod into a 2-quart heavy saucepan. Add pod and remaining ingredients and bring to a boil, stirring occasionally. Reduce heat and simmer, stirring occasionally, until thick, about 20 minutes (jam will continue to thicken as it cools).

Purée jam in food mill set over a bowl, discarding skins and pod. Cool, stirring occasionally.

**Cooks' note:**
- Jam can be made 4 days ahead of assembling trifle and chilled, covered.

## COGNAC SYRUP

*Makes about 1½ cups*
Active time: 5 min   Start to finish: 30 min

1 cup water
½ cup sugar
2 (4-inch) strips fresh orange zest
⅔ cup Cognac or other brandy

Bring all ingredients to a boil in a 1-quart saucepan, stirring until sugar is dissolved. Reduce heat and simmer 5 minutes. Cool.

**Cooks' note:**
- Syrup can be made 4 days ahead of assembling trifle and chilled, covered.

## RICH CUSTARD

*Makes about 5 cups*
Active time: 40 min   Start to finish: 1 hr

¾ cup sugar
3 tablespoons cornstarch
4 cups whole milk
2 teaspoons finely grated fresh orange zest
10 large egg yolks
1 teaspoon vanilla

Whisk together ¼ cup sugar, cornstarch, and a pinch of salt in a 2-quart heavy saucepan. Whisk in ¼ cup milk until smooth, then stir in remaining milk and zest. Bring to a boil over moderate heat, whisking frequently.

Have ready a bowl of ice and cold water. Whisk together yolks and remaining ½ cup sugar in a large bowl. Gradually whisk in hot milk mixture, then transfer custard to saucepan. Cook, stirring constantly, until mixture registers 170°F on an instant-read thermometer, 3 to 4 minutes. (Do not boil.)

Immediately pour custard through a fine sieve into a metal bowl set in ice water. Stir in vanilla. Cool, stirring frequently.

**Cooks' note:**
- Custard can be prepared 3 days ahead and chilled, its surface covered with wax paper and bowl covered with plastic wrap.

## TO MAKE SUGARED CRANBERRIES AND MINT LEAVES

**Makes enough to garnish 1 trifle**
Active time: 20 min   Start to finish: 3 hr

*Though the cranberries look gorgeous, you wouldn't want to eat them—they're extremely tart when raw. The mint leaves, however, are positively delicious. Fresh raw cranberries yielded the most attractive garnish; thawed frozen berries may collapse and shrivel. Feel free to increase the amounts we've provided here if you'd like to make your decoration more elaborate.*

1 tablespoon powdered egg whites
1 tablespoon warm water
9 raw cranberries
6 fresh mint leaves
¼ cup sugar

Slowly whisk together powdered egg whites and water until dissolved. Lightly coat cranberries and both sides of mint leaves with egg mixture using your fingers or a pastry brush, then sprinkle with sugar. Transfer to a lightly oiled rack and dry 2 to 3 hours.

Cooks' note:
• Mint leaves will darken if not used within a few hours, but cranberries will keep, uncovered, 1 day.

## APRICOT-ALMOND GRATINS

**Serves 4**
Active time: 15 min   Start to finish: 25 min

*These clafoutis-like puddings are best served warm. This dessert can be made using a 9-inch pie plate instead of the gratin dishes.*

24 dried apricots, quartered
2 tablespoons brandy
1 cup sliced almonds (4 oz)
½ cup granulated sugar
1 tablespoon all-purpose flour
⅛ teaspoon salt
3 large eggs
¾ cup heavy cream
Confectioners sugar for dusting

*Special equipment:* 4 (6-inch) shallow gratin dishes

Preheat oven to 400°F. Butter gratin dishes and put in a shallow baking pan.

Soak apricots in brandy 10 minutes, then drain, reserving brandy.

Reserve 2 tablespoons almonds. Pulse remaining almonds, granulated sugar, flour, and salt in a food processor until almonds are finely chopped. Add eggs and cream and pulse until smooth. Stir reserved brandy into almond cream. Pour almond cream into gratin dishes and sprinkle with apricots and reserved almonds.

Bake gratins in middle of oven until puffed and golden brown, 18 to 20 minutes. Dust with confectioners sugar.

## ETON MESS

**Serves 4**
Active time: 30 min   Start to finish: 3 hr

*This dessert is simple and delicious, especially when made with very ripe strawberries and thick Devonshire cream (sources on page 264).*

4 large egg whites
1 cup plus 1 tablespoon sugar
¾ lb strawberries
2 tablespoons sweet Sherry
⅔ cup heavy cream

Preheat oven to 225°F.

Beat egg whites with a pinch of salt in a large bowl with an electric mixer until they just hold soft peaks. Gradually add 1 cup sugar, beating, then beat until meringue holds stiff, glossy peaks. Spoon meringue into 4 mounds on a parchment-paper-lined baking sheet and spread each into a 3½-inch round, smoothing tops.

Bake in middle of oven until crisp and firm, about 1½ hours. (If weather is humid, cooking time may be longer.) Cool meringues completely on baking sheet in turned-off oven or on a rack and carefully peel off parchment.

Halve some small strawberries for garnish. Slice remaining strawberries and stir together with Sherry and remaining tablespoon sugar in a small bowl. Macerate 20 minutes. Drain strawberries in a sieve set over a bowl, reserving syrup. Beat cream in a chilled bowl until it just holds stiff peaks and beat in reserved syrup.

Spoon cream mixture over meringues and top with strawberry slices. Garnish plates with halved berries.

Cooks' note:
• Meringues can be made 1 week ahead, wrapped well individually, and kept at cool room temperature.

## MANGO FOOL WITH CHOCOLATE-ANISE STRAWS

*Serves 6*
Active time: 20 min   Start to finish: 8½ hr

*Canned mangoes are excellent in this dessert if ripe fresh ones are unavailable. Use a drained (1-lb 14-oz) can of mango slices in syrup (sources on page 264). If the canned fruits you buy are Alphonso mangoes (our favorite variety of mango), add an additional ½ cup cream.*

1¼ teaspoons unflavored gelatin (less than 1 envelope)
1½ tablespoons fresh lime juice
3 large very ripe mangoes, flesh coarsely chopped (4 cups)
¼ cup sugar, or to taste depending on sweetness of mangoes
¾ cup heavy cream

*Accompaniment:* chocolate-anise straws (recipe follows)

Sprinkle gelatin over juice in a small heatproof cup and let stand 1 minute to soften. Purée mangoes with sugar in a blender until very smooth and force through a sieve into a large bowl. Melt softened gelatin in cup in a pan of simmering water or in a microwave and stir into purée. Beat cream with an electric mixer until it just holds stiff peaks and gently fold into purée.

Chill fool, covered, at least 8 hours.

Cooks' notes:
• Mango fool can be kept, chilled and covered, up to 2 days.
• There are two ways of getting to the flesh of a mango. The safest way is to cut the two wide, fleshiest sides of the mango as close to the pit as possible. Score cut sides of the pieces in a crosshatch pattern, turn them inside out, then cut the flesh from the skin. You can also remove the skin first with a vegetable peeler, then cut the flesh from the pit with a sharp knife. (Take care if you use this method; the mango's slipperiness can be tricky.)

PHOTO ON PAGE 30

## CHOCOLATE-ANISE STRAWS

*Makes 12 straws*
Active time: 20 min   Start to finish: 1 hr

1 teaspoon anise seeds
1½ oz fine-quality bittersweet chocolate (not unsweetened), chopped
2½ tablespoons sugar
3 (17- by 12-inch) phyllo sheets
3 tablespoons unsalted butter, melted

Preheat oven to 375°F.
Finely grind anise in an electric coffee/spice grinder or with a mortar and pestle. Finely chop chocolate with anise and sugar in a food processor.
Cut phyllo sheets in half crosswise to form 6 sheets. Cover with 2 overlapping sheets of plastic wrap and then a dampened kitchen towel. Place 1 sheet of phyllo with long side nearest you on a work surface (keep remaining sheets covered) and lightly brush lower half of sheet with butter. Spoon a heaping tablespoon of chocolate mixture lengthwise across center of sheet. Fold phyllo sheet in half, enclosing chocolate, and brush lightly with butter. Starting with chocolate side, roll up pastry tightly to form a 12-inch straw. Transfer straw, seam side down, to a baking sheet, then make 5 more in same manner.
Bake straws in upper third of oven until golden, 12 to 14 minutes, and cool on a rack. Break in half to form 12 straws.

Cooks' note:
• Straws keep in an airtight container 2 days.

dissolved. Stir in rum, sugar, and mint, then simmer, stirring occasionally, 5 minutes. Remove from heat and let stand, uncovered, while mint steeps, 20 minutes.

Stir in lime juice and remaining cup water, then pour through a fine sieve into baking dish and chill, covered, until firm, at least 8 hours.

While jelly chills, halve limes lengthwise and scoop out all flesh, reserving it for another use. Chill lime bowls, wrapped in plastic wrap.

Place a cutting board over baking dish and invert jelly onto board. Peel off plastic wrap and cut jelly into ½-inch cubes. Spoon into lime bowls.

**Cooks' note:**
- **Jelly and lime bowls can be chilled, separately, up to 24 hours.**

each serving about 142 calories and less than 1 gram fat

## PAAL PAYASAM

### RICE PUDDING WITH PISTACHIOS, RAISINS, AND SAFFRON

*Serves 6*
Active time: 1¼ hr   Start to finish: 1¾ hr

2 qt whole milk
¾ cup jasmine rice
1 cup sugar
6 green cardamom pods, lightly crushed
¼ teaspoon crumbled saffron threads
2 tablespoons *ghee* (page 107 or sources on page 264)
½ cup shelled natural pistachios
½ cup golden raisins

Simmer milk with rice, sugar, cardamom, and saffron in 7- to 8-quart heavy pot, stirring often, until reduced by half, 45 to 50 minutes. Discard cardamom.

Heat *ghee* in a heavy skillet over moderate heat until melted, then cook pistachios and raisins, stirring, until nuts are lightly browned, about 2 minutes.

Stir half of pistachio mixture into payasam and sprinkle remainder on top. Serve warm or chilled.

**Cooks' note:**
- **You can make *payasam*, without pistachio mixture, 1 day ahead and chill, covered. Cook nut mixture just before serving.**

PHOTO ON PAGE 13

## MOJITO JELLY

*Serves 6*
Active time: 15 min   Start to finish: 8¼ hr

*We serve our remake of the Mojito—a Cuban cocktail—in lime bowls, but Martini glasses would also look sleek.*

4 teaspoons unflavored gelatin (less than 2 full envelopes)
1¾ cups water
¾ cup amber rum
½ cup sugar
½ cup fresh mint
6 tablespoons fresh lime juice
6 limes (optional)

Line the bottom and sides of an oiled 8-inch square glass baking dish with a piece of plastic wrap, smoothing out wrinkles.

Sprinkle gelatin over ¾ cup water in a 2-quart saucepan and let stand 1 minute to soften. Heat mixture over low heat, stirring occasionally, until gelatin is

## TAPIOCA PUDDING WITH COCONUT CREAM AND PALM-SUGAR SYRUP

### Serves 6
Active time: 30 min   Start to finish: 1 hr

*For information on specialty ingredients, see sources on page 264.*

6¼ cups water
1 cup (¹⁄₁₆-inch) pearl tapioca (not quick-cooking)
1 *pandan* leaf, thawed if frozen (optional)
½ cup grated or crumbled dark palm sugar (4 oz)
   or packed dark brown sugar
1 (14-oz) can unsweetened coconut milk
   (do not shake)

*Make pudding:*
Bring 6 cups water to a boil in a large saucepan and add tapioca in a slow stream, stirring constantly. Gently boil, stirring frequently, 5 minutes. Remove from heat and let stand, covered, until tapioca is translucent, about 15 minutes.

Add 3 cups cold water to tapioca, then drain in a large sieve. Transfer tapioca to a large bowl. Add cold water to cover by 2 inches and swirl tapioca to remove excess starch. Drain tapioca in sieve and repeat rinsing. Drain tapioca again and divide among 6 serving dishes. Chill, loosely covered, 10 minutes, or until set.

*Make syrup:*
Tear *pandan* leaf into strips and tie strips together in 1 knot. Simmer *pandan* with palm sugar and remaining ¼ cup water in a small saucepan, stirring until sugar is dissolved, until slightly thickened, about 5 minutes. Discard *pandan* and pour syrup through a fine sieve into a small bowl. Cool to room temperature.

*Make coconut cream:*
Scoop out thick layer of coconut cream from top of can, reserving thin liquid in bottom. Whisk ½ cup coconut cream until smooth, whisking in 1 to 1½ tablespoons thin coconut liquid if necessary to get a pourable consistency.

Drizzle some of syrup over tapioca and top with some coconut cream. Serve remaining syrup and cream on the side.

Cooks' notes:
• For this particular recipe, we prefer A Taste of Thai, Royal Blossom, Thai Kitchen, or Ka-Me brand of coconut milk because the thin liquid and the creamlike layer are distinctly separated.

• Syrup may be made 1 day ahead and chilled, covered. If syrup is too thick to drizzle, bring to room temperature.

PHOTO ON PAGE 38

## BLOOD ORANGE JELLY WITH BRANDIED WHIPPED CREAM

### Serves 6
Active time: 1 hr   Start to finish: 9 hr

2 (¼-oz) envelopes unflavored gelatin
½ cup water
4 cups strained fresh blood orange juice
   (from about 2 dozen blood oranges)
3 tablespoons sugar

*Accompaniment:* brandied whipped cream
   (recipe follows)
*Special equipment:* a 1-quart glass, ceramic, or
   stainless-steel mold

Sprinkle gelatin over water in a large bowl and let soften 1 minute.

Bring 1 cup juice just to a boil and add to gelatin mixture. Add sugar and a pinch of salt, stirring until sugar and gelatin are dissolved. Stir in remaining 3 cups juice. Pour mixture into mold and chill, uncovered, until set, about 8 hours.

To unmold, dip mold into a bowl of hot water for just a few seconds. Shake mold from side to side, then invert onto a serving plate.

Cooks' note:
• Blood oranges can be expensive. To cut costs, you could substitute 2 cups strained regular orange juice for 2 cups blood orange juice.

PHOTO ON PAGE 72

## BRANDIED WHIPPED CREAM

### Makes about 4 cups
Active time: 5 min   Start to finish: 5 min

2 cups heavy cream
2 tablespoons confectioners sugar, or to taste
2 tablespoons brandy, or to taste

Beat cream with confectioners sugar with an electric mixer until it holds soft peaks. Fold in brandy.

## CREAMY RICE PUDDING WITH TROPICAL FRUITS

**Serves 4**
Active time: 20 min   Start to finish: 30 min

¾ cup long-grain white rice
1½ cups water
1 cup heavy cream
6 tablespoons sugar
¼ teaspoon vanilla
⅛ teaspoon salt
2 cups diced mixed fresh tropical fruits such as
   pineapple, mango, and papaya

Boil rice in water in a 1½-quart heavy saucepan, uncovered and undisturbed, until steam holes appear on surface, about 8 minutes.

Reduce heat to very low and cook, covered and undisturbed, 12 minutes more. Stir in heavy cream, sugar, vanilla, and salt and simmer, stirring, 2 minutes. Stir 1 cup mixed fruit into pudding and serve topped with remaining fruit.

## VANILLA BEAN FLAN

**Serves 4**
Active time: 30 min   Start to finish: 3½ hr

1¼ cups 1% milk
1 vanilla bean, split lengthwise
¼ cup sugar
1 large egg
1 large egg yolk
¼ cup nonfat sweetened condensed milk

*Special equipment:* 4 (5- to 6-oz) deep custard cups
   or ramekins

Preheat oven to 350°F.

Heat 1% milk with vanilla bean halves in a small saucepan over moderate heat until hot. Remove from heat, cover, then steep 20 minutes.

Cook sugar in a 6-inch nonstick skillet over moderately low heat, swirling skillet to help sugar melt evenly, until melted and pale golden. Continue to cook, swirling skillet, until deep caramel, 1 to 2 minutes. Immediately pour into custard cups, tilting cups to coat bottom. Let caramel cool.

Whisk together whole egg, yolk, condensed milk, and a pinch of salt until smooth. Discard vanilla bean pod from steeped milk and gradually whisk milk into egg mixture.

Divide custard among cups and bake in a water bath, loosely covered with a sheet of foil, in middle of oven until custard is set but still trembles slightly, 35 to 40 minutes.

Remove cups from water bath and cool on a rack. Chill, uncovered, at least 2 hours. Unmold flans by running a knife around edges and inverting onto plates.

**Cooks' note:**
- **Flans can be made 1 day ahead and kept chilled in custard cups, uncovered.**

each serving about 169 calories and 3 grams fat

# BEVERAGES

## PISCO SOURS

**Makes 2 drinks**
Active time: 20 min   Start to finish: 35 min

*In South America, this cocktail is traditionally made with Pisco, a brandy distilled from Muscat or Mission grapes; bitters (omitted here); and egg white, a classic ingredient in a number of old-fashioned cocktails that gives drinks a foamy head. This is chef Mary Sue Milliken's version.*

3 oz Pisco (about ⅓ cup)
3 oz sweet-and-sour mix (about ⅓ cup; recipe
   follows)
1 teaspoon powdered egg white (do not reconstitute)
   or 1 egg white

Combine all ingredients in a cocktail shaker with crushed ice and shake vigorously until egg white is incorporated. Strain into Martini glasses.

Cooks' note:
• If there is a problem with salmonella in your area, using raw egg white instead of powdered may be of concern.

PHOTO ON PAGE 55

## SWEET-AND-SOUR MIX

**Makes about 3 cups (enough for 16 drinks)**
Active time: 20 min   Start to finish: 30 min

¾ cup sugar
¾ cup water
1 cup fresh lemon juice
½ cup fresh lime juice
½ cup fresh orange juice

Bring sugar and water to a boil, stirring until sugar is dissolved. Transfer to a metal bowl set in a larger bowl of ice and cold water to chill syrup quickly. Stir together 1 cup syrup and remaining ingredients in a pitcher.

Cooks' note:
• Sweet-and-sour mix can be made 1 day ahead and chilled, covered.

## CITRON MARTINI WITH BLACK SAMBUCA

**Makes 1 drink**
Active time: 3 min   Start to finish: 3 min

½ teaspoon black Sambuca
   (such as Opal Nera)
1 lemon twist
⅓ cup Absolut Citron vodka or
   regular vodka (about 3 oz)

*Special equipment:* a cocktail shaker

Pour black Sambuca into a chilled Martini glass. Run lemon twist around rim and add to glass. Fill cocktail shaker with ice and add vodka. Shake well, then strain chilled vodka into glass.

Cooks' note:
• Up to 3 Martinis can be made in shaker at one time.

## ELDERBERRY-FLOWER MIMOSAS

**Makes 8 drinks**
Active time: 5 min   Start to finish: 5 min

*We recommend using a good-quality California or Spanish sparkling wine for this recipe. Both are widely available and less expensive than Champagne. You may want to garnish these drinks with fresh elderberry flowers; if so, make sure the blossoms you buy are unsprayed (nontoxic).*

1 cup elderberry-flower syrup (sources on page 264)
2 (750-ml) bottles chilled dry sparkling wine

Put 2 tablespoons elderberry-flower syrup in each of 8 stemmed glasses and top off with sparkling wine. Stir gently to combine.

PHOTO ON PAGE 50

## MULLED WINE

**Serves 8**
Active time: 20 min   Start to finish: 40 min

2 navel oranges
1 small lemon
2 (750-ml) bottles dry red wine such as Côtes du
  Rhône
1 cup sugar
10 black peppercorns
8 whole cloves
4 whole star anise
¼ teaspoon freshly grated nutmeg

*Garnish:* orange slices studded with cloves

Remove zest from oranges and lemon with a vegetable peeler and remove any white pith from zest. Squeeze juice from zested oranges and lemon.
  Bring wine, zest, juices, sugar, peppercorns, cloves, star anise, and nutmeg to a simmer, stirring until sugar is dissolved, and simmer 2 more minutes. Pour mulled wine through a fine sieve into a heatproof pitcher.

**Cooks' note:**
• **You can make and strain mulled wine 1 day ahead, then cool it completely and chill, covered. Reheat before serving.**

PHOTO ON PAGE 15

## FROZEN PAPAYA AND PASSION-FRUIT RUM COCKTAILS

**Makes 6 drinks**
Active time: 15 min   Start to finish: 20 min

1¼ cups light rum
4½ cups chopped peeled papaya (2 lb)
1 cup thawed passion-fruit purée (sources on
  page 264)
¼ cup superfine granulated sugar, or to taste
4 cups ice cubes

Blend rum, papaya, passion fruit, sugar, and ice in 2 batches in a blender until smooth. Serve immediately.

PHOTO ON PAGE 30

## HOT CIDER WITH RUM

**Makes 1 drink**
Active time: 1 min   Start to finish: 5 min

*For a cold version of this cocktail, pour rum over ice in a large glass and top off with apple juice or sparkling cider.*

6 to 8 oz apple cider or juice
1 oz dark rum (2 tablespoons)

*Garnish:* thinly sliced apples

Heat apple cider until hot and pour into a mug. Stir in dark rum.

NON-ALCOHOLIC

## ATOLE DE PIÑA

### HOT PINEAPPLE DRINK

**Makes about 1½ quarts (serving 6 to 8)**
Active time: 30 min   Start to finish: 30 min

*These nourishing atoles—fruit-flavored drinks thickened with corn tortilla flour—are served much like hot chocolate in Mexico. They are warming on cold mornings or evenings.*

½ cup *masa harina* (tortilla flour; sources on
   page 264)
5 cups water
1½ cups chopped fresh pineapple
⅔ cup sugar

Whisk together tortilla flour and 2 cups water in a 3-quart heavy saucepan.

Purée pineapple with sugar and remaining 3 cups water in a blender until smooth and pour through a sieve into flour mixture. Stir together with a wooden spoon and simmer, stirring constantly, 15 minutes.

## CINNAMON HOT CHOCOLATE

**Serves 8**
Active time: 20 min   Start to finish: 30 min

¾ lb fine-quality bittersweet chocolate
   (not unsweetened), chopped
4 (3-inch) cinnamon sticks
8 cups skim milk

Put chocolate in a heatproof pitcher with cinnamon sticks. Bring milk and a pinch of salt just to a simmer in a 4-quart saucepan. Immediately pour into pitcher and stir until chocolate is melted.

## PEACH NECTAR WITH LIME

**Serves 8**
Active time: 10 min   Start to finish: 10 min

6 (11½-oz) cans peach nectar, chilled
½ cup fresh lime juice, or to taste
3 limes, halved

Stir together peach nectar, lime juice, and lime halves and serve over ice.

PHOTO ON PAGE 44

Dramatic hills, valleys strewn with wild-
flowers and long green grasses, Mount Etna's
active volcano, spectacular cliffs that plummet
to sandy beaches, and sparkling azure waters—
all are reason enough to visit Sicily, but there
is so much more. Her location, only a few miles
off the toe of Italy's boot-shaped mainland,
destined her to be the stepping-stone to Europe,
and more than 2,000 years of conquerors—
including the Greeks, Romans, Byzantines,
Arabs, Normans, and Spanish—came and left
their mark. Scattered throughout the island are
ruins of Greek temples and theaters hewn out
of mountaintops with panoramic views that
stretch to the sea. There are Roman villas,
Norman castles, time-worn walled towns with
exquisite piazzas, and narrow city alleyways
that occasionally reward the inquisitive with
wisteria-laden gates and glimpses of neglected
courtyards and crumbling palaces. Magnificent
medieval cathedrals and baroque churches—
some abandoned, some with priceless sculp-
tures, paintings, and mosaics—number in the
hundreds. The sheer volume of visual history
is overwhelming, and often layers of civiliza-
tions can be seen at one site. And then there are
the awesome festivals, the most lavish during
Holy Week, when crowded cobblestone streets
set the stage for well-rehearsed pageantry and
melodrama. Glorious food, as always, plays a
central role during these occasions, and one
easily succumbs to the temptations.

Mount Etna

Unfortunately, everyday life is not without its difficulties. Although Sicily has gained more autonomy since the end of World War II, it has also faced many obstacles—an intrusive bureaucracy, Mafia interference, lingering ties with a defunct feudal system, and devastating earthquakes—that have hampered progress and economic stability. Even the climate can be harsh—torrential rains punctuate the mild winters, jeopardizing crops, as do the summer droughts laced by searing sirocco winds from the Sahara. It is no wonder that Sicilians, though extremely hospitable, are known to be reserved and pessimistic. Collapsed villas and cathedrals left in ruin mirror feelings of despair and futility, and anyone who has witnessed a Sicilian funeral knows just how somber this culture can be. To make ends meet many women now work outside of the home and depend on family (usually a grandmother) to look after the children. Yet urban Sicilians are struggling to hold onto traditional ways. Many prepare homemade meals and drive to the country to buy wine, olive oil, and fresh vegetables from local growers. Those with country houses often have a garden and preserve their harvests for year-round consumption. Fortunately, national holidays follow the church calendar, and the family celebrates these cherished days together.

Regardless of economic circumstances, all Sicilians consider food a priority; they demand quality and often, especially during the holidays, turn a blind eye to cost. Back at the turn of the 20th century, wealthy families sent their personal cooks to France to be trained by French masters. These returning *monzù* chefs, as they were called, were treated with great respect, and while only a handful of their apprentices are still alive, they, too, are revered. Today, however, most people prefer a very simple cuisine using the flavors that the bountiful surrounding seas and strong Sicilian sun provide. Naturally, pristinely fresh fish—particularly tuna, swordfish, octopus, squid, sardines, and anchovies—constantly serve as a mainstay of the diet. Tomatoes, ripened to perfection in the intense sunshine, have a powerful full-bodied taste unlike any others, and sauces made with them give distinctive flavor to many favorite pasta and meat dishes. Vine-ripened tomatoes are available most of the year, but they are also sun-dried for the months when they are not. Likewise, olives and grapes are extraordinarily flavorful, and, in recent years, fine Sicilian olive oils and wines have received coveted international prizes.

The history of Sicily's cuisine is as rich and layered as the history of her conquerors who carried with them favorite foods from their homelands as well as from other lands. Aside from their religion and mythology, the Greeks brought olives, honey, and almonds, as well as their knowledge of making Malvasia (very sweet wine made with dried and fresh grapes crushed together), bread, and cheese. The Romans established feudal estates and planted hard durum wheat (the well-known secret of superior pastas), fava beans, and grapes for Mamertino wine. The Arabs, with their advanced irrigation systems, planted their beloved citrus trees and Zibibbo grapes. They also offered saffron, rice, pasta noodles, and couscous, and with their sugarcane, demonstrated how to make sweets. Later still, the Spanish added a host of vegetables from the West, including tomatoes, peppers, squash, zucchini, beans, potatoes, and corn, as well as chocolate. Although Sicily remains a haven for immigrants, the island is noticeably divided by cultural tradition into two sections: The west, centered in Palermo, the capital of Sicily, is considered Arab; the east, with coastal towns of Catania, Syracuse, and Messina, is mainly Greek.

On the following pages you will find three menus developed by *Gourmet* food editors that highlight some of the favorite dishes of Sicily. Mary Taylor Simeti, the celebrated writer of Sicilian cookbooks (*Pomp and Sustenance* and *Bitter Almonds*) as well as travel/Greek mythology (*On Persephone's Island* and *Travels with a Medieval Queen*), acted as consultant and generously allowed us to style many of our recipes on her own. She kept an eye on authenticity and, when we strayed, either applauded our creativity or diplomatically made another suggestion.

Alexis Touchet's Summer Dinner in Palermo includes a few of this city's obligatory dishes, namely fresh tuna, simply grilled, and *panelle*, the famous fried chickpea snacks sold in La Vucciria market. Although *panelle* began as an Arab street food, clever Palermitan restaurateurs have introduced them to the antipasto table; we have followed suit by serving them along with *caponata* and olives. Summer's best eggplant also appears in *pasta alla Norma*, a national favorite, and zucchini is presented in all its glory, simply marinated with a bit of lemon juice, salt, pepper, and basil, then drizzled with extra-virgin olive oil. Peach granita, a twist on the classic lemon- or coffee-flavored favorites, pairs with anise biscotti for a refreshing, light ending.

Carnival Dinner, served on Shrove Tuesday just before Lent begins, is an excuse to eat as much meat as possible, and Lori Powell's Carnival feast is no exception. Once again, pasta is on offer, this time with a succulent pork *ragù*. *Farsumagru*, a braised meat roll made with flank steak, ground beef, and prosciutto follows with pork sausage and sweet meatballs. Such a heavy meal requires a light, fresh-tasting accompaniment and an orange and sweet-fennel creation provides just that. Heavenly cannoli, made with fresh ricotta, defy description and are worth every bit of effort.

Finally, as a bow to the excessive nature of all things Sicilian, we pull out all the stops with a Sweets Table, created by Tracey Seaman. Such a collection of desserts could have come straight out of Giuseppe di Lampedusa's novel, *The Leopard*, where lavish 19th-century aristocratic Palermitan entertaining was punctuated with lavish sweets displays. Despite the fact that such an unusual combination of sweets probably would never appear today, we couldn't resist the chance to try so many wonderful classics. We found them unusual and delightful at the same time. Each is worthy of a dinner party and, in fact, we expect that most of our readers will try them individually. You might want to begin simply with the watermelon pudding or the fig and almond cookies and progress to the much more involved *spongato di nocciola*.

Two primers follow that add further insight to our menus: *Basic Ingredients* describes all the important foods that define this cuisine, while *Sicilian Sweets* unravels the intriguing history of a convent tradition, now dying out, that kept secret recipes alive for hundreds of years.

Sicily certainly is unique. When a Sicilian travels to the mainland he proclaims that he is traveling to Italy. Now we understand the distinction.

# SUMMER DINNER IN PALERMO

*Serves 6*

PANELLE
Chickpea Fritters

CAPONATA
Sweet and Sour Eggplant

OLIVE VERDI
Green Olives

• • •

PASTA ALLA NORMA
Pasta with Eggplant and Tomato Sauce

• • •

TONNO CON MENTA E MANDORLE
Grilled Tuna with Mint-Almond Sauce

INSALATA DI ZUCCHINI
Zucchini Salad

Regaleali Bianco Sicilia, Conte Tasca di Almerita, 1999

• • •

GRANITA DI PESCA
Peach Granita

BISCOTTI ALL'ANICE
Anise Biscotti

Summers can be extremely hot in Palermo, so dinner must be light, refreshing, and easy to prepare. We begin with a few regional snacks—*panelle* (fried chickpea fritters) and large green olives, both sold in Palermo's Vucciria market, as well as *caponata,* this one made with bell peppers along with the usual eggplant. (The *caponata* should be made a day ahead to allow the flavors to blend, and, while the *panelle* must be fried and served immediately, the chickpea mixture can be prepared and chilled the day before as well.) Then, because we appreciate the Sicilian passion for eggplant, our pasta course features *pasta alla Norma,* the national dish that combines the freshest eggplant, tomatoes, garlic, and basil with plenty of grated *ricotta salata.* Pristine tuna steaks, the pride of Sicily, follow. These are simply grilled and topped with a fresh mint and almond sauce for a lovely main course. Ultra-fresh, no-cook zucchini salad is the perfect accompaniment. For dessert, icy-cold peach granita soothes the palate, while anise biscotti provide yet another delicate touch of sweetness. Both finales can be made ahead of time.

## CAPONATA

SWEET AND SOUR EGGPLANT

***Serves 6***
Active time: 1 hr   Start to finish: 13 hr

*Caponata is generally served as a salad, side dish, or relish. It's traditionally made with eggplant, but we've added some bell peppers for more color.*

2 lb eggplant
1 (28-oz) can whole plum tomatoes including juice
1¼ cups extra-virgin olive oil
2 large red or yellow bell peppers, cut into ½-inch pieces
1 large onion, coarsely chopped
4 celery ribs, cut into 1-inch pieces
1 cup green olives, pitted and cut into ¼-inch-wide slivers
3 tablespoons capers, rinsed and drained
¼ cup red-wine vinegar
2 tablespoons sugar

Cut eggplant into 1-inch cubes and put in a colander. Sprinkle generously with salt and toss, then drain 1 hour.

While eggplant is draining, simmer tomatoes with juice in a 4- to 5-quart heavy saucepan, breaking up tomatoes and stirring occasionally, until thickened, 25 to 30 minutes.

Rinse eggplant and pat dry with paper towels. Heat 1 cup oil in a 10-inch heavy skillet over moderately high heat until hot but not smoking, then fry eggplant in 4 batches, turning occasionally, until browned and tender, 3 to 5 minutes. Transfer with a slotted spoon to paper towels to drain.

Cook bell peppers in remaining ¼ cup oil in cleaned skillet over moderately low heat, covered, stirring occasionally, until just tender but not browned, about 4 minutes, and transfer with slotted spoon to a bowl. Cook onion and celery in oil remaining in skillet over moderately low heat, covered, stirring occasionally, until celery is tender but not browned, about 10 minutes.

Add onion mixture, olives, capers, vinegar, and sugar to tomatoes and simmer, stirring occasionally, 5 minutes. Add eggplant and bell peppers and simmer, stirring occasionally, 5 minutes. Stir in salt and pepper to taste and cool to room temperature. Chill, covered, at least 12 hours and up to 2 days for flavors to develop. Serve cold or at room temperature.

## PANELLE

CHICKPEA FRITTERS

***Serves 6 (makes about 60)***
Active time: 50 min   Start to finish: 4 hr

*Panelle are best eaten right after frying; they will toughen if made ahead and reheated.*

3 cups water
2 cups chickpea flour (sources on page 264)
½ teaspoon salt
¼ cup minced fresh flat-leaf parsley
4 cups extra-virgin olive oil

Line a lightly oiled 8½- by 4½-inch loaf pan (6-cup capacity) with plastic wrap.

Whisk together water, chickpea flour, salt, and pepper to taste in a 2½- to 3-quart heavy saucepan until smooth. Cook over moderately low heat, whisking constantly to prevent lumps from forming, until mixture is very thick and pulls away from side of pan, 10 to 12 minutes. Stir in parsley, then pour hot mixture into pan, smoothing top. Cool chickpea mixture and chill, surface of mixture covered with plastic wrap, until firm, at least 3 hours.

Lift chickpea mixture out of pan, holding plastic wrap, and transfer to a work surface, then turn over and discard plastic. Pat dry with paper towels. Cut crosswise into ¼-inch-thick slices, then halve slices lengthwise.

Preheat oven to 300°F.

Heat oil in a deep 10-inch heavy skillet or pot until it registers 375°F. Fry *panelle* in 6 batches, turning occasionally, until golden and slightly puffed, 3 to 5 minutes. Drain on paper towels and season with salt. Keep warm on a baking sheet in oven while frying remaining batches. Serve immediately.

**Cooks' notes:**
- If you choose a different size frying pan, use enough oil to measure 1 inch deep.
- Chickpea mixture may be chilled up to 1 day ahead.

*Opposite, clockwise from upper left: Zucchini Salad; Caponata; Grilled Tuna with Mint-Almond Sauce; Pasta alla Norma*

## Pasta alla Norma

### Pasta with Eggplant and Tomato Sauce

**Serves 6**
Active time: 50 min   Start to finish: 1¼ hr

2 lb eggplant
2 garlic cloves, finely chopped
1 cup plus 1 tablespoon extra-virgin olive oil
3 lb plum tomatoes, chopped
¼ cup finely chopped fresh basil
1 lb spaghetti
1 cup freshly grated *ricotta salata* cheese or
    pecorino (2½ oz)

*Garnish:* fresh basil sprigs
*Special equipment:* a food mill fitted with fine disk

Cut eggplant lengthwise into ½-inch-thick slices and layer in a colander, sprinkling each layer generously with salt. Let stand 1 hour.

Cook garlic in 1 tablespoon oil in a 5- to 6-quart heavy saucepan over moderate heat until pale golden. Add tomatoes and simmer, stirring occasionally, until thickened, 30 to 40 minutes. Force mixture through food mill into a bowl. Return sauce to pan and stir in basil and salt and pepper to taste.

Rinse eggplant and pat dry with paper towels. Heat remaining cup oil in a large heavy skillet over moderately high heat until hot but not smoking, then cook eggplant in 3 or 4 batches, turning once, until browned and tender, 5 to 6 minutes. (If eggplant begins to brown too quickly, lower heat to moderate.) Transfer to paper towels to drain. Cool and cut crosswise into ¼-inch strips.

Cook pasta in a large pot of boiling salted water until al dente, then drain well. Toss pasta with half of sauce, half of eggplant, and ¾ cup cheese.

Serve pasta topped with remaining sauce, eggplant, and cheese.

Cooks' notes:
· Tomato sauce may be made 1 day ahead and chilled, covered. Reheat before serving.
· Eggplant may be cooked and cut into strips 1 day ahead and chilled, covered. Reheat on a baking sheet in a 350°F oven before proceeding.

*Top of a column in Monreale*

## Tonno con Menta e Mandorle

### Grilled Tuna with Mint-Almond Sauce

**Serves 6**
Active time: 30 min   Start to finish: 30 min

*For sauce*
½ cup extra-virgin olive oil plus additional
    for brushing
6 garlic cloves, finely chopped
¼ cup white-wine vinegar
½ cup finely chopped fresh mint
¼ cup sliced almonds, toasted and cooled

2½ lb (1-inch-thick) tuna steaks

*Make sauce:*
Heat oil in a small heavy saucepan over moderate heat until hot but not smoking, then cook garlic and vinegar, stirring, until garlic is pale golden, about 1 minute. Remove from heat and cool to room temperature. Stir in mint and salt and pepper to taste. Stir in almonds just before serving.

Prepare grill for cooking.

Brush tuna lightly with oil and season with salt and pepper. Grill on a rack set over glowing coals until just cooked through, 3 to 4 minutes on each side.

Serve tuna with sauce.

Cooks' note:
· Sauce may be made (without mint and almonds) 4 hours ahead and chilled, covered. Bring to room temperature and stir in mint and almonds before serving.

## INSALATA DI ZUCCHINI

### ZUCCHINI SALAD

**Serves 6**
Active time: 15 min   Start to finish: 45 min

4 medium zucchini (1½ lb)
2 tablespoons strained fresh lemon juice
⅓ cup finely chopped fresh basil
2 tablespoons extra-virgin olive oil, or to taste

*Garnish:* fresh basil sprigs
*Special equipment:* a *mandoline*

Cut zucchini into very thin rounds with *mandoline.* Layer rounds on a platter and sprinkle each layer with lemon juice, basil, and salt and pepper to taste. Let stand at least 30 minutes and up to 1 hour.

Just before serving, drizzle with oil and toss to coat. Serve immediately.

## GRANITA DI PESCA

### PEACH GRANITA

**Makes about 8 cups**
Active time: 20 min   Start to finish: 3¼ hr

2½ cups water
½ cup sugar
1¼ lb ripe peaches, pitted and chopped
   (do not peel; 2¾ cups)
1 tablespoon fresh lemon juice

Bring water, sugar, and peaches to a boil in a 2- to 3-quart heavy saucepan, stirring until sugar is dissolved. Simmer, covered, until peaches are soft, 5 to 6 minutes, then cool. Drain peaches over a bowl, reserving syrup. Pureé peaches with ½ cup syrup in a food processor, then force through a fine sieve into bowl with remaining syrup, pressing hard on solids. Stir in lemon juice.

Transfer mixture to an 8- to 9-inch metal baking pan and freeze, stirring and crushing the lumps with a fork every 30 minutes, until firm but not frozen hard, 2 to 3 hours. Transfer to a shallow airtight container.

Before serving, scrape with a fork to lighten texture.

**Cooks' note:**
• Granita can be made 1 day ahead. Let stand at room temperature 10 minutes before serving, then scrape to lighten.

## BISCOTTI ALL'ANICE

### ANISE BISCOTTI

**Makes about 60 biscotti**
Active time: 30 min   Start to finish: 1 hr

*"Biscotto" means "twice cooked" in Italian, which explains the cooking procedure of these delicious cookies.*

1 tablespoon plus 1 teaspoon anise seeds
1⅔ cups all-purpose flour
½ teaspoon baking powder
½ teaspoon baking soda
⅛ teaspoon salt
3 large eggs
1 cup sugar
½ teaspoon vanilla

*Special equipment*: a pastry bag fitted with a ½-inch
   plain tip and parchment paper

Coarsely crush anise seeds with edge of a heavy plate or by pulsing in an electric spice/coffee grinder.

Preheat oven to 375°F. Line 2 large baking sheets with parchment paper.

Sift together flour, baking powder and soda, and salt into a bowl. Beat together eggs and sugar in another bowl with an electric mixer at high speed until batter ribbons when beater is lifted, 8 to 10 minutes, then beat in vanilla. Fold flour mixture into egg mixture until combined well, then fold in anise seeds.

Spoon half of batter into pastry bag, then pipe batter onto 1 baking sheet to form 3- by 2-inch rectangles, about 1 inch apart. Pipe remaining batter onto second baking sheet in same manner. Bake in upper and lower thirds of oven, switching position of sheets halfway through baking, until pale golden, 15 to 20 minutes total.

Reduce oven to 325°F.

Cool rectangles on sheets on racks just until they can be handled, about 5 minutes, then cut diagonally into ¾-inch-thick slices. (There will be end pieces.)

Bake slices, a cut side down, on ungreased baking sheets in upper and lower thirds of oven, turning biscotti over and switching position of sheets halfway through baking, until lightly browned, about 10 minutes total. Transfer to racks to cool.

**Cooks' note:**
• Biscotti keep in an airtight container at room temperature 1 week.

# CARNIVAL DINNER

*Serves 8 to 10*

PERCIATELLI CON RAGÙ DI MAIALE
Pasta with Pork Ragù

• • •

POLPETTE DOLCI
Sweet Meatballs

FARSUMAGRU
Braised Meat Rolls

INSALATA DI ARANCE E FINOCCHIO
Citrus Salad with Sweet Fennel

Murgo Etna Rosso, 1997

• • •

CANNOLI

On Shrove Tuesday, just before Lent begins, Sicilians indulge in a meat-filled feast. Here the tradition lives on with a meal so hearty and soul-satisfying that fasting afterwards seems the only logical thing to do. The dinner begins with a toothsome pasta topped with a long-simmered pork *ragù* and continues with a plate of tender meatballs, sausages, *farsumagru* (braised meat roll) slices, and a refreshing citrus salad. Our cannoli—so light and ethereal and almost otherworldly—are definitely worth the little bit of extra effort they take to prepare. Try them once and you'll soon banish from memory any of the heavy, cloyingly sweet ones you've tasted before.

If you cannot afford to devote an entire day to cooking, you can divide the work into the following stages:

Two days ahead:
• Make shells for cannoli

One day ahead:
• Make *farsumagru* and meatballs and cook along with sausages in tomato sauce
• Make filling for cannoli

Day of feast:
• Reheat sauce and meats
• Cook pasta
• Make citrus salad
• Fill cannoli

## PERCIATELLI CON RAGÙ DI MAIALE

### PASTA WITH PORK RAGÙ

**Serves 8 to 10**
Active time: 2¼ hr   Start to finish: 4 hr

*This dish is really two courses in one: The pasta with ragù sauce is served as the first course. The farsumagru (stuffed meat rolls), sausage, and meatballs—which are cooked in the ragù sauce—become the main course. The farsumagru give this ragù a heavenly flavor. However, if you are not making the entire Carnival Dinner, you can omit it and simply make this dish with meatballs and sausages—it's still delicious.*

3 to 4 tablespoons extra-virgin olive oil
Sweet meatballs (recipe follows)
*Farsumagru* (page 233)
12 fresh Italian sausages (2 lb), pricked all over
   with a fork
1 large onion, finely chopped
1 large garlic clove, smashed
2 cups dry red wine
2 tablespoons tomato paste
1 (28-oz) can crushed tomatoes in purée
1 bay leaf
1 cup frozen peas, thawed
1½ lb *perciatelli, bucatini,* or *penne rigate*

*Accompaniment:* citrus salad with sweet fennel
   (page 233)

Heat 1 tablespoon oil in a wide 8- to 9-quart heavy pot over moderately high heat until hot but not smoking, then brown meatballs in batches, about 4 minutes, and transfer to a plate. Add 2 tablespoons oil to pot and brown *farsumagru* rolls in 2 batches, about 5 minutes, transferring to another plate. Brown sausages in pot, about 5 minutes, adding remaining tablespoon oil if necessary, and transfer to another plate.

Cook onions in fat remaining in pot over moderate heat until softened. Add garlic and cook, stirring, 2 minutes. Stir in wine, tomato paste, tomatoes in purée, and bay leaf. Put *farsumagru* in middle of pot with any juices that have collected on platter, then arrange meatballs and sausages, with any juices, around *farsumagru*. Simmer *ragù*, covered, until *farsumagru* is tender, about 1¼ hours. Add peas and simmer, covered, 5 minutes more.

Transfer *farsumagru*, meatballs, and sausages to a heated serving dish with tongs and a slotted spoon and keep warm, covered. Skim fat from sauce, if desired.

Cook pasta in a 6-quart pot of boiling salted water until al dente. Drain well and return to pot. Toss pasta with some sauce and salt and pepper to taste. Serve pasta as your first course.

Remove and discard kitchen string from *farsumagru*, then cut into ¼-inch-thick slices. Drizzle some sauce over *farsumagru*, meatballs, and sausages and serve as a main course with citrus salad.

Cooks' note:
· *Ragù* can be made (before adding peas and tossing with pasta) 1 day ahead. In this case, reduce simmering time from 1¼ hours to 50 minutes. Cool *ragù* completely before chilling, covered. To serve, simmer ragù 15 to 25 minutes, or until *farsumagru* is tender and heated through.

## POLPETTE DOLCI

### SWEET MEATBALLS

**Makes about 36**
Active time: 45 min   Start to finish: 45 min

¾ cup fresh bread crumbs (from Italian bread
   loaves with crusts removed)
¼ cup milk
½ cup whole blanched almonds, toasted
1½ teaspoons sugar
1 lb ground chuck
½ cup finely grated fresh pecorino or parmesan
¼ cup dried currants
¼ cup pine nuts, lightly toasted
2 teaspoons salt
¼ teaspoon cinnamon
1 large egg

Stir together bread crumbs and milk. Pulse almonds with sugar in a food processor until finely ground and add to bread crumb mixture with remaining ingredients, stirring with your hands until just combined. Roll mixture into 1-inch meatballs, transferring to a plate as formed.

Cooks' note:
· Meatballs may be made 1 day ahead and chilled, covered.

## FARSUMAGRU

### BRAISED MEAT ROLLS

*Serves 8 to 10*
Active time: 45 min   Start to finish: 45 min

¼ lb ground chuck
1 large egg
½ cup finely grated fresh *caciocavallo* cheese or
   pecorino
8 large hard-boiled eggs, peeled
1 (2¼-lb) flank steak (10- by 7- by 1-inch)
2 large garlic cloves, finely chopped
4 thin slices prosciutto
4 thin slices mortadella or other cooked ham
½ small red onion, cut into ¼-inch-thick slices
½ cup fresh flat-leaf parsley, finely chopped
2 teaspoons finely chopped fresh rosemary

*Special equipment:* a meat pounder and kitchen
   string cut into 8 (12-inch) lengths and
   2 (30-inch) lengths

Stir together ground chuck, egg, cheese, and pepper to taste. Trim ends from hard-boiled eggs to just expose egg yolks.

Arrange steak with a long side toward you, then halve horizontally (you will have two pieces, each about 10- by 7- by ½-inch). Pound steaks, cut sides up, with the flat side of meat pounder to about ¼-inch thick (be careful not to tear any holes in meat). Trim edges of meat if desired to create a more even piece for rolling.

Rub top of steaks with garlic and season with salt and pepper. Arrange 1 steak, pounded side up, with a long side toward you and top with 2 slices of prosciutto, leaving a 1-inch border on all sides. Top prosciutto with 2 slices of mortadella. Spread bottom half of mortadella with half of ground chuck mixture. Top ground chuck with 4 hard-boiled eggs, lined up end to end (so yolks will show when meat is sliced). Arrange half of onions just above eggs and sprinkle everything evenly with half of herbs. Season with salt and pepper.

Roll up meat tightly, beginning with edge in front of you and using your fingers to keep eggs in place, being careful not to squeeze out filling (ground beef and eggs will be in center of roll). Tie roll tightly crosswise, seam side down, (without squeezing out filling) with 4 (12-inch) lengths of kitchen string. Tie roll tightly lengthwise (do not make roll buckle) with 1 (30-inch) length of string, tucking open ends of meat under when tying, and trim any excess string. Repeat with remaining steak and filling ingredients.

## INSALATA DI ARANCE E FINOCCHIO

### CITRUS SALAD WITH SWEET FENNEL

*Serves 8 to 10*
Active time: 20 min   Start to finish: 40 min

5 juice oranges
1 large fennel bulb
2 tablespoons fresh lemon juice, or to taste
¼ cup extra-virgin olive oil

*Special equipment:* a *mandoline* or other manual
   slicer

Cut a slice from top and bottom of each orange to expose pulp and cut peel and pith from oranges, working from top to bottom. Cut oranges crosswise into ¼-inch-thick slices and transfer to a bowl with any juice.

Trim off fennel stalks flush with bulb and halve bulb lengthwise. Remove most of core from bulb by making an inverted "v" shape, leaving enough core to keep layers intact. Thinly slice bulb lengthwise with a *mandoline* or other manual slicer and toss with oranges, lemon juice, and salt and pepper to taste. Let salad stand, stirring occasionally, until fennel is slightly wilted, about 20 minutes. Drizzle with oil.

*Ruins of the Temple of Apollo in Siracusa*

## CANNOLI

*Makes about 30 cannoli (serving 8 to 10)*
Active time: 1¾ hr   Start to finish: 2¾ hr

*This recipe yields 15 chocolate shells and 15 plain shells. If you would prefer all chocolate or all plain shells, do not divide shell ingredients into 2 bowls. Simply use 1 bowl and omit cocoa powder for plain shells, or double amount of cocoa powder for chocolate shells.*

2 cups all-purpose flour
2 tablespoons sugar
½ teaspoon cinnamon
¼ teaspoon salt
⅛ teaspoon baking soda
2 teaspoons cocoa powder
1 lb lard
1 large egg, separated
8 to 10 tablespoons Marsala
4 cups vegetable oil
*Crema di Ricotta* (page 235)

*Garnish:* confectioners sugar for dusting
*Special equipment:* a 3½-inch round cookie cutter, a pasta machine, 6 metal (5- by 1-inch) cannoli tubes, and a pastry bag fitted with a ½-inch plain tip

Whisk together flour, sugar, cinnamon, salt, and baking soda. Divide mixture between 2 bowls and whisk cocoa powder into 1 bowl. Add 1 tablespoon lard to each bowl and blend in with your fingers until combined well. Stir half of egg yolk and 4 tablespoons wine into each bowl until dough just comes together. (If dough is too dry, add more wine, ½ tablespoon at a time.) Knead each dough separately on a lightly floured surface until smooth and elastic, 5 to 7 minutes. Form each dough into a disk and wrap well in plastic wrap. Let disks stand at room temperature 1 hour.

Unwrap and halve each piece of dough to make 4 pieces total. Rewrap 3 pieces of dough separately in plastic wrap and lightly flour remaining piece of dough. Set smooth rollers of pasta machine at widest setting. Flatten floured dough into a 3¼-inch disk and feed through rollers. Continue to feed dough through rollers, turning dial down 2 notches each time, ending with the narrowest setting. Transfer dough to a lightly floured surface and cut dough with floured cutter into about 7 circles. Keep circles covered with plastic wrap. Repeat with remaining dough.

Heat remaining lard with oil in a 4-quart heavy saucepan over moderate heat until it registers 350°F on a deep-fry thermometer.

While oil is heating, lightly beat egg white. Lightly oil *cannoli* tubes. Wrap a dough circle around each, brushing 1 edge of circle with egg white and overlapping other end (stretching slightly), pressing it to seal. Repeat with remaining tubes and rounds (keep remaining dough rounds covered with plastic wrap).

Fry dough on tubes, 2 at a time, turning with metal tongs to evenly brown until 1 shade darker, 20 to 30 seconds. Transfer, clamping ends of hot tubes with tongs, to paper towels to drain and immediately ease dough off tube with edge of a wooden spoon (if dough cools it will stick to tube and shatter when trying to remove). Stand tubes on paper towels to cool. Fry all dough circles in same manner.

Spoon some *cannoli* filling into pastry bag and fill 1 end of *cannoli* shell, then fill other end. Repeat with remaining shells and filling.

Cooks' notes:
- Dough may be made 1 day ahead and chilled, wrapped tightly in plastic wrap. Let dough stand at room temperature 1 hour before proceeding.
- Shells may be made 2 days ahead, cooled completely and kept in an airtight container, with paper towels between layers.
- Shells may be filled 4 hours ahead and chilled, loosely covered.

## CREMA DI RICOTTA

### RICOTTA CREAM

*Makes enough to fill about 30 cannoli*
Active time: 20 min    Start to finish: 20 min

*Using fresh ricotta in our cannoli made them far superior to any we had ever tasted. It's worth the effort of seeking out fresh ricotta before resorting to supermarket brands. The addition of fresh orange zest in the filling is strictly a Gourmet invention, not a Sicilian one—authentic cannoli have candied orange peel.*

2 lb fresh ricotta (sources on page 264)
¾ cup superfine sugar
6 oz fine-quality bittersweet chocolate (not unsweetened), finely chopped
1 teaspoon finely grated fresh orange zest
¼ teaspoon salt

Beat together fresh ricotta and sugar with an electric mixer until ricotta is smooth but still grainy (do not overbeat or ricotta will become too loose). Fold in chocolate, zest, and salt until combined well.

Cooks' note:
• Filling may be made 1 day ahead and chilled, covered.

# A SICILIAN SWEETS TABLE

*Serves 12*

SPONGATO DI NOCCIOLA
Frozen Hazelnut Bombe

GELO DI MELONE
Watermelon Pudding

GELATINA DI PERA
Pear Gelatin

CASSATA ALLA SICILIANA
Sicilian Layered Cake

BISCOTTI DI FICO
Fig Cookies

Moscato di Pantelleria, Pellegrino, 1998

Opposite, Frozen Hazelnut Bombe; above, Pear Gelatin

In the true spirit of Sicily's national craving for sweets, we offer an entire dessert menu. We quickly note, however, that any one of these heavenly creations would make an ideal treat for the holidays or for a dinner party. The *spongato di nocciola*—a frozen delight of layered hazelnut gelato, sponge cake, and chunks of the finest bittersweet chocolate enclosed in a cream frosting—is a true showstopper. While it's admittedly time-consuming to prepare, it's well worth the effort (and it can be made a week ahead). And, of course, there is *cassata alla siciliana*—a ricotta-filled layer cake sweetened with Marsala, encased in marzipan, and covered in icing. (Although candied citron is the traditional garnish, a good-quality product is difficult to come by outside of Sicily. In our version, we opt for candied orange peel instead.) On a more casual note, we include *gelo di melone*—a watermelon pudding with dense, smooth texture and a sweet, yet refreshing, flavor. Should you happen to have jasmine blossoms handy, use a few in place of the pistachio and chocolate topping to lend an authentic Sicilian touch. Gelatins are a must, and while lemon, orange, and tangerine are more common, our pear variation is a lovely surprise. Ever-popular fig cookies round out the mix.

## SPONGATO DI NOCCIOLA

### FROZEN HAZELNUT BOMBE

**Serves 12**
Active time: 3½ hr   Start to finish: 8 hr

*For cake layers*
3 large eggs, separated, plus 3 extra yolks
1 cup plus 2 tablespoons sugar
3 tablespoons milk
1 teaspoon vanilla
½ teaspoon salt
¾ cup all-purpose flour
*For hazelnut gelato*
2 cups hazelnuts (8 oz)
5 cups milk
¼ cup cornstarch
1½ cups sugar
½ teaspoon salt
½ vanilla bean, split
*For syrup*
¼ cup water
¼ cup sugar
2 tablespoons hazelnut liqueur such as Frangelico

2 oz semisweet or bittersweet chocolate (not unsweetened), finely chopped
*For frosting*
1 tablespoon plus 1 teaspoon powdered egg whites
2 tablespoons warm water
½ cup sugar
1 cup heavy cream
½ teaspoon vanilla

*Garnish:* semisweet or bittersweet chocolate shavings
*Special equipment:* an 8-cup metal brioche mold or metal bowl

*Make cake layers:*
Preheat oven to 350°F. Butter 2 (9-inch) round cake pans and line bottoms with wax paper. Butter wax paper.

Beat 6 yolks, ½ cup plus 2 tablespoons sugar, milk, vanilla, and salt in a large bowl with an electric mixer until well combined. Beat whites in a separate bowl with clean beaters until foamy, then gradually add remaining ½ cup sugar and continue beating until thick and glossy. Sift flour over yolk mixture in 3 batches and gently fold

in until each addition is just combined. Fold in half of whites to lighten mixture, then fold in remaining whites. Pour batter into cake pans, smoothing tops.

Bake in middle of oven until a tester inserted in centers comes out clean and tops of cakes spring back when touched lightly, about 20 minutes. Cool in pans on a rack 10 minutes, then turn out onto rack and cool completely.

*Make gelato:*
While cake layers cool, toast hazelnuts in a baking pan in oven until golden and skins are blistered, 10 to 12 minutes. Wrap nuts in a kitchen towel and let steam 5 minutes. Rub nuts in towel to remove most of skins. Cool completely and finely grind in a food processor.

Whisk together 1 cup milk and cornstarch in a small bowl. Combine remaining 4 cups milk, sugar, and salt in a large saucepan. Scrape seeds from vanilla bean with tip of a knife and add to milk and sugar mixture with pod. Bring to a boil, whisking, then whisk in milk and cornstarch mixture. Reduce heat and simmer, whisking, until mixture is thickened, 2 to 3 minutes. Stir in ground hazelnuts and cool mixture to room temperature. Chill, covered, at least 6 hours and up to 8.

Just before assembling bombe, remove vanilla pod from hazelnut mixture and freeze mixture in an ice-cream maker.

*Prepare syrup:*
Simmer water and sugar in a small saucepan over moderate heat, stirring until sugar is dissolved. Stir in liqueur and remove from heat.

*Assemble bombe:*
Line brioche mold with long sheets of plastic wrap, allowing excess to hang over edge (you will use plastic wrap to cover bombe and unmold it). Chill mold in freezer until cold, about 5 minutes.

Spoon one third of gelato into mold, smoothing top, and sprinkle with half of chocolate. Top gelato and chocolate with 1 cake layer, trimmed to fit in mold. Brush half of syrup over cake layer. Spoon remaining gelato into mold, smoothing top, and sprinkle with remaining chocolate. Top with remaining cake layer (do not trim), and brush cake with remaining syrup. Wrap bombe well in the overhanging plastic wrap and freeze overnight (8 hours).

*Make frosting:*
Beat together powdered egg whites and warm water with electric mixer until frothy. Gradually add ¼ cup sugar and beat until mixture is fluffy and glossy. Put mixture in freezer while beating cream.

Beat cream, remaining ¼ cup sugar, and vanilla in another bowl with clean beaters just until stiff peaks form. Fold whipped cream into egg-white mixture and put in freezer while unmolding bombe.

*Unmold and frost bombe:*

Soak a kitchen towel with hot water, wringing out excess, and wrap towel around mold. Invert bombe onto a platter, gently pulling on plastic wrap to help loosen. Frost bombe using a rubber spatula and garnish with chocolate shavings.

Cooks' notes:
• Cake layers can be made 1 day ahead, wrapped separately in plastic wrap, and kept at room temperature.
• Unmolded frozen bombe (do not frost) may be made 1 week ahead and kept frozen, covered with plastic wrap.

## GELATINA DI PERA

### PEAR GELATIN

***Serves 6***
Active time: 1¼ hr   Start to finish: 12 hr

*For gelatin*
5 large ripe pears (2 lb)
4⅓ cups water
¾ cup sugar
2 tablespoons fresh lemon juice
2 envelopes unflavored gelatin (about
    2 tablespoons)
*For pear topping*
2 large ripe pears, peeled, cored, and sliced
2 tablespoons sugar
1 tablespoon pear brandy or *grappa*

*Special equipment:* a decorative 6-cup ring mold
*Garnish:* fresh mint sprigs

*Prepare gelatin:*

Trim stem ends of pears (do not peel or core). Quarter pears lengthwise and halve pieces crosswise. Bring pears, 4 cups water, sugar, and lemon juice to a boil in a large saucepan, then reduce heat and simmer until pears are tender, 25 to 30 minutes. Drain well, reserving cooking liquid. Force pears through a food mill fitted with medium disk into a large bowl. Drain purée in a sieve lined with several layers of cheesecloth set over a bowl until you have about 2⅓ cups pear juice, 2 to 3 hours.

Sprinkle gelatin over remaining ⅓ cup water in a small bowl and let stand 5 minutes. Strain pear cooking liquid through a sieve into a large saucepan and boil until reduced to 2 cups, 20 to 25 minutes. Add softened gelatin, stirring until dissolved, then stir in pear juice. Pour into mold and chill overnight (8 hours), covered.

*Make pear topping:*

Just before serving, toss together sliced pears, sugar, and brandy.

Unmold gelatin onto a platter and spoon filling into inside ring.

## CASSATA ALLA SICILIANA

### SICILIAN LAYERED CAKE

**Serves 12**
Active time: 2 hr   Start to finish: 2 days

*For cake*
4 large eggs, separated
⅔ cup granulated sugar
1 teaspoon vanilla
½ teaspoon salt
¾ cup plus 2 tablespoons all-purpose flour
*For syrup*
½ cup granulated sugar
½ cup water
¼ cup Marsala
*For filling*
2 lb fresh ricotta or well-drained packaged ricotta
1 cup superfine sugar
1 teaspoon vanilla
4 oz bittersweet chocolate (not unsweetened),
    finely chopped
*For marzipan*
1 (7-oz) tube almond paste, paste cut in
    ½-inch pieces
¾ cup confectioners sugar
2 tablespoons light corn syrup
Cornstarch for dusting
*For frosting*
4 teaspoons powdered egg whites
2 tablespoons warm water
1½ cups confectioners sugar
1 teaspoon fresh lemon juice

*Garnish:* candied fruit

*Make cake:*
Preheat oven to 350°F. Butter a 9-inch springform pan, then line bottom with a round of wax paper and butter paper.

Beat together yolks and ⅓ cup granulated sugar with an electric mixer until thick and pale, then beat in vanilla. Beat whites with salt in a separate bowl with clean beaters until foamy. Gradually add remaining ⅓ cup granulated sugar and beat until glossy and stiff. Fold whites into yolk mixture in 3 batches, then fold in flour until just combined. Pour batter into pan, smoothing top.

Bake cake in middle of oven until a tester comes out clean, about 40 minutes. Cool cake 10 minutes, then remove from pan and cool completely on a rack.

*Make syrup:*
Bring granulated sugar and water to a boil in a small saucepan. Remove from heat and stir in Marsala. Cool.

*Make filling:*
Stir together all filling ingredients in a large bowl.

*Assemble cake:*
Cut cake horizontally into thirds with a large serrated knife. Line cleaned springform pan with plastic wrap, allowing excess to hang over sides. Invert top cake layer into pan. Brush layer with one third of syrup, then top with half of filling, smoothing top with a spatula. Invert middle cake layer onto filling. Brush layer with one third of syrup, then top with remaining filling, smoothing. Invert last cake layer onto filling and brush with remaining syrup. Wrap cake in overhanging plastic and chill overnight (8 hours).

*Make marzipan coating:*
Process almond paste, confectioners sugar, and corn syrup in a food processor until mixture forms a ball. Remove from processor and knead into a smooth ball.

Unmold *cassata* onto a platter. Dust a work surface with cornstarch. Roll marzipan out into a 14-inch round, dusting with cornstarch as needed to prevent sticking. Gently roll marzipan around rolling pin, then unroll it over top of cake, allowing excess to drape down sides. Smooth top with your hand and gently press marzipan onto sides, easing it into place to prevent tearing and pleating. Cut off excess marzipan at base of cake.

*Make frosting:*
Beat together powdered egg whites and water with an electric mixer at medium speed until frothy. Add confectioners sugar and lemon juice and beat at high speed until mixture becomes very thick and fluffy.

Spread frosting over marzipan layer before garnishing and serving.

Cooks' notes:
- Cake can be baked 2 days ahead and kept, wrapped in plastic wrap, at room temperature.
- Frosted *cassata* can be made 1 day ahead and kept chilled. Decorate with fruit just before serving.

Opposite, clockwise from upper left: Pear Gelatin; Fig Cookies; Sicilian Layered Cake; Watermelon Pudding

## BISCOTTI DI FICO

### FIG COOKIES

***Makes about 36 cookies***
Active time: 1 hr   Start to finish: 1½ hr

*This is an adaptation of Carol Field's fig cookie recipe in* The Italian Baker.

*For dough:*
1¾ sticks (¾ cup plus 2 tablespoons) unsalted
   butter, softened
½ cup granulated sugar
½ teaspoon salt
1 large whole egg
1 large egg yolk
1 teaspoon vanilla
2¼ cups all-purpose flour
*For filling:*
½ cup walnuts, toasted and cooled
½ cup blanched almonds, toasted and cooled
3 oz dried Calimyrna figs, trimmed
3 tablespoons dry red wine
2 tablespoons honey
½ teaspoon unsweetened cocoa powder
1 teaspoon finely grated fresh orange zest

1 cup confectioners sugar

*Make dough:*
Beat butter in a large bowl with an electric mixer until smooth, then beat in granulated sugar, salt, whole egg, yolk, and vanilla. Add flour and beat at low speed until incorporated. Divide dough in thirds and form each into a disk. Wrap each disk in plastic wrap and chill until firm, about 1 hour.

*Make filling while dough chills:*
Finely chop nuts in a food processor and transfer to a saucepan. Finely chop figs in food processor and add to nuts with wine, honey, cocoa, and zest. Cook mixture, stirring, over moderately low heat until thickened, about 8 minutes. Remove from heat and let cool.

Preheat oven to 350°F.

Unwrap 1 disk of dough, keeping remaining dough chilled, and cut into 12 wedges. Working with 1 wedge at a time, roll wedge into a ball and flatten into a 2-inch round. Put 1 teaspoon of cooled filling on top of round. Pull edges up over filling to enclose, pressing to seal, then reroll into a ball. Repeat with remaining wedges.

Transfer cookies to ungreased baking sheet, about 2 inches apart.

Bake in batches until lightly golden, about 25 minutes. Put confectioners sugar in a shallow bowl, then roll warm cookies in sugar. Cool completely on a rack, then reroll in sugar.

Cooks' notes:
· Cookie dough can be made 1 day ahead and chilled, covered.
· Cookies keep in a cookie tin at room temperature 1 week.

## GELO DI MELONE

### WATERMELON PUDDING

***Serves 6***
Active time: 30 min   Start to finish: 3 hr

*For pudding*
1 (5-lb) piece watermelon, rind discarded and flesh
   cut into 1-inch pieces
1 cup granulated sugar
½ cup cornstarch
*For topping*
½ cup heavy cream
2 tablespoons confectioners sugar
½ teaspoon vanilla
¼ teaspoon cinnamon

*Garnish:* chopped pistachio nuts, toasted and
   cooled, and semisweet chocolate shavings

*Make pudding:*
Force watermelon through a food mill fitted with a medium disk into a large bowl (you'll have about 4 cups juice). Transfer juice to a saucepan and bring to a boil with granulated sugar and cornstarch, whisking. Reduce heat and simmer, whisking, until thick, 2 to 3 minutes. Remove from heat and cool 10 minutes, stirring occasionally. Divide pudding among 6 parfait glasses or ramekins and chill until set, about 3 hours.

*Make topping:*
Beat cream with confectioners sugar, vanilla, and cinnamon with an electric mixer until stiff peaks form.

Serve puddings with a dollop of cream.

*Maria Grammatico with her nieces and brother
carrying pastries in Erice, Sicily*

# BASIC INGREDIENTS

The cuisine of Sicily is best described as an amalgam of food and techniques introduced by a host of invaders and the simple, straightforward ingredients and cooking methods of *la cucina povera,* the diet of the poor. Sicilians manage to combine these elements in inventive ways, lending their cooking a subtle sophistication that is evident in the perfect sweet/sour balance of *caponata*, for example, or the multi-layered richness of *pasta con le sarde* (pasta with sardines). Most of what gives the food its character, so distinct from that of mainland Italian cooking, comes from the surrounding sea, abundant with some of the world's most coveted fish, as well as the fruit and olive trees, wheat fields, and vegetable gardens that dot its landscape. Fish serves as the centerpiece of most meals, often plainly prepared and adorned only with olive oil and herbs. The island's relentless sunshine gives its fruits and vegetables intense flavor unlike any others. Robust tomatoes, in particular, mark many classic dishes as Sicilian. Vegetable dishes are commonly derived from ancient recipes using capers, olives, and herbs. Fruits are formed into spectacular desserts or simply enjoyed in their natural splendor. And, of course, wonderful pastas and hearty breads prevail.

Whatever the time of year, visitors to Palermo's bustling markets are bombarded with the freshest foods available, including—depending on the season—fish (some with their swords still attached); succulent figs; glorious eggplants; sweet-smelling basil; plump, perfectly spiced olives; fresh lamb and goats; scarcely-picked wild fennel; fragrant lemons and blood oranges; and much, much more. Below is a brief description of the most prominent ingredients of the Sicilian diet. Most are readily available in American supermarkets; for the more unusual items a quick Internet search of on-line purveyors of Italian foods will yield a surprisingly wide variety of choices.

**Olive oil** is at the heart of the cuisine. Sicilian olive oil is strongly flavored and best appreciated in small doses, usually drizzled over bread, fish, or vegetables. Many families have olive trees and press their own oil at harvest time or bring their olives to a collective press. Sicilian extra-virgin olive oil is among the world's most prized. It is available in the United States for a considerable price from some specialty foods stores and on-line Italian grocers. **Olives** come in a wide range of green and black hues. In Sicily, no dinner table would be complete without a bowl of olives. For our Palermo dinner, we offer a bowl of large green olives as part of an antipasto and sliced green olives also appear in the caponata. Black olives are frequently added to salads with citrus and fennel.

**Wheat** is plentiful and **bread** baking is another vital part of the culture. Elaborately crafted breads, decorated with flowers, leaves, birds, and angels and other religious icons, are offered up to St. Joseph on his feast day. Often **bread crumbs,** either purchased or prepared at home, replace more costly cheese in pasta dishes and are used to stretch meat, another relatively expensive ingredient. The cultivation of hard-durum wheat also accounts for superior **pasta.** Traditional pasta shapes are eaten, but they are more likely to appear in baked dishes than they would on the mainland. *Perciatelli,* a thicker, hollow version of spaghetti, is a favorite, so we paired it with our pork *ragù*; spaghetti is used for our *pasta alla Norma.* **Cuscus,** a version of North African couscous, is made by combining two different grades of ground semolina with dampened fingers, then rolling the grains together into tiny, even clusters. In Sicily it is served with fish stew rather than lamb and seasoned with bay leaves instead of red pepper.

## SEAFOOD

**Swordfish** appears on nearly every menu in coastal cities and towns. Usually it is simply grilled, drizzled with olive oil, and seasoned with salt. In Messina, however, swordfish is simmered in a spicy tomato sauce with onions, olives, and capers. Involtini of swordfish, thin fillets wrapped around various fillings (including herbs, bread crumbs, capers, pine nuts, olives, and/or cheese), are also popular. **Tuna** has its own special place in the cuisine. Each spring since the Arab occupation, fishermen have participated in a ritual tuna killing (the *mattanza*), using elaborate, multi-chambered nets to trap the fish before harpooning them. Usually, tuna is braised, grilled, or pan-fried and served with an uncooked sauce. Bottarga (dried tuna roe) shaved over pasta is another specialty. **Sardines,** once among the most plentiful fish, have dwindled considerably as a result of overfishing in recent years. Nevertheless, they remain strongly identified with the cuisine, most notably in *pasta con le sarde,* the national dish that highlights Arab ingredients (pine nuts, currants, and saffron) as well as wild fennel greens. **Squid** and **octopus** make for very popular street food. Octopus, known as *purpu* in the Sicilian dialect, is often boiled to a dark pink color. Both squid and octopus are also served grilled or fried. **Anchovies** are frequently crushed and dissolved in oil as the foundation for many pasta sauces, with or without tomato. They are commonly used as a topping for pizza and pizzette.

## CHEESE

**Caciocavallo,** the principal cow's milk cheese of modern Sicily, is molded into large bricks with smooth yellow rinds. Fresh *caciocavallo* tastes a bit stronger and saltier than provolone, although the flavor is similar. Aged *caciocavallo* is grated and served with pasta as parmesan is used on the Italian mainland. *Caciocavallo* can be found in cheese shops and Italian markets in the United States; parmesan may be substituted. **Ricotta** is not technically cheese but rather a by-product of cheesemaking, made from sheep's milk whey that is "recooked" (hence its name, meaning just that). Although the ricotta-making process was invented in Sicily, ricotta is now made throughout Italy and abroad. We highly recommend seeking out fresh ricotta, especially for our cannoli and *cassata siciliana,* as supermarket ricottas can't compare with the sweet, light

# SICILIAN SWEETS

Everyone in Sicily loves sweets, and one glance in a *pasticceria* window confirms that the joy of preparing them is very much alive on this enchanting island. For hundreds of years, pastry making was perfected by Sicily's nuns from their cloistered convents. In fact, until very recently, the best place to buy a variety of sweets was the local convent itself. Customers would line up in a special room to place their order—by way of a revolving tray—to the nuns behind the wall. Moments later the tray would return, laden with boxes of scrumptious treats. Sadly, with an aging religious community and few newcomers, this tradition is now nearly extinct. As the last of the Sicilian convents close, valuable trade secrets may be lost forever.

Ironically (considering that pastry making eventually became the livelihood of so many Christian convents), it was the Arabs who helped bring desserts to the Sicilian table. After their conquest in the ninth century, they taught Sicilians to grow sugarcane and introduced them to comfits—sugarcoated seeds, fruit, and spices—as well as almond paste and fruit preserves, all collectively considered after-dinner refreshments. To this day, Sicilians covet fruit conserves, candied rose petals, marzipan, and candied citrus peel. Similarly, many of the desserts we have come to identify as Sicilian classics are actually Arabic in origin, most notably the layered cake, *cassata,* whose name comes from the word *qas' ah,* Arabic for bowl, and *gelo di melone,* a watermelon pudding flavored with cinnamon and jasmine water and topped with pistachios (both appear in our dessert menu on page 237).

It is not clear how pastry making in the convents became such a prominent pastime, then business, but theories abound. Food historian and cookbook author Mary Taylor Simeti explains that "it offered women of very restricted lives a rare outlet for creativity." Most of the pastries were made for the outside world, so their preparation was often a way for the cloistered sisters to illustrate their devotion and piety. In any event, 18th-century convent pastries became something of an obsession. Elaborate banquets of sweets and iced desserts were prepared when a girl took her final vows. At one point, the king tried to abolish these extravagantly excessive festivities, but to no avail. The nuns continued to make pastries and desserts to give to patrons as well as to their families and friends during their frequent visits and at holidays. In fact, many were so busy preparing *cassata* and other pastries for Easter, they sometimes missed Holy Week church services altogether.

Nuns within the same convent worked hard to compete with each other, and similarly, convents competed to see who could produce the most beautiful pastries. Some confections actually carry the names of particular convents. The most well-known example is marzipan fruit, known in Palermo as *frutta di Martorana* after the Monastery of the Martorana, the now defunct convent where it was believed to have been invented. These stunning delights are made from a paste of blanched almonds, sugar, and water, which is shaped by hand or with small plaster molds into fruits, dried, then painted with food coloring. Legend has it that the convent's Mother Superior decided to surprise the visiting archbishop by hanging marzipan fruit from all the trees in the cloister garden. The archbishop marveled at the garden, especially since it was Easter and the trees appeared unseasonably fruitful. Only after he took a bite from a piece of fruit did Mother Superior reveal her cunning secret.

After Garibaldi's expedition and Sicily's union with Italy in 1860, church property was confiscated and many of the religious orders were closed. The ones that remained open were largely impoverished, and pastry making was reserved for major holidays. This is, more than likely, when the nuns started to make pastries available for purchase.

Today, commercial pastry shops carry on the convent tradition of making *frutta di Martorana* (also known as *pasta reale* outside Palermo), especially in preparation for All Souls' Day, when children who have prayed for the souls of the dead are rewarded with these wonderful treats. Although fruit is the most common and traditional form of marzipan, the confection is also shaped to resemble vegetables, seashells, animals, flowers, fish, and other foodstuffs as varied as fried eggs or salami. Lambs are the specialty of Easter, each one adorned with bunches of tiny, curly, white marzipan strips designed to look like fleece. *Pasticcerie* continue to produce other convent specialties, too, although a number of pastries have become extinct, especially those that prove too labor-intensive to sell profitably. Notable exceptions, however, can still be found in a *pasticceria* in Erice owned by Maria Grammatico, a woman raised for several years in a cloistered convent. She continues to sell pastries exactly like the ones she learned to make as a girl. (*Bitter Almonds,* a book written by Mary Taylor Simeti, beautifully recounts Maria's convent story in her own words.) The question remains, however, whether anyone will carry on the traditional methods of pastry making after she and possibly others like her retire.

# COMFORT FOOD

• • •

If you have the good fortune to spend time with great cooks and to listen to them talk about food, you soon realize that their culinary know-how doesn't come from the classroom alone. Many times a day *Gourmet*'s food editors gather-round to taste each other's dishes and to offer helpful advice. Comments like, "My grandmother always added a pinch of sugar to cut the acidity; maybe you should add a pinch to this sauce," and "My mother gets a velvety-smooth soup with her food mill; I'd try it here for that ultra texture" are not rare. And slowly it dawned on us (impressionable book editors) that these exceptional cooks—the progeny of all this remarkable input—must make the most fabulous comfort foods imaginable. And we were right. Below are 24 recipes for comfort food favorites from two *Gourmet* food editors, Shelley Wiseman and Ruth Cousineau. As you might expect, you'll find classics that they've enjoyed (and perfected) since childhood. (Nana, Baba, and the like appear in a few titles that probably are direct hand-me-downs). But, being *Gourmet* food editors, they reveal some surprises, too—ethnic dishes that mirror their heritages and travels as well as recipes borrowed (and embellished) from friends. When it comes to food for the soul, it just doesn't get any better than this.

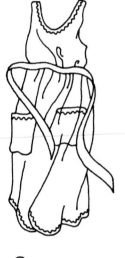

### BRAISED LAMB SHANKS

**Serves 4**
Active time: 30 min   Start to finish: 2½ hr

*Slow-cooked lamb, succulent and savory, is true comfort food. I like to serve this Provençal-inspired braise over polenta.* —Ruth Cousineau

4 lamb shanks (2½ to 3 lb total)
1 tablespoon olive oil
1 large onion, thinly sliced
2 garlic cloves, minced
1 bay leaf
1 teaspoon fennel seeds, crushed with a
    rolling pin
1 teaspoon dried marjoram, crumbled
1 (4- by 1-inch) strip orange zest
1 cup dry white wine
1 (14-oz) can whole plum tomatoes with
    juices, coarsely chopped
1½ tablespoons chopped fresh parsley

Pat shanks dry. Season with salt and pepper.

Heat oil in a heavy 5- to 6-quart pot or a deep heavy 12-inch skillet over moderate heat until hot but not smoking, then brown shanks on all sides, 8 to 10 minutes. Stir in onion, garlic, bay leaf, fennel seeds, marjoram, and zest. Add wine and tomatoes with juice and bring to a boil. Simmer, covered, turning meat halfway through cooking, until shanks are very tender, about 2 hours total.

Transfer shanks to a serving platter and loosely cover with foil. Skim fat from sauce and, if desired, boil sauce over high heat until reduced by about half. Season with salt and pepper and pour over shanks. Sprinkle with parsley.

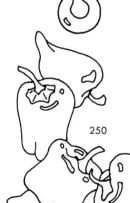

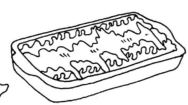

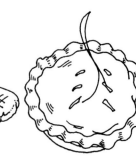

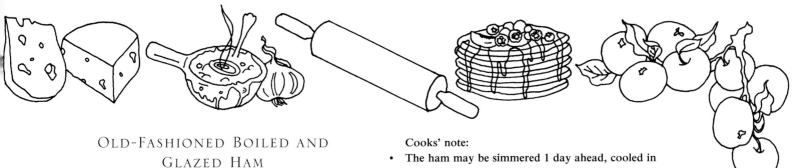

## OLD-FASHIONED BOILED AND GLAZED HAM

**Serves 12**
Active time: 30 min   Start to finish: 7 hr

*Even though most country hams come fully cooked, my grandmother, Eve Norton, always simmered hers in water before glazing for a moist ham with mellow saltiness, as well as a hearty ham "liquor" (as the simmering liquid is sometimes called). This liquor was the basis of much of her cooking.*
*—Shelley Wiseman*

1 (8-lb) bone-in cooked half country ham
¾ cup packed light brown sugar
¼ cup Dijon mustard
¼ cup coarse-grained mustard
1 tablespoon dry mustard
2 tablespoons apricot preserves

*Special equipment:* 1 (12-quart) stock pot

Put ham in pot and add cold water to cover. Bring to a simmer and cook at a bare simmer, covered, until ham reaches desired saltiness, 2 to 3 hours. (Taste after 2 hours.)

Cool ham in liquid, uncovered, 1 to 2 hours. Preheat oven to 350°F.

Drain ham, reserving liquid, and put, cut side down, in a roasting pan just large enough to hold it. Trim off skin and excess fat. Whisk together remaining ingredients and spread glaze over ham (reserve any extra glaze for basting).

Bake ham in middle of oven, basting with reserved glaze halfway through baking, until glaze is bubbling and caramelized and ham is warmed through, 40 to 50 minutes total. Transfer to a cutting board and add 1 cup reserved cooking liquid to roasting pan. Deglaze pan by boiling over moderately high heat, stirring and scraping up brown bits, until slightly thickened, 3 to 5 minutes.

Serve ham with sauce.

**Cooks' note:**
• The ham may be simmered 1 day ahead, cooled in its liquid, uncovered, then chilled, covered.

## RED-COOKED BEEF SHORT RIBS WITH RICE NOODLES

**Serves 6**
Active time: 30 min   Start to finish: 3 hr

*Braised short ribs from any culture provide stick-to-your-ribs comfort. Here is a Chinese version guaranteed to fortify you.   —Shelley Wiseman*

4 lb beef short ribs, cut into large pieces between bones
4 cups water
⅔ cup soy sauce
⅓ cup medium-dry Sherry
¼ cup sugar
1 (1-inch) piece peeled fresh ginger, cut into 4 slices and smashed
2 large garlic cloves, smashed
2 large scallions (white and pale green parts only), smashed
4 whole star anise
2 teaspoons Asian chile paste with garlic
1 lb (¼-inch-wide) flat rice noodles or flat bean thread noodles
¼ cup coarsely chopped fresh cilantro

Bring beef, water, soy sauce, Sherry, sugar, ginger, garlic, scallions, and star anise to a simmer in a 5-quart heavy pot and skim foam from surface. Simmer, partially covered, until beef is tender, 2 to 2½ hours. Remove ginger, garlic, scallions, and star anise and spoon off any fat from surface. Stir in chile paste.

Cook rice noodles in a large pot of boiling water until just tender, about 4 minutes, then drain and rinse briefly under cold running water.

Serve beef and broth over noodles and sprinkle with cilantro.

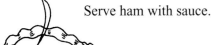

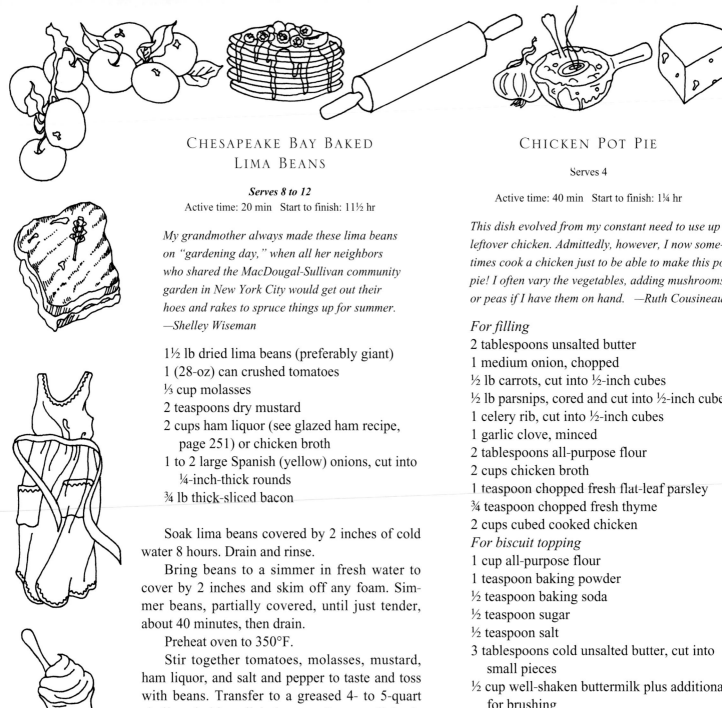

## CHESAPEAKE BAY BAKED LIMA BEANS

**_Serves 8 to 12_**
Active time: 20 min   Start to finish: 11½ hr

_My grandmother always made these lima beans on "gardening day," when all her neighbors who shared the MacDougal-Sullivan community garden in New York City would get out their hoes and rakes to spruce things up for summer._
_—Shelley Wiseman_

1½ lb dried lima beans (preferably giant)
1 (28-oz) can crushed tomatoes
⅓ cup molasses
2 teaspoons dry mustard
2 cups ham liquor (see glazed ham recipe, page 251) or chicken broth
1 to 2 large Spanish (yellow) onions, cut into ¼-inch-thick rounds
¾ lb thick-sliced bacon

Soak lima beans covered by 2 inches of cold water 8 hours. Drain and rinse.

Bring beans to a simmer in fresh water to cover by 2 inches and skim off any foam. Simmer beans, partially covered, until just tender, about 40 minutes, then drain.

Preheat oven to 350°F.

Stir together tomatoes, molasses, mustard, ham liquor, and salt and pepper to taste and toss with beans. Transfer to a greased 4- to 5-quart shallow baking dish (or two 2-quart dishes). Cover bean mixture completely with a layer of onion rounds and top onions with a layer of bacon. Press down on top of mixture with a spatula to moisten onions.

Bake in middle of oven until beans have soaked up half of liquid (there should be 1 inch of liquid remaining) and bacon strips are browned well, about 2½ hours. Pat top with paper towels to absorb excess fat.

## CHICKEN POT PIE

Serves 4

Active time: 40 min   Start to finish: 1¼ hr

_This dish evolved from my constant need to use up leftover chicken. Admittedly, however, I now sometimes cook a chicken just to be able to make this pot pie! I often vary the vegetables, adding mushrooms or peas if I have them on hand._   _—Ruth Cousineau_

_For filling_
2 tablespoons unsalted butter
1 medium onion, chopped
½ lb carrots, cut into ½-inch cubes
½ lb parsnips, cored and cut into ½-inch cubes
1 celery rib, cut into ½-inch cubes
1 garlic clove, minced
2 tablespoons all-purpose flour
2 cups chicken broth
1 teaspoon chopped fresh flat-leaf parsley
¾ teaspoon chopped fresh thyme
2 cups cubed cooked chicken
_For biscuit topping_
1 cup all-purpose flour
1 teaspoon baking powder
½ teaspoon baking soda
½ teaspoon sugar
½ teaspoon salt
3 tablespoons cold unsalted butter, cut into small pieces
½ cup well-shaken buttermilk plus additional for brushing

Preheat oven to 400°F.
_Make filling:_

Heat butter in a large skillet over moderate heat until foam subsides and cook onion, carrots, parsnips, celery, and garlic, stirring frequently, until they begin to soften, 8 to 10 minutes. Stir in flour and cook, stirring, 1 minute. Add chicken broth and herbs and simmer, stirring frequently,

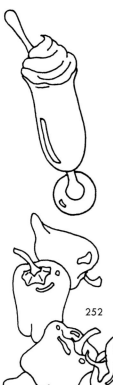

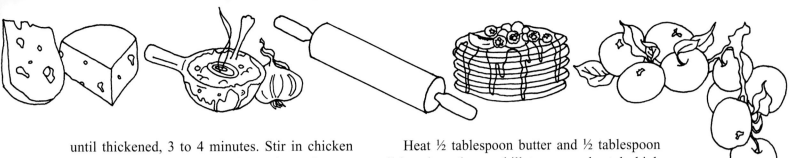

until thickened, 3 to 4 minutes. Stir in chicken and salt and pepper to taste. Spoon into a 2-quart shallow baking dish.

*Make topping:*

Sift together flour, baking powder, baking soda, sugar, and salt. Blend in butter with a pastry blender or your fingertips until mixture resembles coarse meal. Add buttermilk, stirring with a fork until just combined. Drop topping onto filling in large spoonfuls, leaving spaces to allow topping to expand, and brush with additional buttermilk.

Bake pot pie in middle of oven until topping is golden brown and filling is bubbling, about 30 minutes.

## MARY'S CHICKEN AND CREAM

**Serves 4 to 6**
Active time: 30 min   Start to finish: 1½ hr

*My husband remembers sopping up the juices of this dish with warm bread baked by his mother (Mary Cousineau). Clabbering her own cream and using chicken raised on their own farm made the meal even more memorable.  —Ruth Cousineau*

1 (3½-lb) chicken
1 tablespoon unsalted butter
1 tablespoon vegetable oil
1 large onion, slivered
2 garlic cloves, minced
1 cup crème fraîche mixed with 1 cup water
1 tablespoon sweet or hot Hungarian paprika

Preheat oven to 350°F.

Cut off wing tips and remove backbone from chicken. Halve chicken through breast bone, then cut off legs and separate thighs and drumsticks. Halve breasts crosswise through bones, leaving wings attached. Pat chicken dry and season with salt and pepper.

Heat ½ tablespoon butter and ½ tablespoon oil in a large heavy skillet over moderately high heat until foam subsides, then brown chicken on all sides. Transfer to a 3-quart shallow glass or ceramic baking dish.

Add remaining ½ tablespoon butter and ½ tablespoon oil to fat remaining in skillet. Cook onion and garlic, stirring occasionally, over moderate heat until softened. Stir in crème fraîche mixture, paprika, and salt and pepper to taste and bring to a simmer.

Spoon mixture over chicken and bake, uncovered, until cooked through, about 1 hour.

## TUNA MELT

**Serves 2**
Active time: 15 min   Start to finish: 15 min

*When I was a child we walked home from school every day for lunch. These open-faced sandwiches, paired with a bowl of cream of tomato soup (page 258), were my all-time favorite.  —Ruth Cousineau*

1 (6-oz) can light tuna in olive oil, drained
¼ cup finely chopped onion
1 tablespoon finely chopped fresh dill
3 tablespoons mayonnaise
4 slices rye bread, lightly toasted
4 slices Swiss cheese

*Accompaniment:* dill pickles

Preheat broiler.

Stir together tuna, onion, dill, mayonnaise, and salt and pepper to taste and spread on toasts. Top tuna with cheese and transfer to a baking sheet. Broil 5 to 6 inches from heat until cheese is melted, 1 to 2 minutes. Serve immediately.

253

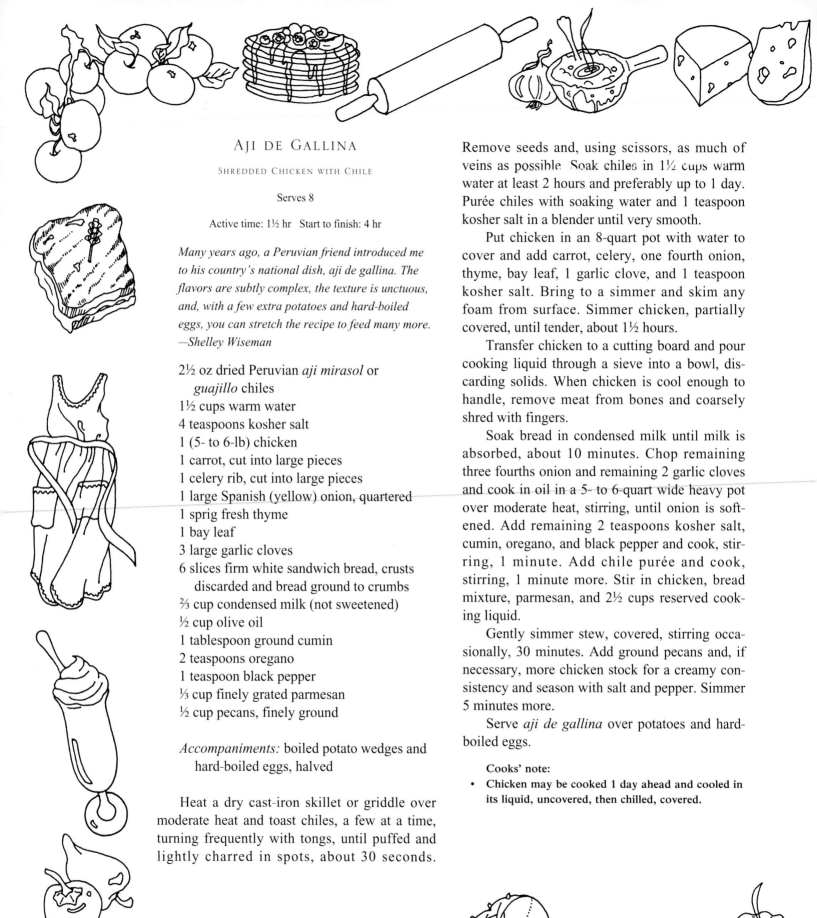

# AJI DE GALLINA

## SHREDDED CHICKEN WITH CHILE

Serves 8

Active time: 1½ hr   Start to finish: 4 hr

*Many years ago, a Peruvian friend introduced me to his country's national dish, aji de gallina. The flavors are subtly complex, the texture is unctuous, and, with a few extra potatoes and hard-boiled eggs, you can stretch the recipe to feed many more.*
*—Shelley Wiseman*

2½ oz dried Peruvian *aji mirasol* or
   *guajillo* chiles
1½ cups warm water
4 teaspoons kosher salt
1 (5- to 6-lb) chicken
1 carrot, cut into large pieces
1 celery rib, cut into large pieces
1 large Spanish (yellow) onion, quartered
1 sprig fresh thyme
1 bay leaf
3 large garlic cloves
6 slices firm white sandwich bread, crusts
   discarded and bread ground to crumbs
⅔ cup condensed milk (not sweetened)
½ cup olive oil
1 tablespoon ground cumin
2 teaspoons oregano
1 teaspoon black pepper
⅓ cup finely grated parmesan
½ cup pecans, finely ground

*Accompaniments:* boiled potato wedges and
   hard-boiled eggs, halved

Heat a dry cast-iron skillet or griddle over moderate heat and toast chiles, a few at a time, turning frequently with tongs, until puffed and lightly charred in spots, about 30 seconds. Remove seeds and, using scissors, as much of veins as possible. Soak chiles in 1½ cups warm water at least 2 hours and preferably up to 1 day. Purée chiles with soaking water and 1 teaspoon kosher salt in a blender until very smooth.

Put chicken in an 8-quart pot with water to cover and add carrot, celery, one fourth onion, thyme, bay leaf, 1 garlic clove, and 1 teaspoon kosher salt. Bring to a simmer and skim any foam from surface. Simmer chicken, partially covered, until tender, about 1½ hours.

Transfer chicken to a cutting board and pour cooking liquid through a sieve into a bowl, discarding solids. When chicken is cool enough to handle, remove meat from bones and coarsely shred with fingers.

Soak bread in condensed milk until milk is absorbed, about 10 minutes. Chop remaining three fourths onion and remaining 2 garlic cloves and cook in oil in a 5- to 6-quart wide heavy pot over moderate heat, stirring, until onion is softened. Add remaining 2 teaspoons kosher salt, cumin, oregano, and black pepper and cook, stirring, 1 minute. Add chile purée and cook, stirring, 1 minute more. Stir in chicken, bread mixture, parmesan, and 2½ cups reserved cooking liquid.

Gently simmer stew, covered, stirring occasionally, 30 minutes. Add ground pecans and, if necessary, more chicken stock for a creamy consistency and season with salt and pepper. Simmer 5 minutes more.

Serve *aji de gallina* over potatoes and hard-boiled eggs.

Cooks' note:
• Chicken may be cooked 1 day ahead and cooled in its liquid, uncovered, then chilled, covered.

## CREAMY POLENTA WITH WILD MUSHROOM AND PEARL ONION RAGOUT

**Serves 4**
Active time: 1 hr   Start to finish: 1½ hr

*Since two of my sisters and many of my friends are vegetarian in one form or another, I am always on the lookout for satisfying meatless dishes. A few years ago, I hit the jackpot when I saw Lidia Bastianich combine wild mushrooms and polenta in a savory dish—I've been recreating it with variations ever since. Creamy polenta is now one of my favorite comfort foods. As for wild mushrooms, they are the essence of the earth itself.*
—Shelley Wiseman

1 oz dried porcini mushrooms
1½ cups hot water
10 oz pearl onions
4 cups cold water
2½ teaspoons kosher salt
1 cup polenta or yellow cornmeal
¼ lb Italian Fontina, coarsely grated
*For ragout*
¼ cup extra-virgin olive oil
3 tablespoons unsalted butter
2 portabella mushrooms (½ lb total), stems
    removed and each cap cut into 8 wedges
½ lb small fresh cremini or white mush-
    rooms, stems trimmed and caps halved
    or quartered if large
3 large garlic cloves, finely chopped
1 teaspoon finely chopped fresh rosemary
1 teaspoon finely chopped fresh thyme
½ cup dry white wine

*Garnish:* chopped fresh flat-leaf parsley

Soak porcini in 1½ cups hot water until softened, 20 minutes. Agitate porcini in water to loosen dirt, then lift mushrooms out of liquid, squeezing slightly. Coarsely chop porcini and reserve. Pour soaking liquid through a sieve lined with several layers of cheesecloth to remove dirt and reserve.

Blanch onions in a large saucepan of boiling water 1 minute, then drain. When cool enough to handle, peel.

Whisk together 4 cups cold water, 1½ teaspoons salt, and polenta in a 4-quart heavy saucepan and bring to a boil, whisking occasionally. Cook polenta over moderate heat, whisking constantly, 2 minutes. Simmer, covered, stirring for 1 minute every 10 minutes, over low heat 45 minutes, then stir in cheese.

*Make ragout while polenta simmers:*
Heat 1 tablespoon each oil and butter in a 12-inch heavy skillet over moderately high heat, then sauté onions, stirring, until golden brown, 3 to 5 minutes. Add remaining olive oil and, when oil is hot, add portabellas and sauté, stirring, until slightly wilted, 3 to 4 minutes. Add cremini and sauté, stirring, 1 minute. Add garlic, rosemary, thyme, and remaining teaspoon salt and sauté, stirring, until mushrooms are wilted, 3 to 4 minutes. Add wine and boil 1 minute. Add porcini and reserved soaking liquid and simmer, uncovered, until onions are tender and about three fourths of liquid has evaporated, about 10 minutes. Cut remaining 2 tablespoons butter into bits and add to mushrooms with salt and pepper to taste, shaking pan until butter is incorporated.

Serve polenta topped with ragout.

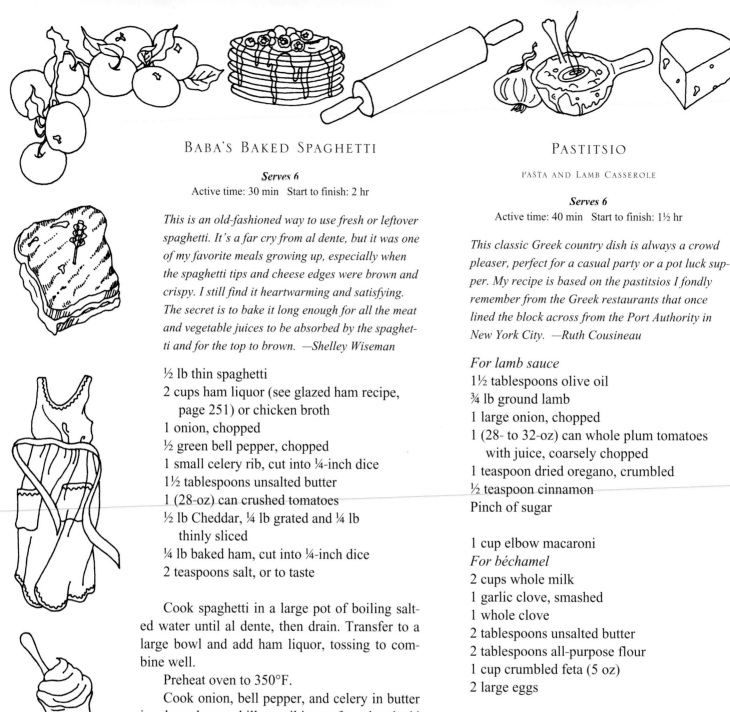

## Baba's Baked Spaghetti

### Serves 6
Active time: 30 min   Start to finish: 2 hr

*This is an old-fashioned way to use fresh or leftover spaghetti. It's a far cry from al dente, but it was one of my favorite meals growing up, especially when the spaghetti tips and cheese edges were brown and crispy. I still find it heartwarming and satisfying. The secret is to bake it long enough for all the meat and vegetable juices to be absorbed by the spaghetti and for the top to brown. —Shelley Wiseman*

½ lb thin spaghetti
2 cups ham liquor (see glazed ham recipe, page 251) or chicken broth
1 onion, chopped
½ green bell pepper, chopped
1 small celery rib, cut into ¼-inch dice
1½ tablespoons unsalted butter
1 (28-oz) can crushed tomatoes
½ lb Cheddar, ¼ lb grated and ¼ lb thinly sliced
¼ lb baked ham, cut into ¼-inch dice
2 teaspoons salt, or to taste

Cook spaghetti in a large pot of boiling salted water until al dente, then drain. Transfer to a large bowl and add ham liquor, tossing to combine well.

Preheat oven to 350°F.

Cook onion, bell pepper, and celery in butter in a large heavy skillet until just softened and add to spaghetti with tomatoes, grated cheese, ham, salt, and pepper to taste. Transfer to a buttered 2½- to 3-quart shallow baking dish and top with sliced cheese.

Bake in middle of oven, uncovered, until liquid is absorbed and cheese and spaghetti tips are browned, about 1½ hours.

## Pastitsio

### PASTA AND LAMB CASSEROLE

### Serves 6
Active time: 40 min   Start to finish: 1½ hr

*This classic Greek country dish is always a crowd pleaser, perfect for a casual party or a pot luck supper. My recipe is based on the pastitsios I fondly remember from the Greek restaurants that once lined the block across from the Port Authority in New York City. —Ruth Cousineau*

*For lamb sauce*
1½ tablespoons olive oil
¾ lb ground lamb
1 large onion, chopped
1 (28- to 32-oz) can whole plum tomatoes with juice, coarsely chopped
1 teaspoon dried oregano, crumbled
½ teaspoon cinnamon
Pinch of sugar

1 cup elbow macaroni
*For béchamel*
2 cups whole milk
1 garlic clove, smashed
1 whole clove
2 tablespoons unsalted butter
2 tablespoons all-purpose flour
1 cup crumbled feta (5 oz)
2 large eggs

*Make sauce:*

Heat 1 tablespoon oil in large heavy skillet over moderately high heat until hot but not smoking, then sauté lamb, breaking up clumps with a fork, until browned. Transfer to a plate with slotted spoon. Add remaining ½ tablespoon oil to fat remaining in skillet and cook chopped onion over moderately low heat, stirring occasionally, until softened. Add plum tomatoes with juice, oregano,

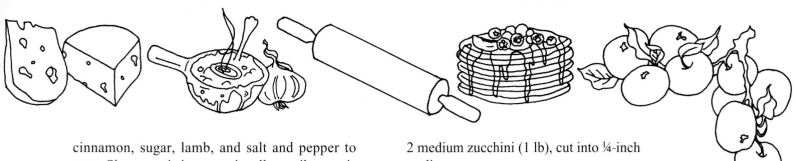

cinnamon, sugar, lamb, and salt and pepper to taste. Simmer, stirring occasionally, until sauce is thickened, about 35 minutes.

*Cook macaroni and make béchamel while sauce simmers:*

Preheat oven to 425°F.

Cook macaroni in a pot of boiling salted water until al dente, about 8 minutes, then drain.

Bring milk with garlic and clove to a simmer. Heat butter in a 2-quart heavy saucepan over moderate heat until foam subsides, then add flour, whisking, 1 minute. Add hot milk mixture, whisking constantly, and simmer until sauce thickens, 3 to 5 minutes. Discard garlic and clove. Stir in cheese and season with salt and pepper. Beat eggs in a large bowl and gradually add sauce to eggs, whisking. Stir in macaroni.

*Assemble pastitsio:*

Spoon lamb sauce into a 2-quart shallow baking dish and top with macaroni mixture.

Bake *pastitsio* in middle of oven until bubbling and top is golden brown, about 45 minutes. Let stand 5 minutes before serving.

**Cooks' note:**
- **Lamb sauce and *béchamel* may be made 1 day ahead and chilled, covered.**

## Vegetable Lasagne

**Serves 6**
Active time: 1 hr   Start to finish: 1¾ hr

*This lasagne—lighter than the usual tomato-and-meat-sauce variety—only needs a green salad for a complete supper.   —Ruth Cousineau*

16 sheets dry no-boil lasagne (¾ lb)
½ stick (¼ cup) unsalted butter
1 onion, chopped
2 large garlic cloves, 1 minced and 1 smashed
2 carrots, peeled and cut into ¼-inch dice

2 medium zucchini (1 lb), cut into ¼-inch dice
1 yellow bell pepper, cut into ¼-inch dice
1 (10-oz) package frozen baby peas, thawed
3 cups whole milk
2 tablespoons all-purpose flour
2 tablespoons chopped fresh basil
2 cups freshly grated parmesan
1½ cups shredded fresh mozzarella

Soak lasagne sheets in hot water to cover until softened, about 30 minutes.

Heat 2 tablespoons butter in a large skillet over moderate heat until foam subsides, then cook onion, minced garlic, carrots, zucchini, and bell pepper, stirring frequently, until softened and browned, 10 to 12 minutes. Transfer to a bowl and stir in peas and salt and pepper to taste. (Do not wash skillet.)

Simmer milk and smashed garlic in a small saucepan 10 minutes.

Heat remaining 2 tablespoons butter in skillet over moderate heat until foam subsides, then add flour and cook, whisking constantly, 2 minutes. Add hot milk and garlic mixture and simmer, whisking occasionally, until sauce is slightly thickened, 3 to 5 minutes. Discard garlic and stir in basil and salt and pepper to taste.

Preheat oven to 425°F.

Spread ½ cup sauce on bottom of a buttered 13- by 9-inch shallow baking dish. Top sauce with 4 drained lasagne sheets, overlapping if necessary. Spread one third of vegetable mixture over sheets. Top with ½ cup sauce and sprinkle with one fourth of each cheese. Make two more layers in same manner. Top with remaining sheets, sauce, and cheeses.

Bake lasagne, covered, in middle of oven 20 minutes. Uncover and bake until top is lightly browned and filling is bubbling, about 15 minutes more. Let stand 10 minutes before serving.

257

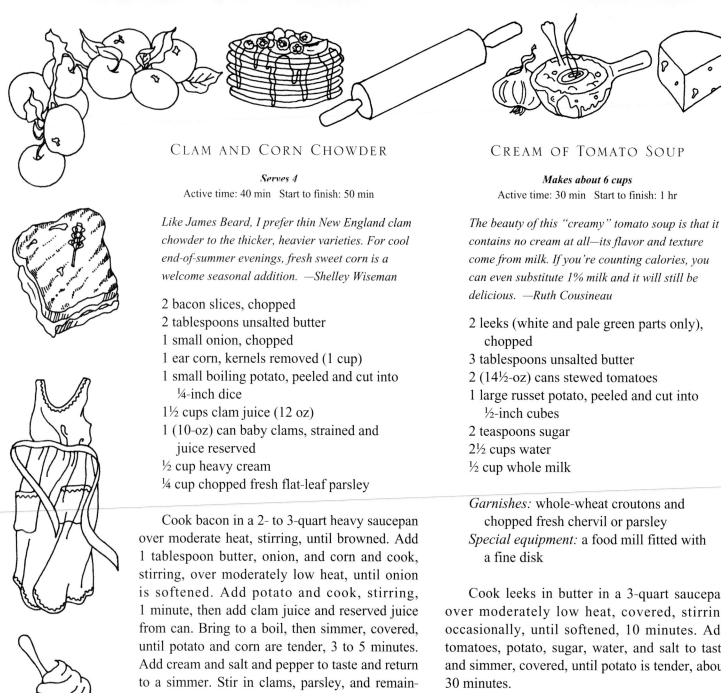

## CLAM AND CORN CHOWDER

**Serves 4**
Active time: 40 min   Start to finish: 50 min

*Like James Beard, I prefer thin New England clam chowder to the thicker, heavier varieties. For cool end-of-summer evenings, fresh sweet corn is a welcome seasonal addition.  —Shelley Wiseman*

2 bacon slices, chopped
2 tablespoons unsalted butter
1 small onion, chopped
1 ear corn, kernels removed (1 cup)
1 small boiling potato, peeled and cut into
   ¼-inch dice
1½ cups clam juice (12 oz)
1 (10-oz) can baby clams, strained and
   juice reserved
½ cup heavy cream
¼ cup chopped fresh flat-leaf parsley

Cook bacon in a 2- to 3-quart heavy saucepan over moderate heat, stirring, until browned. Add 1 tablespoon butter, onion, and corn and cook, stirring, over moderately low heat, until onion is softened. Add potato and cook, stirring, 1 minute, then add clam juice and reserved juice from can. Bring to a boil, then simmer, covered, until potato and corn are tender, 3 to 5 minutes. Add cream and salt and pepper to taste and return to a simmer. Stir in clams, parsley, and remaining tablespoon butter and cook until clams are just heated through, about 1 minute.

Cooks' note:
· Fresh littleneck clams can be substituted for the clams and clam juice in this recipe. Cook about 3 dozen scrubbed clams in 2 cups water or beer. Shell and chop clams and strain cooking liquid through several layers of cheesecloth or a coffee filter to remove any sediment.

## CREAM OF TOMATO SOUP

**Makes about 6 cups**
Active time: 30 min   Start to finish: 1 hr

*The beauty of this "creamy" tomato soup is that it contains no cream at all—its flavor and texture come from milk. If you're counting calories, you can even substitute 1% milk and it will still be delicious.  —Ruth Cousineau*

2 leeks (white and pale green parts only),
   chopped
3 tablespoons unsalted butter
2 (14½-oz) cans stewed tomatoes
1 large russet potato, peeled and cut into
   ½-inch cubes
2 teaspoons sugar
2½ cups water
½ cup whole milk

*Garnishes:* whole-wheat croutons and
   chopped fresh chervil or parsley
*Special equipment:* a food mill fitted with
   a fine disk

Cook leeks in butter in a 3-quart saucepan over moderately low heat, covered, stirring occasionally, until softened, 10 minutes. Add tomatoes, potato, sugar, water, and salt to taste and simmer, covered, until potato is tender, about 30 minutes.

Force soup through food mill (to remove tomato skins and seeds) into a large bowl and add milk. Purée soup in a blender in 2 batches until smooth (use caution when blending hot liquids). Reheat and season with salt and pepper.

Cooks' note:
· Soup may be made 3 days ahead and chilled, covered.

## CREAM OF POBLANO CHILE SOUP

**Makes about 7 cups (serves 6)**
Active time: 1 hr   Start to finish: 1¼ hr

*A chile pepper soup? Its flavor is much gentler than you'd think, especially if you remove the veins as well as the seeds from the chiles. This comforting soup instantly brings me back to the years I lived in Mexico City.   —Shelley Wiseman*

2 lb fresh *poblano* chiles (8 to 10)
1 large onion, coarsely chopped
1 large garlic clove, chopped
2 tablespoons unsalted butter or vegetable oil
4 cups chicken broth
1 cup heavy cream

*Garnishes:* diced Monterey Jack and fried
   tortilla strips (optional)

*Roast poblanos:*
Lay chiles on their sides on racks of burners (1 to 3 to a burner) and turn flame on moderately high. Char chiles, turning with tongs, until skins are blackened, 5 to 8 minutes. Transfer to a bowl and let stand, covered with plastic wrap, until cool enough to handle, then peel and remove seeds and veins. Coarsely chop chiles.

Cook onion and garlic in butter in a 3-quart heavy pot over moderately low heat, stirring, until softened. Transfer to a blender with chiles and 2 cups broth and purée until very smooth. Return mixture to pot and stir in remaining 2 cups broth, cream, and salt and pepper to taste. Simmer 10 minutes.

**Cooks' note:**
- Soup may be made 3 days ahead and chilled, covered. If freezing, do not add cream until reheating.

## FRENCH ONION SOUP GRATINÉE

**Makes 8 cups (serves 6 to 8)**
Active time: 1 hr   Start to finish: 1¾ hr

*Some cooks make French onion soup with water, but I love it made with brown veal stock. For those who don't have veal stock on hand, water and beef Bovril make a surprisingly tasty substitution, as I learned from my friend, Sean O'Donnell.
—Shelley Wiseman*

3 lb onions, thinly sliced
½ stick (¼ cup) unsalted butter
1 teaspoon sugar
1½ teaspoons salt, or to taste
3 tablespoons all-purpose flour
1 cup dry white wine
3 tablespoons beef Bovril
1 bay leaf (not California)
1 sprig fresh thyme
12 to 16 (¾-inch) baguette slices, toasted
12 to 16 thin slices Gruyère (½ lb)

*Special equipment:* 6 to 8 flameproof soup
   bowls, preferably with handles

Cook onions in butter with sugar and salt in a 12-inch heavy skillet over moderately low heat, covered, stirring occasionally, until softened, about 20 minutes. Cook over moderately high heat, uncovered, until caramelized, about 20 minutes more. Add flour and cook, stirring, 3 minutes, then add wine and simmer, stirring occasionally, 3 minutes more.

Transfer mixture to a 4- to 5-quart heavy pot and whisk in 8 cups water and Bovril. Add bay leaf, thyme, and salt and pepper to taste. Bring to a boil, then simmer, covered, 30 minutes.

Preheat broiler. Put bowls on a baking sheet.

Fill bowls with soup and top each with 2 baguette slices. Divide cheese slices among bowls, laying them over toasts and to edges of bowls, and broil soup until cheese is melted and browned in spots.

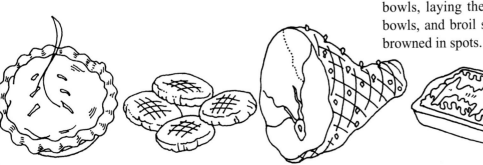

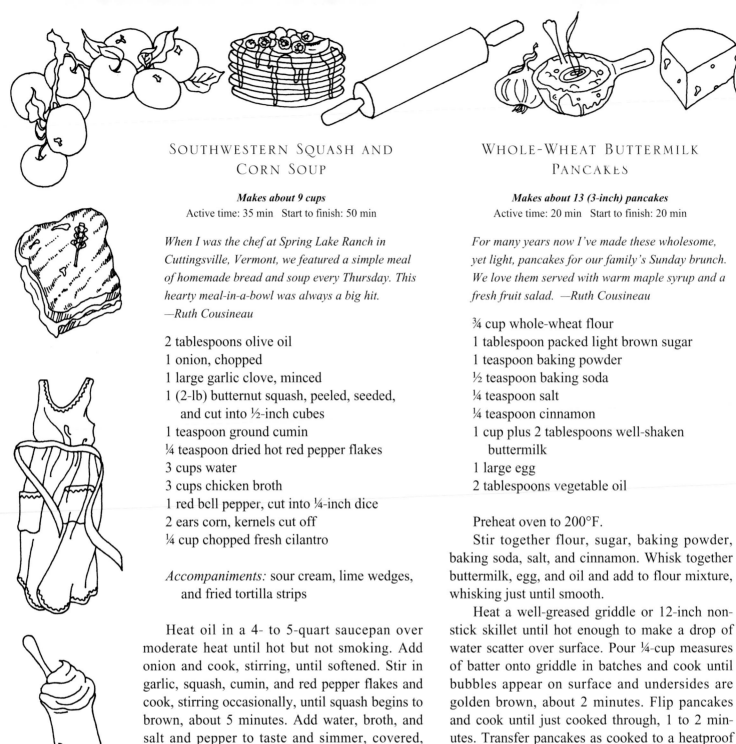

### SOUTHWESTERN SQUASH AND CORN SOUP

*Makes about 9 cups*
Active time: 35 min   Start to finish: 50 min

*When I was the chef at Spring Lake Ranch in Cuttingsville, Vermont, we featured a simple meal of homemade bread and soup every Thursday. This hearty meal-in-a-bowl was always a big hit.*
—*Ruth Cousineau*

2 tablespoons olive oil
1 onion, chopped
1 large garlic clove, minced
1 (2-lb) butternut squash, peeled, seeded,
   and cut into ½-inch cubes
1 teaspoon ground cumin
¼ teaspoon dried hot red pepper flakes
3 cups water
3 cups chicken broth
1 red bell pepper, cut into ¼-inch dice
2 ears corn, kernels cut off
¼ cup chopped fresh cilantro

*Accompaniments:* sour cream, lime wedges,
   and fried tortilla strips

Heat oil in a 4- to 5-quart saucepan over moderate heat until hot but not smoking. Add onion and cook, stirring, until softened. Stir in garlic, squash, cumin, and red pepper flakes and cook, stirring occasionally, until squash begins to brown, about 5 minutes. Add water, broth, and salt and pepper to taste and simmer, covered, until squash is tender, about 10 minutes. Add bell pepper and corn and simmer, covered, 5 minutes. Stir in cilantro.

Cooks' note:
• **Soup may be made 3 days ahead and chilled, covered.**

### WHOLE-WHEAT BUTTERMILK PANCAKES

*Makes about 13 (3-inch) pancakes*
Active time: 20 min   Start to finish: 20 min

*For many years now I've made these wholesome, yet light, pancakes for our family's Sunday brunch. We love them served with warm maple syrup and a fresh fruit salad.* —*Ruth Cousineau*

¾ cup whole-wheat flour
1 tablespoon packed light brown sugar
1 teaspoon baking powder
½ teaspoon baking soda
¼ teaspoon salt
¼ teaspoon cinnamon
1 cup plus 2 tablespoons well-shaken
   buttermilk
1 large egg
2 tablespoons vegetable oil

Preheat oven to 200°F.

Stir together flour, sugar, baking powder, baking soda, salt, and cinnamon. Whisk together buttermilk, egg, and oil and add to flour mixture, whisking just until smooth.

Heat a well-greased griddle or 12-inch non-stick skillet until hot enough to make a drop of water scatter over surface. Pour ¼-cup measures of batter onto griddle in batches and cook until bubbles appear on surface and undersides are golden brown, about 2 minutes. Flip pancakes and cook until just cooked through, 1 to 2 minutes. Transfer pancakes as cooked to a heatproof platter and keep warm in oven, loosely covered with foil.

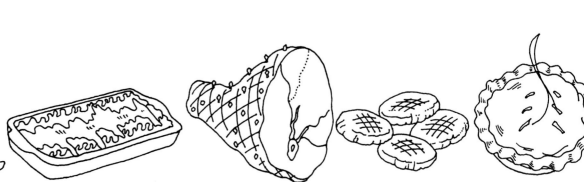

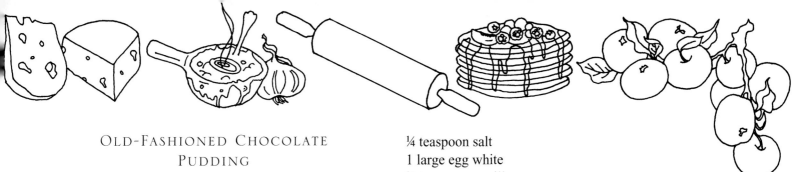

## OLD-FASHIONED CHOCOLATE PUDDING

**Serves 4**
Active time: 20 min   Start to finish: 2½ hr

*Be sure to use fine-quality semisweet chocolate (such as Valhrona or Lindt) in this recipe; regular chocolate just doesn't compare.  —Ruth Cousineau*

¼ cup sugar
¼ cup unsweetened cocoa powder (not Dutch-process)
2 tablespoons cornstarch
2 cups whole milk
1 large egg, beaten
4 oz fine-quality semisweet chocolate, chopped

*Accompaniment:* sweetened whipped cream

Whisk together sugar, cocoa powder, cornstarch, and a pinch of salt in a 2-quart heavy saucepan and gradually whisk in milk. Boil, whisking constantly, until pudding is thick, 3 to 5 minutes. Very gradually whisk pudding into egg, then whisk in chocolate until smooth.

Pour into 4 (6-oz) ramekins or bowls and cover surface with wax paper to prevent a skin from forming. Chill, covered.

## PECAN MACAROONS

**Makes about 40 cookies**
Active time: 30 min   Start to finish: 1¼ hr

*Almond macaroons were never a favorite of mine, but a gift of pecan macaroons really opened my eyes. —Shelley Wiseman*

1¼ cups pecan pieces, finely ground, plus 40 to 50 pecan halves
¾ cup sugar
2 tablespoons all-purpose flour

¼ teaspoon salt
1 large egg white
½ teaspoon vanilla

Preheat oven to 300°F.
Stir together ground pecans, sugar, flour, and salt in a bowl, then stir in egg white and vanilla. Form into ¾- to 1-inch balls and arrange 1½ inches apart on greased baking sheets. Press a pecan half into center of each ball to flatten into 1½-inch disks.

Bake in batches in middle of oven 15 minutes for chewy cookies or 20 minutes for crisp cookies. Transfer to a rack to cool.

## RUTH'S RICE PUDDING

**Serves 6 to 8**
Active time: 40 min   Start to finish: 1 hr

2 cups water
¼ teaspoon salt
2 tablespoons unsalted butter
½ teaspoon freshly grated lemon zest
1 cup long-grain rice
1 qt whole milk
½ cup sugar
½ vanilla bean, split lengthwise
1 cup raisins
Cinnamon for dusting

Boil water, salt, butter, and zest in a 3-quart heavy saucepan and stir in rice. Return to a boil and simmer, covered, over very low heat until water is absorbed, about 15 minutes.

While rice is cooking, heat milk, sugar, and vanilla bean over low heat. Add rice mixture and raisins and simmer, stirring frequently, over low heat until most of milk is absorbed and rice is creamy, about 20 minutes. Discard vanilla bean and transfer pudding to a bowl. Dust with cinnamon and cool until just warm.

261

## PEAR AND BRANDY CLAFOUTIS

**Serves 6**
Active time: 20 min   Start to finish: 1½ hr

*Clafoutis is an easy dessert to whip up with whatever fruit is in season and any brandy, liqueur, or wine that complements the fruit. The French classic, clafoutis limousin, is made with cherries and kirsch. Other favorites are blackberries and cassis, and peach and white wine or brandy. Here the pears are first sautéed to cook off some juice—a good idea when using peaches as well. For cherries and blackberries simply macerate the fruit with the sugar and brandy or liqueur (omit butter) for 20 minutes before adding mixture to the baking dish. —Shelley Wiseman*

*For pears*
1½ tablespoons unsalted butter
2 tablespoons sugar
1 lb firm-ripe Bartlett pears (2 to 3), peeled
    and cut into 16 wedges
¼ cup plus 1 tablespoon brandy
*For custard*
1 cup whole milk
4 large eggs
1 tablespoon vanilla
½ cup sugar
½ cup all-purpose flour
4 tablespoons unsalted butter, melted

*Garnish:* confectioners sugar

Preheat oven to 325°F and butter a 5- to 6-cup shallow baking dish.
*Cook pears:*
Melt butter in a large heavy skillet over moderate heat and sprinkle evenly with sugar. Cook pear wedges in 1 layer, undisturbed, until sugar begins to caramelize and undersides are golden, 3 to 5 minutes. Shake pan to loosen pears, then turn over and brown other side. Remove pan from heat and add ¼ cup brandy, shaking pan to combine and dissolve any caramelized juices stuck to pan. Simmer pears over moderate heat, shaking pan, until about half of liquid evaporates, about 1 minute. Pour pear mixture into baking dish, spreading evenly.
*Make custard:*
Blend together all ingredients in order listed in a blender just until smooth.
Pour custard over pears and bake in middle of oven until puffed and golden, 50 minutes to 1 hour. Transfer *clafoutis* to a rack to cool slightly.
Dust with confectioners sugar and serve immediately.

## CRISP PEANUT BUTTER COOKIES

**Makes about 48 cookies**
Active time: 20 min   Start to finish: 65 min

*As a 70s mom, I was always trying to get some whole grains into my children's diet, and these crunchy peanutty cookies did the trick. I soon found they were a hit with adults, too, so they're still a regular item in my cookie jar. —Ruth Cousineau*

2½ cups whole-wheat flour
1 teaspoon baking soda
2 sticks (1 cup) unsalted butter, softened
1 cup chunky peanut butter
1 cup packed light brown sugar
½ cup granulated sugar
2 large eggs
1 teaspoon vanilla
1 cup chopped salted peanuts

Preheat oven to 350°F and butter 3 baking sheets.
Stir together flour and baking soda. Beat together butter, peanut butter, sugars, eggs, and

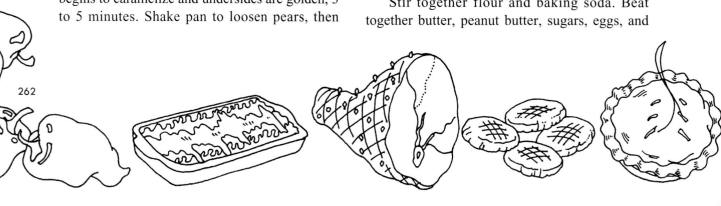

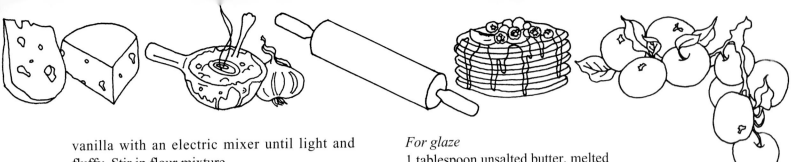

vanilla with an electric mixer until light and fluffy. Stir in flour mixture.

Drop dough by level tablespoons 2 inches apart on baking sheets. Press a crosshatch design on top of each cookie with a fork dipped in flour and sprinkle with peanuts.

Bake cookies in batches in middle of oven until browned around edges, 13 to 15 minutes. Cool 1 minute on sheet, then transfer to a rack to cool completely.

## OLD-FASHIONED APPLE PIE

**Serves 8**
Active time: 1 hr   Start to finish: 2½ hr

*For this pie, I've resurrected an old-fashioned hot-water crust. I'm in love with its unusual flakiness and hope to see it come back into fashion.*
—Shelley Wiseman

*For crust*
3 cups all-purpose flour
¼ teaspoon salt
1 stick (½ cup) cold unsalted butter, cut
    into bits
⅔ cup cold vegetable shortening, cut into bits
½ cup boiling-hot water
*For filling*
2½ lb Granny Smith apples, cored, peeled,
    and each cut into 16 wedges
1 tablespoon fresh lemon juice
⅓ cup granulated sugar
⅓ cup packed light brown sugar
¾ teaspoon ground cinnamon
¼ teaspoon freshly grated nutmeg
¼ teaspoon allspice
2 tablespoons all-purpose flour
2 tablespoons cold unsalted butter, cut
    into bits

*For glaze*
1 tablespoon unsalted butter, melted
2 teaspoons granulated sugar

*Make crust:*
Stir together flour and salt in a large bowl. Make a well in center and add butter and shortening. Pour in boiling-hot water and quickly stir together butter, shortening, and water with a fork until combined and softened, then incorporate flour into mixture just until evenly distributed (do not overwork or pastry will be tough). Gather dough loosely into a ball and transfer to a lightly floured work surface. With heel of your hand, smear dough 2 to 4 times in a forward motion to help distribute fat (each smear should be with a different part of the dough). Divide dough into 2 pieces, one slightly larger than the other, and form into disks. Chill, wrapped separately in plastic wrap, 1 hour.

*Prepare filling while dough chills:*
Toss apples with lemon juice in a large bowl and add remaining filling ingredients, except butter, stirring to coat.

Preheat oven to 400°F.

Roll out larger piece of dough into a 13-inch round on a lightly floured surface and fit into a 10-inch glass pie plate. Mound filling over dough and dot with butter.

Roll out remaining piece of dough into an 11- to 12-inch round and drape over apples. Press edges together to seal, then trim and crimp decoratively. Cut several slits in crust to allow steam to escape.

*Glaze crust:*
Brush butter over crust and sprinkle with sugar. Bake on a baking sheet in middle of oven until golden, 50 minutes to 1 hour. Transfer pie to a rack to cool at least 30 minutes.

263

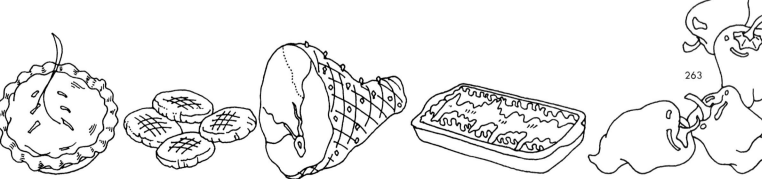

# GUIDES TO THE TEXT

## SOURCES

Below are sources for the sometimes hard-to-find ingredients and cookware used in the Recipe Compendium.

**Achiote** (or annato) **paste** is made from the ground seeds of a tropical tree and used as a yellow or reddish coloring agent. It is available at Latino markets or from Kitchen/ Market, (888) 468-4433 (ask for El Yucateco or Sabora brands).

**Amaranth** is highly nutritious and, when popped, or puffed, looks like tiny popcorn kernels. Puffed amaranth is available in natural foods stores and by mail order from Nu-World Amaranth, (630) 369-6819.

Dried **apricots** should be soft and pliable with deep orange color. Look for them in specialty foods shops, natural foods stores, and some supermarkets.

White **arepa flour** (precooked cornmeal) such as *masarepa* or *areparina* is available in Latino markets and some supermarkets or by mail order from Kitchen/ Market, (888) 468-4433.

**Asafetida**, an extremely smelly spice from the dried gum resin of giant fennel plants, gives depth and balance to Indian dishes. It is available at Kalustyan's, (212) 685-3451

or www.kalustyans.com. Ask for the Vandevi brand.

**Baba au rhum molds** can be mail-ordered from Bridge Kitchenware, (800) 274-3435 or (212) 838-1901.

Ground **buffalo** can be found at some butcher shops and supermarkets and by mail order from Denver Buffalo Company, (800) 289-2833.

**Chickpea flour** may be ordered from Dean & DeLuca, (800) 221-7714 or (212) 226-6800.

Most of the **chiles** called for in these recipes, including **poblanos**, **anchos** (dried **poblanos**), dried **New Mexico** chiles, **guajillos**, **pancos**, and canned **chipotles** in **adobo**, can be found in Latino markets or some supermarkets or by mail order from Chile Today— Hot Tamale, (800) 468-7377 or Kitchen/Market, (888) 468-4433. **Indian red chile powder**, made from a variety of hot red chiles native to India, should not be confused with cayenne pepper or chili powder. It's sold at Kalustyan's, (212) 685-3451 or www.kalustyans.com. Hot red

**Thai chiles** are available by mail order from Uwajimaya, (800) 889-1928 or www.EthnicGrocer.com, (800) 523-1961.

Fresh **curry leaves**, slightly bitter, almond-shaped, dark green leaves, are used in savories throughout South India. They can be ordered from Kalustyan's, (212) 685-3451 or www.kalustyans.com.

A **3/4-inch round cutter** can be ordered from Sweet Celebrations, (800) 328-6722 as part of an 11-piece set.

**Dals** are any dried legumes such as lentils, beans, or peas and the vast array of dishes made from them. The actual legumes differ in size, shape, color, flavor, texture, and cooking time. They are sold whole or split, and hulled (skinned) or unhulled. In general, don't substitute whole *dals* for split ones in a recipe; it will affect the end result. **Chana dal** is a variety of small Indian chickpea also known as Bengal gram bean. It looks more like a yellow split pea than what we think of as a chickpea. **Toovar dal** are usually described as yellow lentils, although they are actually a variety of pigeon pea (and virtually indistinguishable from *chana dal*); also known as *toor dal* and *arhar dal*. **Urad dal** are commonly called black lentils but are more closely related to mung beans; they are also known as *urd* or black gram beans. You can find all these varities of *dals* (and many more) at Kalustyan's, (212) 685-3541 or www.kalustyans.com.

**Devonshire cream** is available in many specialty foods shops and by mail order from Dean & DeLuca, (800) 221-7714 or (212) 226-6800.

**Dried shrimp** offer saltiness and a hint of fish flavor to dishes. They are available by mail order from Kalustyan's, (212) 685-3451.

**Edamame**, tender young soybeans in the pod, can be found in Japanese or other Asian markets, natural foods stores, or the freezer sections of large supermarkets and by mail order from Uwajimaya, (800) 889-1928.

**Elderberry-flower syrup** is sold in some specialty foods shops and by mail order from Scandia Food and Gifts, (203) 838-2087.

Dried **epazote**, a pungent herb used in Mexican cookery, is available from Kitchen/Market, (888) 468-4433.

Chinese **five-spice powder**, the fragrant combination of star anise, Sichuan peppercorns, fennel, cloves, and cinnamon, is available at Asian markets and some supermarkets or from Uwajimaya, (800) 889-1928.

**Flax seeds** impart a mild, nutty flavor. They can be found at natural foods stores and some specialty shops.

Many of the recipes in this volume call for edible **flowers**. Indian Rock Produce, (800) 882-0512, stocks most of what you'll need, including fresh nontoxic **flowering fresh chives**, **nasturtiums**, and **violets**. **Flowering pea shoots** are also available from Indian Rock, or in season at Chinese markets (ask for *dau miu*). Dried, untreated **lavender** can be mail-ordered from Dean & DeLuca, (800) 221 7714 or (212) 226-6800. Dried **hibiscus**, also known as *flores de jamaica*, is available at Latino markets and by mail order from Kitchen/Market, (888) 468-4433.

French green **lentils** are sold at specialty foods shops and some supermarkets.

**Ghee**, Indian clarified butter, is available at Kalustyan's, (212) 685-3451 or www.kalustyans.com.

Crystallized **ginger**, pieces of gingerroot that have been cooked in sugar syrup and coated with granulated sugar, can be purchased at some supermarkets, specialty foods shops, and by mail order from Williams-Sonoma, (800) 541-2233. Pickled **ginger** is available at Japanese and other Asian markets, some specialty foods shops, and by mail order from Uwajimaya, (800) 889-1928.

**Ice pop molds** can be found at supermarkets and housewares shops and by mail order from Williams-Sonoma, (800) 541-2233.

**Japanese slicers** are excellent alternatives to more expensive *mandolines*. We like the Benriner slicer found at Williams-Sonoma, (800) 541-2233.

**Katsuo bushi**, dried bonito (a member of the tuna family) flakes, are available at Japanese and other Asian markets, natural foods stores, and by mail order from Uwajimaya, (800) 889-1928.

**Kombu**, dried kelp that comes packaged in lengths that are easily cut with scissors, is available at Japanese and other Asian markets, natural foods stores, and by mail order from Uwajimaya, (800) 889-1928.

**Madras curry powder** is available at Indian markets and from www.EthnicGrocer.com.

Canned **mango** is sold in most supermarkets (look for the Ka-Me brand); Ratna brand (with a more intense flavor) may be ordered from Kalustyan's, (212) 685-3451 or www.kalustyans.com.

**Masa harina**, sometimes called tortilla flour, is made from dried corn kernels treated with cal (the mineral lime), then dried and powdered. (Do not subsitute cornmeal.) Look for it at Latino markets and some supermarkets and by mail order from Kitchen/Market, (888) 468-4433.

**Mirliton**, commonly known as chayote, is a culinary chameleon. You may also see it labeled as *christophine*, *chocho*, *chuchu*, and vegetable pear. Many Latino and Asian groceries sell mirlitons as do some large supermarkets.

Dried **morels** can be mail-ordered from Dean & DeLuca, (800) 221-7714 or (212) 226-6800.

Black **mustard seeds**, popular in South Indian cooking, are actually reddish brown. They're available at Kalustyan's, (212) 685-3451 or www.kalustyans.com.

**Nigella seeds** are not black onion seeds though they're often labeled as such. You can mail-order them from Penzeys Spices Ltd., (800) 741-7787.

**Palm sugar** is made from the sap of a variety of palms that's boiled down, then formed into cylinders or cakes. **Pandam leaves** are those of the *pandan*, or screw pine. Look for both from Uwajimaya, (800) 889-1928 or www.EthnicGrocer.com, (800) 523-1961.

**Paneer**, Indian fresh cheese, can be found at Kalustyan's, (212) 685-3451 or www.kalustyans.com.

**Panko**, Japanese bread crumbs, is available in Japanese or other Asian markets, many fish stores, and by mail order from Uwajimaya, (800) 889-1928.

**Pappadams**, Indian lentil wafers, can be found at Kalustyan's, (212) 685-3451 or www.kalustyans.com. Try deep-frying store-bought *pappadams* in about 5 cups of oil to give them extra crispness.

**Passion-fruit purée** is available in the freezer sections of most Latino markets and some supermarkets. Look for Goya and La Fe brands.

**Pearl tapioca** has larger granules than typical supermarket tapioca and must be soaked before using. It is available by mail order from Uwajimaya, (800) 889-1928 or www.EthnicGrocer.com, (800) 523-1961.

**Pierogi**, Eastern European dumplings, are sold fresh and frozen in supermarkets in many parts of the country. Like premade egg rolls, they've become a convenience food for cooks with limited time. If pierogi aren't sold in your supermarket, try a local Polish or Eastern European deli.

Sweet, meaty **sugar pumpkins** are smaller, darker, and smoother than carving pumpkins and can be found at farmers markets and most supermarkets.

Hulled green **pumpkin seeds** can turn rancid quickly, so purchase them from a source with a high turnover. We had the best luck at natural foods shops; they're also available at Latino markets, specialty foods shops, and some supermarkets. Store them in your freezer once purchased.

Japanese short-grain **rice** is available in Japanese and other Asian markets, some specialty foods shops, and by mail order from Uwajimaya, (800) 889-1928.

**Rice paper rounds** are available in Asian markets or by mail order from www.EthnicGrocer.com, (800) 523-1961; ask for "spring roll skins."

Seasoned **rice vinegar** is found in Japanese and other Asian markets, some specialty foods shops, and by mail order from Uwajimaya, (800) 889-1928.

Fresh **ricotta** can be purchased (and shipped overnight anywhere in the continental U.S.) from Citarella, (212) 874-0383.

Asian **sesame oil**, used primarily as a flavoring in China, Japan, and Korea, is available through www.EthnicGrocer.com, (800) 523-1961. We recommend the Kadoya brand.

Toasted black **sesame seeds** are used whole to dramatic effect as a garnish in both Japanese and Chinese cooking. They can be found in Japanese and other Asian markets, some specialty foods shops, and by mail order from Uwajimaya, (800) 889-1928.

**Shiro miso** is also known as white miso, although its actually pale yellow or golden in color. It is the mellowest of a wide range of misos (feremented-soybean pastes) used in Japanese cooking. You can buy it at Japanese and other Asian markets, natural foods stores, and by mail order from Uwajimaya, (800) 889-1928.

**Shiso** belongs to the same family as basil and mint, and is also widely known as perilla. Small green shiso leaves are sold fresh in the summer and fall at Japanese and other Asian markets, natural foods stores, and by mail order from Uwajimaya, (800) 889-1928.

**Sichuan peppercorns** are the dried pods (not the inner seeds) of the prickly ash, which is botanically related to citrus fruits, not to black and white pepper. They are available in Asian markets or by mail order from Kalustyan's, (212) 685-3451.

A **Silpat** or **Exopat pad** is a reusable liner treated with silicone to give it an ultra-nonstick finish. Silpat is one of several brands available at specialty cookware shops and by mail order from Bridge Kitchenware, (800) 274-3435 or (212) 838-1901.

**Spaetzlemakers**, used to make the German dumplings known as *spaetzle* (*shpets*-leh) are available from Bridge Kitchenware, (800) 274-3435 or (212) 838-1901, and Otto's, (818) 845-0433.

Ground **sumac** blended with toasted sesame seeds and fresh thyme make a very popular Middle Eastern seasoning called *za'atar*. Look for sumac at Middle Eastern markets and by mail order from Kalustyan's, (212) 685-3451 or www.kalustyans.com.

**Tamarind concentrate** and **tamarind paste**—both derived from the pulp of fresh tamarind-tree pods—are available from Kalustyan's, (212) 685-3451 or www.kalustyans.com.

**Thai red curry paste** can be found at Asian markets, some specialty foods shops and supermarkets, and by mail order from Uwajimaya, (800) 889-1928.

Fresh black **truffles** are available seasonally at specialty foods shops; both fresh and canned truffles and **truffle oil** are available from Marché aux Delices, (888) 547-5471.

Unió is our favorite brand of **Spanish olive oil**. To mail order, call La Tienda, (888) 472-1022.

**Wakame** is a deep green seaweed used in Japanese cooking. It is sometimes found fresh in Asian markets but more commonly available in its dried form in Japanese and other Asian markets, natural foods stores, and by mail order from Uwajimaya, (800) 889-1928.

**Wasabi paste** and **wasabi powder** are both derived from the wasabi plant, a relative of horseradish. They are used widely in Japanese cooking and available in Japanese and other Asian markets, natural foods shops, and by mail order from Uwajimaya, (800) 889-1928 or www.EthnicGrocer.com, (800) 523-1961.

**Won ton wrappers** are sold in Asian markets, some specialty foods shops, supermarkets, and by mail order from Uwajimaya, (800) 889-1928 or www.EthnicGrocer.com, (800) 523-1961.

**Yuca** (pronounced "*yoo*-ka") is sometimes referred to as cassava or manioc, and serves as the basis for tapioca. Fresh yuca has an appealing texture—similar to that of potato—when cooked and mashed. You can find yuca at Latino markets and many supermarkets. Choose those that are free of mold, soft spots, or an ammonia-like smell. When you cut into the flesh, it should be pure white, with no black veins. Frozen, peeled yuca pieces are also available in the freezer sections of many supermarkets.

# GENERAL INDEX

Page numbers in *italics* indicate color photographs
☺ indicates recipes that can be prepared in 45 minutes or less
☺+ indicates recipes that can be prepared in 45 minutes but require additional unattended time
🍃 indicates recipes that are leaner/lighter

To avoid duplication below of table setting information within the same menu, the editors have listed all such credits for silverware, plates, linen, and the like under "Table setting."

Any items in the photograph not credited are privately owned.

### Back Jacket

*Table setting*: See table setting credits for Provence's Grand Aïoli.

### Table of Contents

*Man sitting in chair* (page 6, left): Shirt—Paul Smith, (212) 627-9773. Cotton pants—Gap, (800) 427-7895. *Salmon-Wrapped Poached Eggs* (page 6, right): See table setting credits for Meet Us in the Country: Brunch: The Long Good-Bye.

### The Menu Collection

*Table setting* (page 11): See table setting credits for From the Terrace: A Late Summer Vegetarian Dinner.

### A Picnic in the Snow

*Snowshoeing in the woods* (page 14): Orange jacket—Patagonia, (800) 638-6464. All other clothing—Hind, (800) 952-4463. Poles and man's snow-shoes—ATLAS, (800) 654-7463. Women's snowshoes—Tubbs Snow-shoe Company, (800) 882-2748. *Spicy Red Pork and Bean Chili* (page 15, upper right): Handmade bowl—Luna Garcia, (800) 905-9975. *Mango Jícama Chopped Salad* (page 15, lower left): Handmade plate and tray—Luna Garcia, (800) 905-9975.

### The Generous Table: An American Potluck Supper

*Buffet setting* (page 16): Madrone salad bowl and servers—Cookworks, (800) 972-3357. "Sausalito" oval bowl—Pottery Barn, (800) 922-5507. Fringed napkins—Material

Possessions, (312) 280-4885. Flatware—Boda Nova, (800) 351-9842. Oval gratin baker—Emile Henry, (302) 326-4800. Round plates and marble bowl (with *focaccia*)—Tuscan Square, (212) 977-7777. Rectangular serving dish, wineglasses, square plates, silver-plated serving set, and stone-colored napkins—Banana Republic, (888) 277-8953. *Herbed Lima Bean Hummus* (page 17, upper): Metal dish—Bed, Bath & Beyond, (800) GOBEYOND. Oval ceramic dish—Pottery Barn, (800) 922-5507. Napkins—Gracious Home, (888) 452-2285. *Hundred-Corner Shrimp Balls* (page 17, lower): Footed bowl—Pottery Barn, (800) 922-5507. *Apple Crumb Tart; Hungarian Chocolate Mousse Cake Bars* (page 19): Sommeliers wineglasses—Riedel, (800) 642-1859.

### Dinner by the Fire

*Table setting* (page 24): Green throw (on sofa)—ABH Design, (212) 688-3764. Wineglasses—Villeroy & Boch, (800) 845-5376. Striped cashmere and wool blanket with fringe (on table)—Meg Cohen, (212) 473-4002. Tall glass vase (with tropical palm leaves)—The Terence Conran Shop, (212) 755-9079. *Poached Pears with Spiced Caramel Sauce* (page 25, upper): Blue dessert plates—Ad Hoc, (888) 748-4852. *Coriander- and Chile-Rubbed Lamb Chops* (page 25, lower): "Zenit"

stainless-steel flatware—Royal Scandinavia, (800) 433-4167.

### Paradise at Home: A Casual Caribbean Dinner

*Frozen Papaya and Passion-Fruit Rum Cocktails* (page 30, upper left): Tulip wineglasses—Simon Pearce, (800) 774-5277. *Mango Fool with Chocolate-Anise Straws* (page 30, lower left): Bamboo tray—Jamson Whyte, (212) 965-9405. *Table setting* (page 31, lower): Teak dining table and side chairs, bench, and bamboo mats—Jamson Whyte, (212) 965-9405. Vintage sterling beakers—F. Gorevic & Sons, (212) 753-9319. "Classique" ceramic dinner plates—Crate & Barrel, (800) 996-9960. Thomas by Rosenthal wineglasses, Ralph Lauren stainless-steel flatware—Ad Hoc, (888) 748-4852. Palm trees, crickets (on napkins), and woven fruit bowl—Caribbean Cuts (to the trade), (212) 924-6969. Cotton voile napkins—Dransfield & Ross, (212) 741-7278.

### La Dolce Vita: An Italian Fantasy

*Green-Pea Ravioli in Lemon Broth* (page 32): Bowl—Ralph Lauren Home Collection, (800) 578-7656, ext. 8700. *Crispy Artichoke Flower with Salsa Verde* (page 33): "Marqueterie" plates—Versace, (800) 804-8070. White marble pedestal—Malmaison, (212) 288-7569. *Roasted Double Veal Chops; Carrot*

*and Squash Ribbons* (page 34): Flowers and vase—L'Olivier Floral Atelier, (212) 774-7676. "Stella" wineglasses and "Thistle" highball glasses—Cristal Saint-Louis, (800) 238-5522. "Arcantia" flatware—Christofle, (877) 728-4556.
*Grappa Semifreddo with Espresso Sauce* (page 35): "Carat" dessert plates and demitasse cup and saucers (all by Philippe Deshoulières)—Lalique, (800) 993-2580.

### The Celebration Table

*Shrimp Satés with Spiced Pistachio Chutney* (page 36, upper left): Wineglasses and carafe—Ad Hoc, (888) 748-4852.
*Miso-Marinated Salmon with Citrus and Shiitakes* (page 36, upper right): Ceramic fish platter—Dean & DeLuca, (800) 221-7714. Linen napkins—ABH Design, (212) 688-3764.

### Prime Time: Father's Day Cookout

*Buffet setting* (page 40): "Hampton" wood picnic table—Williams-Sonoma, (800) 541-2233. Acrylic cooler (with flowers) and acrylic pitcher—Crate & Barrel, (800) 323-5461. Serving fork and spoon and acrylic charger (with steaks)—Banana Republic, (888) 277-8953. "Teema" ceramic platter (with potato salad) by Arabia—Ad Hoc, (888) 748-4852. Acrylic pepper grinder—Gracious Home, (212) 517-6300. Linen napkins—ABH Design, (212) 688-3764. "Cambridge" acrylic flatware—Mariposa, (800) 788-1304.
*Tropical-Fruit Splits with Rum Sauce and Chile-Macadamia Brittle* (page 41, lower): Ceramic plates—Dean & DeLuca, (800) 221-7714. Shot on location at Hope Springs Resort, Desert Hot Springs, CA, (760) 329-4003.

### Meet Us in the Country: Friday Night Supper

*Walking to house* (page 42): Woman's clothing—Anthropologie, (800) 309-2500.
*Mango Tart* (page 43): Platter—Crate & Barrel, (800) 996-9960.

*Buffet setting* (page 43, lower): White platter, ceramic plates, and salt and pepper shakers—The Terence Conran Shop, (212) 755-9079. Ceramic salad plates—Smith & Hawken, (212) 925-1190. Silverware—Crate & Barrel, (800) 996-9960. White ceramic vase and perforated vases—Jonathan Adler, (212) 941-8950. Wineglasses—Simon Pearce, (800) 774-5277. Taupe linen napkins—Ad Hoc, (888) 748-4852.

### Saturday Morning

*Table setting* (page 45): Glass cake plate, spiral metal egg cups, glass pitcher, bowls, and silverware—Crate & Barrel, (800) 996-9960. White linen placemats and napkins—Ad Hoc, (888) 748-4852. White porcelain plates, cups, and saucers—Nicole Farhi, (212) 223-8811. Footed glasses and basket—Simon Pearce, (800) 774-5277.

### Lunch: A Movable Feast

*Walking to beach* (page 46): Women's sweaters—Anthropologie, (800) 309-2500.
*Grilled Chicken; Corn, Tomato, and Scallion Salad; Haricots Verts with Hot Pepper Relish; Potatoes with Vinegar and Sea Salt* (page 47, lower): Chinese take-out boxes—GSD Packaging, (800) 486-0490 (shown: Bio-Pak #6 holding two Bio-Pak #1's and two pint-size Microwave Food Pails).

### The Big Night

*Table setting* (page 48, lower): Glass decanter, wineglasses, cream plates, silverware, and tablecloth—Crate & Barrel, (800) 996-9960. "Bag" vase—Smith & Hawken, (212) 925-1190. Wood chargers—Global Table, (212) 431-5839. Hurricane lamps—Anthropologie, (800) 309-2500. Water glasses—The Terence Conran Shop, (212) 755-9079. Cream Napkins—ABC Carpet & Home, (212) 473-3000.
*Vegetable Bulgur Salad* (page 49, upper left): Cream-colored bowl—Crate & Barrel, (800) 996-9960.
*Lime Ice on Watermelon; Lime Sugar Cookies* (page 49, lower left): Square plate—ABC Carpet & Home, (212) 473-3000.

### Brunch: The Long Good-Bye

*Table setting* (page 50): Glass bowls, teapot, and Champagne flutes—The Terence Conran Shop, (212) 755-9079. Glass pitcher and silverware—Crate & Barrel, (800) 996-9960. Pillows—Calvin Klein Home, (877) 256-7373.
*Salmon-Wrapped Poached Eggs* (page 51, lower): White plate with border—The Terence Conran Shop, (212) 755-9079.

### Sunday in the Park

*Table setting* (page 52): Table, goblets, highball glasses, and bowls—Crate & Barrel, (800) 323-5461. Basket—Sur La Table, (800) 243-0852. Ice bucket—One Beach Road, (310) 887-3920. Flatware—Banana Republic, (310) 273-8953. Salt and pepper shakers and napkins—Gearys of Beverly Hills, (310) 273-4741. Napkin rings—Pottery Barn, (800) 922-5507. Plates—Sur La Table, (800) 243-0852.

### Summer Splash: Poolside Dinner with Mary Sue Milliken

*Chile-Glazed Salmon with Orange Salsa; Quinoa-Fennel Pilaf* (page 55, lower right): Dinner plates—Calvin Klein, (877) 256-7373. Flatware—IKEA, (626) 912-1119.
*Roasted Orange Cakes* (page 55, lower left): Bowls—Crate & Barrel, (800) 323-5461.

### Provence's Grand Aïoli

*Table setting* (pages 58-59): Pine table (circa 1850)—Country Gear, (631) 537-1032.

### From the Terrace: A Late Summer Vegetarian Dinner

*Table setting* (page 60): "Sand" plates, lime Murano glasses (with wine), water glasses, decanters, and large oval dish (as centerpiece)—Nicole Farhi, (212) 223-8811. "Prism" flatware—Georg Jensen, (212) 759-6457. Celadon stoneware bowl (with salad)—Ad Hoc, (888) 748-4852. Brushed-silver platter (under salad bowl), pillows, candle pillars, and various throws—Calvin Klein, (877) 256-7373. Square napkin rings—Felissimo, (212) 247-5656. Silk napkins—Bergdorf Goodman, (212) 753-7300.

*Oat Biscuits with Triple-Crème Cheese and Grapes* (page 61, lower): Dark oak charger—Calvin Klein, (877) 256-7373. Cheese knife—Felissimo, (212) 247-5656.

### Thanksgiving: An American Gathering

*Pear and Dried-Cherry Tart; Ginger-Pecan Roulade with Honey-Glazed Pecans* (page 66): Coffeepot—Bergdorf Goodman, (212) 753-7300. Cups and saucers—Bernardaud, (800) 884-7775. Cake plate—Lalique, (800) 993-2580 for store locations. Bench (circa 1815)—Florian Papp, (212) 288-6770.

*Beet Soup in Roasted Acorn Squash; Cornmeal-Cayenne Grissini* (page 67, upper): Chargers—Lalique, (800) 993-2580 for store locations.

*Buffet with flowers* (page 67, lower): 19th-century cabinet—William Lipton, Ltd., (212) 751-8131. Gold vases—Gordon Foster, (212) 744-4922.

*Table setting* (pages 68-69): Tablecloth and water goblets—Barneys New York, (212) 826-8900. Wineglasses and water pitcher—Cristal Saint-Louis, (800) 238-5522 for store locations. Flatware—Hermès, (800) 238-5522 for store locations. Candlesticks—Baccarat, (212) 826-4100. Flowers and votive candle holders—Takashimaya, (212) 350-0100. Pepper mills—Dean & DeLuca, (800) 221-7714. Napkins—ABH Design, (212) 688-3764. Carving set—James Robinson, (212) 752-6166. Chargers by Puiforçat and dinner plate

by J. L. Coquet—Lalique, (800) 993-2580 for store locations. Glass bowl—Calvin Klein, (800) 294-7978 for store locations.

### Deborah Madison's Santa Fe Christmas

*Roasted Capon with Chile-Cilantro Rub and Roasted Carrots; Potato-Green Chile Gratin; Cavolo Nero with Cilantro* (page 72, lower left): Green plates and candlesticks—The Clay Angel, (505) 988-4800.

*Date, Dried-Cherry, and Chocolate Torte* (page 73): Plates—The Clay Angel, (505) 988-4800.

### Holiday Cocktail Party

*Sesame Rice Balls with Red Pepper Dipping Sauce* (page 74, upper): Platter and dishes—Felissimo, (800) 565-6785. Champagne flute—Barneys New York, (212) 826-8900. Top and skirt—Calvin Klein, (212) 292-9000.

*Truffled Quail Eggs* (page 74, lower): Plate and bowl—Bergdorf Goodman, (212) 753-7300.

*Peppery Beef Kebabs with Braised Pearl Onions* (page 75, top left): Glass plate—Crate & Barrel, (800) 323-5461.

*Caviar Moons; Tapenade on Jícama Stars* (page 75, top right): Square wooden tray—Takashimaya, (800) 753-2038.

*Scallop Ceviche on Black Pasta Cakes with Cilantro Salsa* (page 75, lower left): Frosted plate—Felissimo, (800) 565-6785.

*Coconut Macadamia Truffles; Candied Grapefruit Peel; Chocolate Star Anise Truffles* (page 75, lower right): Tray

with four dishes—Takashimaya, (800) 753-2038.

### Elegant Holiday Dinner

*Herbed Rib Roast; Parmesan Roasted Potatoes; Celery and Fennel with Bacon* (page 77, lower): Handblown 18th-century wineglasses—Aero Studios Ltd., (212) 966-4700. Blanket chest—Les Pierres Antiques, (212) 243-7740.

### Low-Fat: Spicy Cool Dinner

*Peruvian-Style Beef Kebabs with Grilled Onion and Zucchini; Quinoa and Grilled-Pepper Salad* (page 81, lower): "Dalton" wineglass—Calvin Klein Home, (877) 256-7373. Ceramic plate—The Terence Conran Shop, (212) 755-9079.

### Summer Dinner in Palermo

*Chickpea Fritters; Sweet and Sour Eggplant; Green Olives* (page 222): Deruta Square Dinner Plate and Tuscan Vegetable Bow—Tavola, (908) 273-0040.

### Carnival Dinner

*Cannoli* (page 235): Ceramic Cake Stand—Tuscan Square, (212) 977-7777.

### A Sicilian Sweets Table

*Frozen Hazelnut Bombe* (page 236): Peltro Pewter Round Tray—Tuscan Square, (212) 977-7777.

*Fig Cookies* (page 241, upper right): Peltro Pewter Expresso Cups—Tuscan Square, (212) 977-7777.

*Sicilian Layered Cake* (page 241, lower right): Peltro Pewter Flatware—Tuscan Square, (212) 977-7777.

# CREDITS

We gratefully acknowledge the photographers listed below. With a few exceptions, their work was previously published in *Gourmet* magazine.

**Melanie Acevedo:** The Generous Table: An American Potluck Supper, pp. 16–19. All photographs © 2000.

**Quentin Bacon:** A Picnic in the Snow, p. 14; Summer Splash: Poolside Dinner with Mary Sue Milliken, pp. 54–55; Dinner in France with Ken Hom, pp. 62–65; Holiday Cocktail Party, pp. 74-75. All photographs © 2000.

**Ernesto Bazan:** Mount Etna, Sicily, pp. 218–219 © 2000.

**Beatriz da Costa:** Spain's Melting Pot, pp. 20–23. All photographs © 2000.

**Miki Duisterhof:** Salmon-Wrapped Poached Egg, p. 6, right; Meet Us in the Country, pp. 42–51. All photographs © 2000.

**Mark Ferri:** Man with basket of fruit, p. 7, right; Woman picking fruit, p. 229; Ruins of the Temple of Apollo in Siracusa, p. 232; Van with flowers,

p. 239; Maria Grammatico with her nieces and brother carrying pastries in Erice, Sicily, p. 243. All photographs © 1994.

**John Kernick:** Provence's Grand Aïoli, pp. 56–59; A Recipe Compendium, p. 84; Back jacket; endsheets. All photographs © 2000.

**Rita Maas:** Elegant Holiday Dinner, pp. 76–79. All photographs © 2000.

**Maura McEvoy:** Taglierini with Morels, Asparagus, and Nasturtiums, p. 7, left; The Promise of Easter Blooms, pp. 26–29; Thanksgiving: An American Gathering, pp. 66–69. All photographs © 2000.

**Victoria Pearson:** Sunday in the Park, pp. 52–53. All photographs © 2000.

**Dan Peebles:** Alaska King Crab "Nachos," p. 6, left; Prime Time: Father's Day Cookout, pp. 40–41. All photographs © 2000.

**Alan Richardson:** Fragrant Feast: A Taste of India, pp. 12–13; Low-Fat: Hearty Winter Dinner, p. 80. All photographs © 2000.

**K. F. Schmidt:** Top of a column in Monreale, Sicily, p. 226 © 2000.

**Ellen Silverman:** One-Dish Dinner, p. 83 © 2000.

**Lisa Charles Watson:** Hot and Cool Comfort: A Taste of Malaysia, pp. 38–39. All photographs © 2000.

**Jonelle Weaver:** The Menu Collection, p. 10; From the Terrace: A Late Summer Vegetarian Dinner, pp. 60–61. All photographs © 2000.

**Anna Williams:** La Dolce Vita: An Italian Fantasy, pp. 32–35; Deborah Madison's Santa Fe Christmas, pp. 70–73. All photographs © 2000.

**Romulo Yanes:** Frontispiece, p. 2; A Picnic in the Snow, p. 15; Dinner by the Fire, pp. 24–25; Paradise at Home: A Casual Caribbean Dinner, pp. 30–31; The Celebration Table, pp. 36–37; Low-Fat: Spicy Cool Dinner, p. 81; One-Dish Dinner, p. 82; Summer Dinner in Palermo, pp. 222–223, p. 225; Carnival Dinner, p. 228, p. 231, 235; A Sicilian Sweets Table, pp. 236–237, p. 241. All photographs © 2000.

We also would like to gratefully acknowledge chefs **Ken Hom, Deborah Madison,** and **Mary Sue Milliken** for their menus, which previously appeared in *Gourmet* magazine.

If you are not already a subscriber to *Gourmet* magazine and would be interested in subscribing, please call *Gourmet*'s toll-free number, (800) 365-2454.

If you are interested in purchasing additional copies of this book or other *Gourmet* cookbooks, please call (800) 438-9944.